W9-DBQ-687

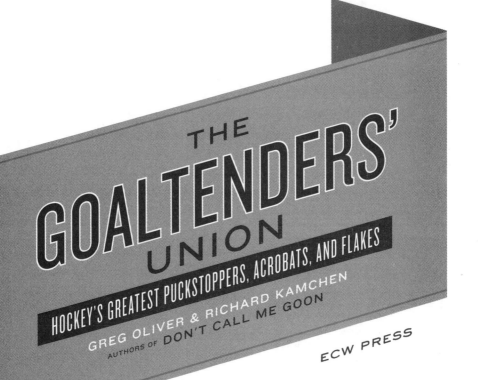

THE GOALTENDERS' UNION

HOCKEY'S GREATEST PUCKSTOPPERS, ACROBATS, AND FLAKES

GREG OLIVER & RICHARD KAMCHEN

AUTHORS OF DON'T CALL ME GOON

ECW PRESS

Published by ECW Press
2120 Queen Street East, Suite 200
Toronto, Ontario, Canada M4E 1E2
416-694-3348 / info@ecwpress.com

We acknowledge the financial support of the
Government of Canada through the Canada
Book Fund for our publishing activities,
and the contribution of the Government
of Ontario through the Ontario Book
Publishing Tax Credit and the Ontario
Media Development Corporation.

LIBRARY AND ARCHIVES CANADA
CATALOGUING IN PUBLICATION

Oliver, Greg, author
The goaltenders' union : hockey's greatest
puckstoppers, acrobats, and flakes /
Greg Oliver and Richard Kamchen.

(Hockey's greatest series)
Issued in print and electronic formats.
ISBN 978-1-77041-149-4 (pbk.)
978-1-77090-585-6 (PDF)
978-1-77090-584-9 (ePUB)

1. Hockey goalkeepers—Biography.
2. Hockey players—Biography.
3. National Hockey League.

I. Kamchen, Richard, 1974–, author
II. Title.

GV848.5.A1044 2014   796.962092'2
C2014-902558-0   C2014-902559-9

Editor for the press: Michael Holmes
Cover design: David Gee
Front cover photos: Shack: © Graphic
Artists/Hockey Hall of Fame; Quick: ©
Brad Rempel/Icon SMI
Back cover photo: Courtesy David Arrigo
Text design: Tania Craan
Printing: Marquis   5   4   3   2   1

PRINTED AND BOUND IN CANADA

To our favourite goalies growing up.

For Greg, it was easily Ken Dryden, though Michel "Bunny" Larocque was always a close second—he was stuck behind Dryden on the Canadiens' bench and had an unforgettable nickname.

For Richard, it was Bob Essensa of the Jets, whom he got to interview for this book; special mention goes to the chirpy and positive Allan Bester, Toronto's acrobatic underdog—the complete opposite of Richard, who is decidedly more Ron Hextall–like.

THE GOALTENDERS' UNION is not an imaginary code or a joke shared among forwards and defencemen. It's an unofficial but very real brotherhood and support group for those who put themselves in harm's way as they bravely and stoically guard their teams' net.

"We all got along real well. We got together, had a beer, and discussed the shooters," Chuck Rayner, the star goaltender of the New York Rangers in the 1940s and early '50s, said of the small circle of goalies in his era.

Terry Sawchuk, a staunch admirer of Rayner, saw his hero in top form from the other end of the ice as he shut out Detroit in a 1-0 victory. Sawchuk skated over to congratulate Rayner at the final buzzer.

"Chuck Rayner is the best, that's all. It's a great thrill playing against a man you used to idolize, and when he comes up with that kind of performance, well, you just feel you've got to say something," Sawchuk said.

The Montreal Canadiens' Gerry McNeil refused to take over from Bill Durnan when the latter pulled himself from the nets in a semifinal series against Rayner and his Rangers in 1949–50: "I didn't want to take his place. Dick Irvin said, 'You're playing,' and I said, 'I'm not playing unless Bill tells me to play.' So Bill told me. At first I'd thought he was getting kicked out. But it was him that didn't want to go out."

Cesare Maniago said he always respected his peers, perhaps not to the point of celebrating one of their big saves against his own team, but he did not find happiness if they let in a soft goal either: "There would usually be a few words between goalies when you

Roberto Luongo of the Panthers chats with Jose Theodore of the Canadiens during an All-Star game practice in 2004. (George Tahinos)

were skating around during the warm-up. Or you'd be standing beside each other and you'd say things like, 'How's it going? I've had a good week, or a lousy week.'"

No fiercer competition existed than that between the Canadian and Russian National Teams, especially in the early days of North American All-Star competition against the Red Army. And yet, before the first game of the '72 Summit Series, retired Montreal Canadiens great Jacques Plante, accompanied by a translator, discussed with Soviet netminder Vladislav Tretiak the shooting habits of the NHLers he'd be facing that night in Montreal.

"To help me visualize it, Plante showed me everything on a blackboard. Then he said goodbye and left," Tretiak wrote in his eponymous memoir. "I will always be very grateful to Jacques Plante, whose suggestions helped me so much."

In 1974, Tretiak and the Soviets met another team of All-Stars, this time those of the competing World Hockey Association (WHA). Then, it'd be Canadian starter Gerry Cheevers who'd offer encouragement. "Before the game, he would come over and hit me on the pads with his stick, his way of wishing me good luck," Tretiak wrote.

Goalies' friendships also continued past their playing days and into the world of the goalie coach, where Jeff Reese, in Philadelphia, would call up Sean Burke, in Phoenix, for advice on dealing with Ilya Bryzgalov. "He didn't know him, so he was just, at times, looking more for what is his personality like . . . is he joking about that? It takes a little time to get to know Bryz," said Burke.

After a hard night for one of their peers, even the seemingly nastiest, most competitive of goalies have offered their condolences and encouraging words. After a horrendous night for the Toronto Maple Leafs, who left a young Allan Bester hung out to dry against the mighty New York Islanders, Billy Smith came calling. That would be the same Smith who wouldn't shake hands in the playoffs if his team had been eliminated, and the same Smith who used his heavy lumber as a weapon against anyone who got too close to his crease.

After the game, Bester was sitting dejected in an empty visitors' dressing room still wearing half his equipment when Smith stopped by to check in on him. It's a memory Bester recalls vividly to this day:

> All of a sudden, I heard, "Allan! Get your head up!" And I looked up and it was Billy Smith standing in the doorway. "Allan, don't you hang your head. We should have scored 17 goals tonight. Not we could have scored 17, we *should* have scored 17. You stood on your head! Don't you ever hang your head after playing like that." That's the International Goaltenders' Union for you. People don't think of Billy Smith as having that type of sportsmanship. . . . But he took the time out to stand around and wait for me, and then when he didn't see me come out, he walked into our dressing room

and came in to tell me, a young kid of 19 years who's trying to break into the league, to get your head up and don't you ever hang your head. That was special. That's one of the things I'll always remember.

"It's such a unique position," said Corey Hirsch, who bounced between the American Hockey League to the NHL from 1992 to 2003 and was recently the goaltending coach for the St. Louis Blues. "It's not like being a player, it's not like being a defenceman. It's a completely different position. You're not scoring goals, you're making saves, so I think that's why we feel a connection to each other. We know what the pressure is, we know what it feels like to be in those situations. And we know what it feels like to be the goat, and we know what it feels like to be the hero. There's no in-between about a goalie."

WHO *ARE* THESE MASKED MEN?

Goaltenders have reputations as solitary, mercurial figures. This reputation isn't without foundation and is, in some cases, well earned.

In his autobiography, Glenn Hall wrote, "We were always considered loners. I was a loner because I couldn't relate to anybody. I'd go for walks by myself to get ready for a game, going over the other team and its players . . . I liked it best when nobody recognized me. Before a game, I kept to myself because I was so miserable I didn't think anyone would want me around."

Tony Esposito, who succeeded Hall in Chicago, wouldn't talk to anyone before games either, preparing himself to play from the time he got up in the morning. After going through the same ritual each and every time for a home game—morning skate, laying out his equipment, returning home to eat and nap—his wife would drive him to Chicago Stadium.

"I used to tell Marilyn, my wife, to be ready to leave at 5 o'clock, or else," Esposito told Dick Irvin for his book *In the Crease*. "We never talked in the car going to the game, never. Even when the kids started to drive down with us, no talking. If I was going to fail, it wasn't going to be because I wasn't mentally prepared. On the road I usually roomed by myself. But if I ever had a roommate, it was the same thing. No talking."

Cesare Maniago explained, "Before the game is when I would say most goalies, including me, weren't just one of the boys. When it's getting near game time you want to be left alone. The other guys talk, defenceman with defencemen, forwards with forwards. But the goalie wants to be by himself."

Rhyming off the habits of the goaltenders who played under him in his numerous NHL stops, former coach Mike Keenan is almost wistful, the descriptions spiriting him back to the dressing rooms of the 1980s and '90s.

Ron Hextall would take off only one pad and rock back and forth. Grant Fuhr was a rocker too. Mike Richter was a silent enigma. Pelle Lindbergh would sit between periods with all his gear on, including his helmet and gloves. And then there's Eddie "the Eagle" Belfour: "Eddie used to spend a couple of hours a day sharpening his skates on game day. It was just totally a mental routine. It had nothing to do with his skates. It was just his way of focusing and getting ready," said Keenan.

Superstitions were nothing to take lightly, and Islander Billy Smith would go berserk if anyone tampered with how he'd laid out his equipment. Jacques Plante could play worse than a green Junior B third stringer if someone interfered with his preparations. In *Without Fear: Hockey's 50 Greatest Goaltenders*, Johnny Bower said: "He was great on the ice, but off the ice, Jacques was one of the most superstitious people I'd ever met. When he came to Toronto in the early '70s, you'd walk into the dressing room to find his equipment laid out on the floor in the order that he would put it on. If anyone accidentally touched or moved the equipment, you might as well have left him on the bench for the rest of the night because his focus would have been disrupted."

Jean Beliveau shoots on Glenn Hall. (IHA/Icon SMI)

Maybe the greatest of them all, Terry Sawchuk needed continual reassurance and comforting. Near the end of his career, when he was with the Rangers, he rarely saw any action, but when he did, he'd nervously ask reporters afterwards if he'd embarrassed himself. Even in his salad days with the Red Wings, he needed convincing he hadn't let anyone down.

"You always had to be careful with Terry. He became more sensitive every year," teammate Benny Woit said in *Shutout: The Legend of Terry Sawchuk*. The peculiarities, odd habits, and phobias of goalies were easy fodder for the press. How does one ignore Plante knitting in the dressing room? Or Gary "Suitcase" Smith taking off all his gear—including a dozen pair of socks, which was a whole other story—between periods for a quick shower? The most popular stories, however, involved recounting Glenn Hall's penchant for throwing up before games.

"I've heard more galdarn stuff about that, and the writers, they'd say I had a pail there beside me," complained Hall, who stressed the oft-repeated tales of his nervous stomach were overblown. "Holy Christ, what a crude bunch of bastards. What the hell did they think they were dreaming up?"

But Hall's teammate Al Arbour, who played defence in front of him in numerous cities, believed Hall's genuine habit signalled to teammates a great performance ahead.

"I think he was the greatest goalie of all. He was so quick, he was so fast. But he'd get sick. Ugh. Every night. We got used to it. In Chicago, we'd cheer, 'Oh, oh! He's going to throw up! He's going to throw up! Oh! Oh!' We'd cheer, 'We'll win tonight! We're all set!'" said Arbour

Frank Brimsek, the U.S.-born Hall of Famer, was another odd duck, a hypochondriac who dragged around a medicine chest filled with drops, pills, and fizzy powders from town to town. The team expected him to do well in net if he was feeling crummy. "The nights when Brimsek complained of a rising temperature and spots before the eyes were quite apt to be the night he turned in a netminding masterpiece," wrote Tom Fitzgerald in the *Boston Globe*.

The most celebrated eccentric among them all, of course, was Gilles Gratton, a.k.a., Grattoony the Loony.

When Gratton was a Toronto Toro, he did a naked spin around the ice at practice. He firmly believed in astrology and asked out of games based on the misalignment of stars. He also believed he'd been reincarnated many times and would fall to the ice when, say, the puck smashed against an old sword wound.

"He did a 15-minute program of calisthenics before each game and practice, including a series of upside-down push-ups. Dressed in full goaltending toggery, Gilles stood on his head in a shower stall and raised and lowered himself by his arms," wrote Trent Frayne in *Maclean's* magazine in 1993. In response, Gratton said that the workout "clears the brains" and that "sometimes I bring the body to the rink, but the head she is somewhere else."

The modern day Grattoony would have to be Ilya Bryzgalov. A Vezina Trophy nominee with the Phoenix Coyotes, Bryzgalov's thoughts about life, the universe, and everything else went mostly under the radar—until he signed a nine-year, $51 million contract with hockey-mad Philadelphia. From then on, the spotlight has been on this iconoclast. While viewers might have enjoyed his antics on HBO's *24/7* series, Flyers management most decidedly did not, and Bryzgalov, who once praised Stalin, soon wore out his welcome.

Bob Froese, a netminder from 1982 to 1990, was the polar opposite of the likes of Gratton and Bryzgalov. Serene and thoughtful, it is little wonder he sought answers in the ministry and is now a pastor in upstate New York. The one-time Flyer believed that the wackier players "really hurt their teams. They never last very long. I think as a goalie, what you want to do, you want to give your team a sense of assurance, a sense of calm, not a sense of 'What's this idiot going to do next?' But I think a lot of it has to do with pressure. There's tremendous pressure on a goalie."

Could some of the more outrageous characters have been putting on an act? Perhaps.

"Sometimes, as goaltenders, we perpetuate that notion that we are a little bit nutty, and we're not as nutty as we pretend to be," said Bobby "the Chief" Taylor, who turned his few NHL years, mainly with the Flyers, into decades as an analyst. Erratic behaviour might result in a little more room around the crease as an oncoming forward second-guessed the consequences of getting too close.

Kelly Hrudey, who led the Los Angeles Kings to the 1993 Stanley Cup Final, believes the days of the flake in goal are mostly a thing of the past, but he understands why the antics existed in the first place. "When the guys first played, nobody wore a mask, so I'd be pretty uptight too. You look at some of the gruesome injuries that the goalies suffered, boy, on top of that with the pressure, I think you could easily explain that that's why those guys were different than everybody else. They were afraid—who wouldn't be under those circumstances?" said the *Hockey Night in Canada* analyst.

MAKING THE GRADE

The stereotype of the bad skater or chubby kid in net had some truth to it at one point. The idea of the little brother being stuck in net because he wants to play with the big kids will never go away; Phil Esposito needed Tony as a target, after all.

In *In the Crease*, Gump Worsley said, "I started playing goal mainly because of my size. I played outdoor hockey in Point Saint Charles for a man named Phil Walton. He said if I wanted to play in the league, I'd have to be a goalie because I was too small to play anywhere else. I was 4-foot-11 at the time. I never got much taller, but I got fatter."

The days of bad, overweight skaters blocking shots are past. The physical challenge of being a top-level professional goaltender eliminates all but the best-conditioned and hungry athletes; the mental stresses remorselessly push others aside.

"The goalies that think the least [about pressure] are probably going to have the most success," said Darren Jensen, who faced tremendous pressure after being called up to the Philadelphia Flyers in November 1985 after the death of Vezina Trophy–winner Pelle Lindbergh. "Sometimes it literally comes down to a game or a practice whether you make a team or not. You have to have a real short-term memory. Probably the most important thing you have to have as a goaltender—really as an athlete—if you don't have self-confidence, you're done. I don't care how talented you are, if you question yourself at all, you will not succeed. That's pretty well life."

It is simple to Glenn Hall: "The mind is the most important part of playing a goal."

Accountability and anxiety are at the start of the goalkeeper's alphabet.

"If a goalie plays bad for four games, he can't hide, whereas a forward, if he's having a bad stretch, he hides. They just sit him on the bench," said Kevin Hodson, who backed up Chris Osgood when the Detroit Red Wings won the Stanley Cup in 1998. According to Hodson, "Wins are such a huge thing because it means people have jobs, it means managers have jobs, and coaches have jobs. You're always being measured on performance, and you're always being measured on getting wins."

The stakes are now even higher. "I think mentally that probably the game is a little tougher in the sense that there's so much more money involved in it," said Bobby Taylor. Think of it as a trickle-down effect: the goalie's performance not only affects the team but also the management, arena staff, agents, media, fans, and his own family and friends.

Or, as Gump Worsley once cracked, "the only job worse is a javelin catcher at a track and field meet."

Minor hockey outfits generally discourage players from specializing until at least age eight or 10; instead, a few sets of the expensive goalie equipment are shared among the young players. Hall of Famer Ed Giacomin's brother, who is five years older than him, was also a goalie. The younger Giacomin recalled, "There would be times that we'd have a game on the same night, and he'd say, 'Well, your game is more important than mine.' I would use the equipment instead, because we only had the one set of equipment."

Emulating the stars of one's childhood in the driveway or the schoolyard, getting peppered with tennis balls instead of pucks, can lead to dreams of stardom.

Gold medal–winning Canadian goaltender Sami Jo Small always tuned into *Hockey Night in Canada*. "I used to draw their pictures every Saturday night and pretend that I was them," she said.

Growing up, Marty Turco looked up to the likes of Patrick Roy, Ron Hextall, and Eddie Belfour. He explained that it was a gradual process of wanting to become a goaltender. "You started to get to the tip of the iceberg of what goalies meant to the team, the fun, the glory, the aches and pains," he said. With time, the equipment and masks become fascinating, and soon posters of your favourites are on the wall in your room. "All those things helped gravitate [me] toward being a goaltender."

Given their gladiator-outfits as they bravely head into battle, it's actually a wonder that more kids these days don't demand to be goalies.

"I'll tell you, it's really the best position in today's game and it's probably the safest position. It was not for a long time; it was the worst position in sport," said Hall.

Not everyone, however, is cut out to carry the load.

In relative terms, the two-goaltender system has not been around that long. It started during the 1965 playoffs and was instituted league-wide for the 1965–66 season. It was a decision by the National Hockey League, and while there was an initial outcry by teams about paying another player, in reality, it was a move necessitated by television. The delay dictated by stitching up the unmasked netminder could not be tolerated when there was a broadcast schedule to adhere to.

Alex Delvecchio saw dozens of colleagues get stitched up during his Hall of Fame career as a centre. "A goaltender would get hit and you'd have to stop play. He'd go in and get stitches. You might be just loafing around out on the ice for 10 or 15 minutes while the goaltender was coming back. The one I remember was Eddie Shack—he'd do some figure skating while we were waiting," he said.

Before the two-goalie system, the men in net were hard as nails and expected to return to action after being fixed up in the dressing room. Often, it was a crude stitching job by the trainer (without painkillers), and the intention was to do a better sewing job post-game. Gerry Cheevers's famed mask with all the stitches is both a tribute to the goalies of the past and a reminder of what his face *could* have looked like had he played in a different era. Charlie Hodge (who played from 1954 to 1971) distinctly remembers when he didn't return to the net: "Twice I didn't return to the game, and

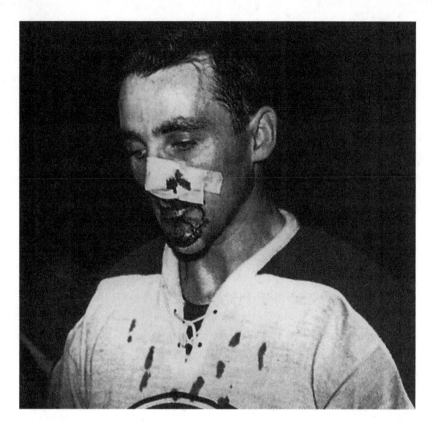

Jacques Plante leaves the ice after a puck to the face, courtesy of Andy Bathgate of the New York Rangers, on November 1, 1959. Later, he returned to the ice wearing a mask. (IHA/Icon SMI)

they had to find somebody out of the stands. I got my mouth split open with a skate. I didn't come back on that one. When I broke my jaw, I didn't come back on that one either."

Hockey lore, and the accompanying game reports, are sprinkled with tales of trainers or the local junior goaltender hastened to the dressing room to don the pads—sometimes to play for the opposition. Most famously, Lester Patrick, at age 45, strapped on the pads while coaching the New York Rangers in April 1928. His star goalie, Lorne Chabot, had taken a puck between the eyes in the first period. Patrick, a former defenceman, hadn't played a competitive game in seven years and had never been in net. Somehow Patrick and the

Rangers beat the Montreal Maroons and went on to win the Stanley Cup (with Chabot back between the pipes).

Wilfred Cude was the patron saint of backups. Originally from Barry, Wales, Cude learned to play hockey in Winnipeg and was plucked from the Saskatchewan senior circuit in 1930 to play pro in Pittsburgh. The Pirates became the Philadelphia Quakers, and when that squad folded, the league kept him on as a spare goalie for all the teams. The Boston Bruins "borrowed" him for two games in 1932, and the Blackhawks used his services once. Properly acquired in a trade by the Montreal Canadiens on October 19, 1933, he played one game there before being loaned to the Detroit Red Wings for the remainder of the season. Even when he did get a real shot in Montreal, from 1934 to 1940, he wore three different jersey numbers, 4, 17, and 24.

Why the backup system didn't come into practice earlier is harder to explain. The Bruins platooned "Sugar" Jim Henry and "Long" John Henderson in 1955 to decent success. When an injury befell the starter, the backup had to drop his bag of peanuts and scurry down to the locker room to get ready.

Speaking to *The Hockey News*'s Roger Barry that season, Harold Cotton, the Bruins' chief scout, said, "The day is coming when goaltenders will be two-platooned, virtually alternated on a game-to-game basis. Years ago the most durable player on most teams was the goaltender. He generally outlasted all the other players on his team. But those days are gone. Today the strain on a goaltender is so great that any goalie can benefit from periodic rests. That situation is especially noticeable this season, with every regular goalie in the league being out of the lineup at one time or another."

How the teams choose their goaltending tandem determines a lot. There is no tried-and-true rule for how the pairings go, but more often than not, it seems that a team will combine a seasoned pro with a young up-and-comer. In some cases, the elder statesman is the starter and the neophyte his apprentice. Occasionally the latter usurps the former, or an old hand might play a supporting role for the young number one. In today's NHL, the decision is usually made with salary-cap implications.

Regardless of the set-up, there is still just one net.

"I think it's a lot easier for a veteran guy, that's played around the league as a starter, and all of a sudden he's relegated to a backup time, where he's only going to play 25 or 30 games. He can prepare himself a little better than a rookie," said Bruins veteran Eddie Johnston, who would parlay his playing career (1962–1978) into a head coaching job.

But not everyone is cut out to be a mentor. "Some guys don't like to do it, or they figure some guy's taking their job and that, but it's a team game and you can help the guy. I always thought that was important, that I try to help the guy that was working with me," said Johnston.

Sharing the duties is easier for some than others. For guys like Rick DiPietro or Tom Barrasso, it just didn't come naturally, according to Glenn "Chico" Resch, veteran of 571 NHL games and now a Devils broadcaster: "Those guys were so good their whole career that again, it's not criticism, it's just their environment and the way they grew up, they were always top dog. They never really had to think about sitting on the bench—'Sharing? What's that? I don't do that. I just play all the time. I play whenever I want and I'm the best.' For them, maybe they didn't understand that mentality."

"Great goaltenders just don't make great backup goaltenders. Great backup goaltenders have the ability to focus on team first. Great backup goaltenders have the ability to put on perhaps a brave face or become a good actor, and take pride in other people's success. You have more of the emotions that a coach would, because at that point your job is done. All you can do is cheer and support, and you can't actually make a difference on the ice," said Sami Jo Small.

It is important to keep a positive outlook and be a team player. "You've got to be ready to go in. It's like being a closer in pitching, I guess, a backup quarterback—you've got to be ready to go," said Curt Ridley (who played from 1975 to 1981).

Jason LaBarbera, who played for the Oilers in 2013–14 before going to Chicago at the trade deadline, has been satisfied making a career out of being a backup. "It's my job to help him along for whatever he needs, and to be a cheerleader. And when I do get a chance to play, it's to go out and give the guys a chance to win," said LaBarbera.

In practice, the backups are key.

"A backup goalie has a huge role on a team," said Keith Yandle, assistant captain for Phoenix. "They can't have a bad day. They've got to come in every day and have a smile on their face, be ready to go, take shots all practice long, take 'em high and hard." Knowing that they are a target, some goaltenders will actually wear a thicker glove in practice for added protection.

Kevin Hodson, who backed up Chris Osgood in Detroit, boiled it down: "Ozzie would get the shots from the waist down, I'd get the shots from the waist up in practice. That was standard. You've got to just suck it up and take your lumps."

THE EVOLUTION OF THE GOALIE COACH

For the longest time, becoming a top-notch goaltender was a matter of trial and error. Coaches couldn't help. *I don't care how you stop it, just stop it. I'd rather you look bad stopping it than good letting it in* was a common life lesson.

"All the coaches were like, 'I don't know anything about goaltending. You just stop the puck.' You heard that over and over," said Pat Riggin, who played from 1978 to 1988. He followed his father into the game, so at least he had someone to talk to about goaltending.

Dick Irvin Jr. trailed his father into hockey too, but he became a Hall of Fame broadcaster instead of a head coach. Through his dad and his own job, he has met just about every player of the past 70 years. One was Gump Worsley.

Irvin recounted, "Gump used to tell a story, he came to Montreal and he thought, 'God, I've finally got a coach I can talk about goaltending to.' Toe Blake. The first game that they played, something went wrong, so he approaches Blake to ask him about it. Blake says, 'I don't know anything about it, I don't know anything about it! I can't talk to you about it!' And he walked away."

Irvin Sr. was equally ignorant about the mysteries of the net. Irvin revealed, "My dad was my hero, coaching in the National Hockey League, and the day he told me he knew absolutely nothing about goaltending, I was shattered. I thought he knew everything about everything when it came to hockey."

Goalie coaches started in the 1970s, but often their main task was taking their charge for coffee and talking about the game. Slowly, the role changed to on-ice advice, off-ice discussions, and study of video. Like quarterback or offensive line advisors in football, goalie coaches play important roles on their teams.

The first acknowledged goalie coach was Denis DeJordy, who played with the 1974–75 Detroit Red Wings. He had essentially been pushed to the sidelines to make way for a couple of promising keepers. Terry Richardson, the 11th overall draft pick out of New Westminster, BC, was one of them. "I don't really recall a whole lot of coaching going on. I don't think he was the happiest guy in that part of his career," said Richardson, now a scout for the Washington Capitals.

DeJordy, who will forever be remembered as the man who replaced Glenn Hall in the Chicago net to end Mr. Goalie's incredible streak of 502 regular season starts (or, if you use Hall's sum, 1,024 starts, which includes his consecutive junior and minor-pro matches, with playoffs), knew his job in Detroit. "They had two young goaltenders. That's why they decided to just have somebody in charge of the goaltenders," he said.

His real difficulty was knowing what to teach. Another young charge for DeJordy in his second year as a goalie coach was Jim Rutherford. DeJordy said, "He had a style of his own, and at that time, it was tough. I was a stand-up goaltender and Jimmy was a butterfly style, so I could not really work with butterfly because I believe in stand-up goaltenders."

Rutherford, the general manager in Pittsburgh, after two decades running the Hartford Whalers/Carolina Hurricanes, has given the role of goaltender coach more thought than most.

"I think in those days, it was an idea that they felt was right, but the guys that worked at it in those days didn't do as much coaching as the guys do today," he said.

The first full-time goalie coach was Warren Strelow. He'd played goal as a youth and befriended Herb Brooks, who hired Strelow to work with the keepers at the University of Minnesota, a perennial powerhouse in NCAA hockey. Brooks took Strelow along when he coached Team USA at the 1980 Lake Placid Olympics, including their "Miracle on Ice" win. He took Strelow along again in 2002, when Brooks led the collection of pros to a silver medal, losing to Canada in Salt Lake City.

In 1983, the Washington Capitals gave Strelow the task of mentoring the goalies in the system. One of them was Bob Mason, now the goalie coach with the Minnesota Wild. After Strelow's death in 2007, Mason recalled, "He was my goalie coach for four years in Washington. He had this image of being a gruff guy but, with his goalies, he was always positive."

With the Caps and during his subsequent years with New Jersey and San Jose, Strelow worked with a who's who of goaltending: a rookie Martin Brodeur, Miikka Kiprusoff, Evgeni Nabokov, Sean Burke, Al Jensen, Pat Riggin, Pete Peeters, Clint Malarchuk, Mason, Craig Billington, Chris Terreri, Corey Schwab, Johan Hedberg, and Vesa Toskala.

In simple terms, there are two things for a goalie coach to work on: mental and physical conditioning. Some believe they go hand in hand, like Carter Hutton, who was given the reins in Nashville in 2013–14 after years in Chicago's system. "For me, personally, I stay away from the mental side of it. I think you take care of yourself, and hard work and the technical side of it will take care of the mental side. Because the better you feel, confident in net, the more it'll help your play, which will help you mentally," he said.

The head coach has to know when to step in and when not to, according to former Coach of the Year Mike Keenan. He said, "When you're in there coaching, [goaltending's] probably the most critical position so you have to try and manage them and help them get ready, help them learn to get ready and prepare to play and to win. I think there's a lot of technical skill involved in their prep, but there's probably a lot more mental skill than anything."

Kirk Muller, the new coach for the Hurricanes in the 2012–13 season, asked his GM, Rutherford, to back him in limiting the amount of on-ice time for the goalie coach. "He doesn't want our goalie coach on the ice every day, like we've had over the last few years. He wants Greg Stefan around probably half the time with the big team, and then working with our guys in the AHL and the prospects," confirmed Rutherford.

On the ice, the goalie coaches vary from former players to the professional goaltending gurus whose expertise has risen in demand over the past 20 years. The Allaire brothers, François and Benoit, are probably the most well known of the gurus. François gained fame working with Patrick Roy and Jean-Sébastien Giguère, and he preaches a very rigid system.

"He had an answer for every save, and you really weren't able to do much else. He's very strict and very structured in his guidelines," said Corey Hirsch, a former pupil who's adapted some of Allaire's techniques to his own teachings.

Rick St. Croix replaced François Allaire, working with the goaltenders in Toronto in September 2012. "Work with what they have, that's always been my philosophy," said St. Croix, adding, "I don't come in and say these are the parameters, this is how you're going to play. That's not the way I feel it should be handled."

Mitch Korn is exhibit A in the new school of goalie coaches. While coaching NCAA Division I hockey at Miami of Ohio, he made the fortuitous decision to lend a hand at a hockey camp one summer in Buffalo. Then–Sabres coach Rick Dudley happened to walk in on the session, where Korn had a videotape playing and was quizzing the students on what the goalie should do next. Dudley decided that depth of analysis would benefit his team, and within a year Korn had come aboard part-time, for the 1991–92 season.

Was he in over his head? Of course. "Remember the commercial for the deodorant 'Never Let Them See You Sweat'? That was the approach. You can't show weakness. Be yourself," Korn said.

Replacing veteran Doug Favell in Buffalo, Korn brought a new attitude: "A lot of the goalie guys coached on instinct and what they did as a player, whereas I had a chance to hone my skills at the university level with a little more science, and got a chance to get my philosophies in place before I got to pro hockey."

And then along came Dominik Hasek, with his unorthodox style of stopping the puck with his helmet or the butt of his stick. Korn was up for the challenge, once the Sabres let him near the newcomer: "Hasek had unbelievable skills, but in my opinion, he didn't have any order. My job was to take the 1,000-piece jigsaw puzzle that it takes to play goal—Dom had all the pieces. A lot of guys, if it's a 1,000 pieces, they have 800 pieces, 900 pieces, the guys that don't make it have 300 pieces. Dom had all 1,000 pieces, they just weren't put together yet."

Like Korn (who is now with Nashville), Dave Prior of the Washington Capitals didn't have any background as a goaltender himself. His years as a hockey scout honed his ability to deal with players, and his low-key demeanour and quiet voice—the Goalie Whisperer?—have been positive attributes, starting with the Winnipeg Jets in 1990.

But unlike Korn or François Allaire, Prior doesn't necessarily promote change. He explained:

I've always worked with what the goaltender wants himself. I'm not one who implements a certain way of playing. We ask all of our guys to work and train in a certain way, but how they stop the puck is not something I dictate to them. I've come to feel that you have a much better chance of developing guys if you are willing to accept them as they are and work with what they bring to their game. When you're talking about pros, many of those kids when they come into the NHL or the American League, are pretty established in how they're playing the game. It's correcting what isn't working for them. I tell all our guys, 'Even if you do something that I don't agree with, if it's working for you, I'm not going to ask you to change just to satisfy me.' In that way, I think I've always been more tolerant maybe than some of the modern-day goaltending coaches.

In the end, it's about relationships. The goalie coach can act as a buffer between the keepers and the head coach (and management). Bruce Racine, who played 11 NHL games in 1995–96, likened it to having a lawyer in your corner. They are bound by client confidentiality, but they can also advocate on your behalf with the coaches or GM. "Maybe I had a bad game or something, he would be the go-between, and be my lawyer to go to the head coach and explain why it was a bad game or why it was a goal, or what happened on that goal, or why I should start the next game," he said.

Trust in your goalie coach, preached Keith Allain, who has worked with goalies in the U.S. national program, St. Louis, and Washington and is now the head coach at Yale. "If you're halfway decent as a goalie coach, it's a relationship where you get them to understand that all you want is for them to enhance their career. You're clearly there to help them every step of the way," said Allain. "Sometimes as a head coach, there can be some adversarial aspects to it, or conflict. But usually with a goalie coach, if they understand you're there for their benefit, you're a tool that can help their career, it does lead to a great relationship."

The goaltending coach is a confidant who builds confidence.

"There's a lot of good players and everyone can work on the same things technically and go out on the ice and teach the same sort of things, but at the end of the day, the goalie that's the most

Chris Mason seeks the counsel of the Predators' goalie coach, Mitch Korn, in April 2004. (Courtesy Mitch Korn)

confident that believes in himself has the best chance of succeeding," said Sean Burke, a Canadian Olympian and NHL-veteran turned goalie coach in Phoenix.

In his four years mentoring goalies in Buffalo, Favell drew on his own experiences in the nets. He said, "It's all about keeping your goaltender's confidence up. I remember, God, at times you're struggling. My second year in Philly, I was struggling. When you're going great, the puck looks like a beachball, and when you're going bad, it looks like an Aspirin. I can simplify goaltending into that."

CHAPTER 1

THE EARLY DAYS

THERE IS NO single position in professional sports that has changed more than that of the hockey goaltender; the rules have been amended, the equipment has been adjusted both for safety and puckstopping, and the styles have evolved from strictly stand-up to butterflying to a hybrid of the two.

For all the differences in the ways Georges Vezina and George Hainsworth played versus modern-day netminders, they would still be able to empathize with the basic pressures the Jonathan Quicks and Marty Brodeurs of today face. It doesn't matter when you stood in goal; you're the last line of defence and sole protector of the six-by-four goal. That being said, neither they nor Clint Benedict, the first goalie to wear a mask, would recognize the armoured warriors flopping to the ice in the current game, the equipment's changed that much.

Organized ice hockey has been around in some form since the 1870s, and the "Montreal Rules" were laid down in 1886, establishing consistency in the game. In the 15 rules of the world's first hockey league, the Amateur Hockey Association of Canada, it was stated that "the goal keeper must not, during the play, lie, kneel or sit up on the ice, but must maintain a standing position."

There was no special equipment. The net used to be two 6-foot high posts, 6 feet apart, marked by flags. Later, the height was lowered to 4 feet and a crossbar was added.

Like the game itself, which changed from seven players aside to six, added forward passing, and allowed substitutions, the evolution of goaltending did not happen overnight. Goaltender pads—cricket pads, really—made their way into the sport in the early 1890s; after George "Whitey" Merritt of the Winnipeg Victorias wore pads in a Stanley Cup challenge against the Montreal Victorias, their use became widespread.

Goalies and defencemen have been allowed thicker blades on their sticks for years, but that changed too, and it was the netminders who stuck with the bigger weapons; the formation of the National Hockey League, for the 1917 season, established the paddle blade width at 3½ inches. Depending on a keeper's playing style, the "lie" of the blade—the angle of the "L" portion between the shaft and paddle—could be modified as well.

With the guardians of the cage not allowed to handle the puck, there was no need for gloves. By the 1910s, thicker gloves became the norm for all players. Over time, a padded glove on the dominant hand became a blocker, designed to protect the hand and wrist that were controlling the stick. The other hand held a trapper, a glove that was initially based on the idea of a baseball catcher's glove but that has evolved into a streamlined instrument for nabbing pucks in the air.

Other objects in the air were more difficult to defend against. In the early days, goalies were prime targets for fans—opposition or disgruntled homers—who hurled everything from empty bottles to batteries in their direction, often timed to force a misplay on a shot.

You had to watch opposing players for projectiles too. In a 1969 interview, Jake Forbes told a Toronto newspaper, "Newsy Lalonde came around the net and caught me in the eye with his stick. I went . . . to protest to the referee . . . He said he had not seen the incident and sent me back to the net. The next time Lalonde came down to my end of the ice, I went out to stop him, using a high stick if possible. He skated to the side and spat his tobacco juice in my face and, when I fell, skated around me to score."

Also alien to the modern fan would be the early day rinks.

"I've seen them lining up at six o'clock in the morning for a game that night at Quebec's Grand Alley rink," said Paddy Moran in 1944 of his days with the Quebec Bulldogs from 1910 to 1916. "We played to gas-light. The rink held only 1,400 but sometimes there would be 2,000 there." In the *Montreal Star* article Moran also figured his total earnings throughout his career was $4,000, with the average wage for a season being $500.

In 1939, Redvers "Red" Mackenzie wrote a series of articles for the *Washington Post* that introduced the game of hockey to the area. He noted how difficult it was to compare the past to the action he was watching at the time. "George Vezina was great. He never went to his knees or fell to the ice to smother a shot, but he never played in the days when forward passing was allowed in the attacking zone, and this is a different age," wrote Mackenzie, citing Frank Brimsek, Charlie Gardiner, and Dave Kerr as the top trio of his day.

The March 14, 1938, edition of *Time* magazine tried to explain both hockey and the lonely men in the nets to the masses: "Target of whizzing pucks, he must be nimble as a squirrel, sharp-eyed as a hawk. And since a perfect performance for him is a shut-out, he works for naught on the scoreboard."

In 1918, an amendment to the rules permitted goalies to leave their feet to make a save, with Frank Calder, president of the National Hockey League, decreeing that "they can fall on their knees, or stand on their heads" while trying to stop the puck. But it wasn't until the 1930s that a goaltender was actually allowed to catch—and hold onto—the puck.

Most of the credit for that change goes to Clint Benedict. In his *Globe and Mail* column "On the Highways of Sport," M.J. Rodden wrote, "Goaltending has changed a lot since the days when Benedict broke in. Net-guardians then were not permitted to fall down when stopping shots, but Benedict never bothered much about that rule, and he became hockey's greatest stumbler. The 'praying goalkeeper' they called him, and Benedict often served sentences for such offences, until finally the magnates ruled that goalkeepers could do as they pleased."

Benedict may have also been the first to add some showmanship to his position. "In contrast to Georges Vezina, who played his position standing straight and without any antics," wrote Charles L. Coleman in his 1964 epic, *The Trail of the Stanley Cup*, "Benedict put on a continuous show in the nets. His proclivity of hopping to the ice when the pressure was on necessitated a rule change. The officials claimed that the game would become a farce with frequent penalties to Benedict for going to the ice to make saves."

The 1890s saw the debut of specialized skates just for goalies, but today's blades allow for movement forward, backward, and sideways that could not have been imagined then.

"You've got to be the best skater on the team," said '70s goalie Paul Harrison, adding that the ability to skate well has always been an overlooked skill for a goaltender. "All of your agility, timing, reflexes, all your skills come from your ability to skate. That's certainly your balance."

Today's better skates and lighter equipment have allowed goalies to venture farther afield, into the corners, and act like a third defenceman.

The defence and the goaltender have to work together, and Percy LeSueur's advice in his 1909 book, *How to Play Hockey*, still rings true today: "Have your defense play what is known as the open game—as that gives the goal-keeper a much better chance to see the puck and follow its movements."

The changes to the rest of the equipment are pretty obvious. Brave men who stood in net without a mask and wearing rudimentary pads stuffed with deer hair, a homemade protective cup, and maybe a little felt sewn into a jersey gave way to masked men who hacked away at the gear that the skaters wore to create functional gear to fit the action. Today, the outcry over the size of the lightweight, scientifically engineered goaltending equipment—the pads, the catching mitt, the blocker, specialized skates—is a regular topic for fans and pundits and is brought up at the general manager meetings.

Those equipment changes allowed goalies to adapt their style in the net as well. The ban on going to the ice resulted in stand-up goaltending, sure, but think about the simple principle of human nature and fear. Today's keepers can drop to their knees in the butterfly position, legs splayed to cover the entire bottom of the net, without a worry in the world. Without a mask, who in their right mind would purposely put their face in the way when the brunt of the shot could be absorbed by their legs or arms instead?

Time to find out.

THE FIRST NAMES IN GOALTENDING

GEORGES VEZINA The Vezina Trophy, presented to the NHL's top goaltender, is an award that is familiar to all hockey fans. It's named after Georges Vezina of the Montreal Canadiens, who played from 1910 until 1925 and died in 1926 of tuberculosis at age 39. The Chicoutimi, Quebec, native made his National Hockey Association debut in the Canadiens net in 1910–11 and stayed there until illness knocked him out. Four months after the disease forced him from a game, he was dead. He was consistently one of the top keepers in the NHA/NHL, establishing the standard for stand-up goaltending, and helped the Canadiens to one Stanley Cup, losing out on a couple of other challenges—plus he was the guardian during the 1919 Cup Final against the Seattle Metropolitans, which was cancelled due to an influenza epidemic.

GEORGE HAINSWORTH

GEORGE HAINSWORTH A

less well-known award is the George Hainsworth Memorial Trophy. Hainsworth played in the NHL from 1926 to 1937, and in some ways he surpassed the great Vezina—beyond being the goaltender who replaced the legend in the Canadiens' net. Born in Toronto in 1893, Hainsworth spent his early hockey years in Berlin (now Kitchener), Ontario, playing his junior and senior hockey there. After a couple of seasons with the Western Canada Hockey League's Saskatoon Crescents, Hainsworth was brought up to the NHL. Suitably, he won the first three Vezina Trophies.

Hainsworth played in Toronto from 1933 to 1936, finishing up with a final four games with the Canadiens after signing as a free agent in December 1936. His greatest season, and maybe the greatest ever for a goaltender, statistically speaking, came in 1928–29, when he recorded 22 shutouts in a 44-game season, with only 43 goals getting past him all season.

Upon his death in October 1951, the George Hainsworth Memorial Trophy, the hardware having been donated by the barnstorming Carling-Kuntz touring softball team in April 1951, was established by the Ontario Hockey Association to honour the "hockey player chosen as most valuable and sportsmanlike from among OHA teams competing in Kitchener and Waterloo arenas."

Hainsworth—who was an alderman in Kitchener and helped spearhead the construction of the city's showcase rink, where the OHL's community-owned Kitchener Rangers still play—was inducted into the Hockey Hall of Fame in 1961.

In March 1950, Hainsworth told the *Toronto Star*'s Milt Dunnell, "I have three of those Vezina replicas in my attic. The winning goalie gets a thousand bucks now, and the club duplicates that. So those three little trophies would be worth $6,000 at today's rates. There was no cash award when I won them. Leo Dandurand of the Montreal club told me the actual value of the replica was $60. So, after I'd won it once, I suggested he give me the $60 and put a little shield on the original trophy for each of the two additional wins. Leo didn't like the idea."

Vezina, the "Chicoutimi Cucumber," and "Little" George Hainsworth are just two of the significant names—with some great nicknames—from the early years of the NHL, which was established in 1917.

Others in the Hockey Hall of Fame from the pre–Original Six era (which began in 1942) include the players profiled here.

CLINT "PRAYING BENNY" BENEDICT (1892–1976)

In the spirit of Benedict's nickname, the Holy Trinity of goalkeeping of the early years was Vezina, Hainsworth, and Benedict. And while Vezina's name lives on through the trophy, Benedict's influence on the game was certainly his most important contribution. Not only did he force the change that allowed goaltenders to drop to the ice to stop the puck—"You had to do something," he said in the *Ottawa Citizen* in 1965. "Quite a few of the players could put a curving drop on a shot, and the equipment wasn't exactly the greatest in those days"—but he was the first to wear a mask in a game. The set-up to the mask was January 7, 1930, and Benedict was in net for the Montreal Maroons against the Canadiens. Benedict told the *Citizen*, "It isn't too hard to recall it. Jimmy Ward accidentally screened me and Howie Morenz hit me right on the bridge of the nose with a drive from 25 feet. I woke up in hospital and I wasn't right for a month."

Though he recovered from the shattered cheekbone, his vision remained clouded and never improved. Over the final games of his career, Benedict tried out a couple of models: a Boston firm designed a heavy, awkward leather mask for him, and another was closer to that of a baseball catcher's mask. The Maroons didn't think he would get better and released him outright in November 1931. Benedict spent a final season with the team's farm club in Windsor, Ontario, winning the International Hockey League title, a nice complement to his four Stanley Cups (three with the Ottawa Senators and one with the Maroons, during which he counted three shutouts in a four-game victory over the Victoria Cougars in the 1926 final). He tried refereeing but eventually settled into life as a municipal clerk in Ottawa. He was inducted into the Hockey Hall of Fame in 1965. For the final two decades of his life, he was confined to a wheelchair.

ALEX "THE OTTAWA FIREMAN" CONNELL

(1900–1958) When Connell died, teammate Tommy Gorman recalled "the greatest goalkeeping performance in the history of hockey." The game was in Toronto in 1935.

"It was in the Stanley Cup playoffs when the Maroons were two men short. For three minutes, Connell put on an astounding effort against the Leafs and the Maroons went on to win the Cup," said Gorman.

As great as it was, consider that Connell also holds the NHL record for consecutive shutouts, with six from January 31 to February 18, 1928, or 460 minutes and 49 seconds. He had 81 career shutouts and won two Stanley Cups, playing primarily for the first incarnation of the Ottawa Senators but also for the Detroit Falcons, New York Americans, and Montreal Maroons. Connell, who usually wore a black cap while in net and was a notorious prankster, excelled in baseball as a catcher, playing in the Interprovincial League, and in lacrosse, helping Ottawa win successive Eastern Canadian League championships in the 1920s. He coached the Ottawa Senators of the Quebec Hockey League in the 1940s but gave it up in 1949 because of ill health. As for his nickname, he worked for the Ottawa fire department from 1921 to 1950, as a secretary to a succession of fire chiefs.

"SMILING" CHARLIE GARDINER *(1904–1934)*

A triumph and a tragedy, the flashy Gardiner went out on top. His best season was 1933–34, when he served as the captain of the Chicago Black Hawks, claimed the Vezina Trophy as the NHL's best goaler, and won the Stanley Cup. Eight weeks later, he was dead at 29; he collapsed on a street in his hometown of Winnipeg, Manitoba, and died on the operating table as doctors attempted to remove a tumour from his brain. He had a remarkable 42 shutouts over 316 games through seven NHL seasons and another five in 21 playoff games, on some not-so-great teams.

"He grinned his way through the toughest going with a team in front of him that could hardly be called good for major league competition," wrote Redvers "Red" Mackenzie, adding, "He had his angles down pat and never seemed to bog down or give up even when his team failed to give him the protection that a junior goalie would expect."

In *A Breed Apart*, Elmer Ferguson expressed how Gardiner "bounced and dived around, shouted an endless flow of encouragement or advice to his teammates, occasionally exchanged jovial repartees with nearby customers, and often shouted jibes at opposing players as they bore in on him." Gardiner was inducted into the Hall in 1945.

HARRY "HAP" HOLMES *(1888–1941)* "Few men gave

as much of their lifetime to professional hockey as a player, as a coach, and as a manager as Aurora [Ontario]'s quiet-talking, conscientious Hap," wrote Vern DeGeer, the sports editor of the *Globe and Mail*, upon Holmes's passing. Holmes was the first man to claim the Stanley Cup with four different teams (Toronto Blueshirts, Seattle Metropolitans, Toronto Arenas, Victoria Cougars) and challenged for the Cup on three other occasions. He finished off his career with two seasons on an expansion NHL team, the Detroit Cougars

Tiny Thompson stops a shot against the Maple Leafs at the Boston Garden, circa 1938. (Courtesy Trustees of the Boston Public Library, Leslie Jones Collection)

(now the Red Wings), before coaching and managing in Kitchener, Ontario, and then introducing professional hockey to Cleveland, Ohio. The Hall enshrined him in 1972.

CECIL "TINY" THOMPSON *(1903–1981)* When
Phil Esposito of the Bruins took on brother Tony, who was in the Chicago net, in the 1970 Stanley Cup playoffs, writers sought out the story of Paul and Tiny Thompson, the only other brother goalie-forward combination to face each other in the Stanley Cup playoffs. At that point, Tiny was a scout in Western Canada for the Hawks. "When I played goal for Boston against Paul and [the] New York Rangers in the final of 1929, he was just a rookie. It was really no contest. We beat them two straight in a best-of-three series," Tiny said in a *Toronto Star* article. The nickname "Tiny" was ironic, as

he was 5-foot-10 and about 170 pounds. His early hockey was in Minnesota, until the Boston Bruins bought his rights.

"Almost unpassable if given any chance to save. Has an eye like a hawk and moves to meet a puck with lightning-like rapidity. Uses wonderful judgment in clearing," reads a *Lethbridge Herald* story on him. He played 553 NHL games, for a 284-194-75 record, with 81 shutouts; in the playoffs, he was 20-24-0, with 7 shutouts. The Hall called Thompson in 1959. "It goes without saying that I am both happy and proud to become a member of such a select group," Thompson wrote back to the Hall's Bobby Hewitson.

ROY "SHRIMP" WORTERS *(1900–1957)* There is
a scrapbook that was kept by Worters's grandson on file at the Hockey Hall of Fame (which inducted Worters in 1969). It is full of delightful stories on "a veritable hockey pygmy" who is "scarcely larger than a beer stein" from years gone by. One story describes how "Worters has such small and delicate hands that he seldom catches the puck and tosses it aside like so many of the other goalies, but contents himself with batting it, or pushing it away." In another, Worters himself tells Frank Graham that his size, 5-foot-3, was not a factor:

> It always has seemed to me that talent, rather than size, makes a man a good goalie and that there is no reason why he should succeed or fail according to his size. The greatest goaltender that ever lived was Vezina, who was 6-foot-2 inches tall, and next to him John Ross Roach, who is about 5-feet-4. If a big man can make saves simply by moving his stick an inch or two or putting out his hand, as Vezina did, a small man who is agile can do the same by moving quickly and with just a little energy, as Roach always has done.

While Worters himself brought energy to the cage, he was on

woeful teams like the Pittsburgh Pirates and New York Americans, though he did force an unheard-of $8,000 salary from the latter in 1928. He earned it, being named the Hart Trophy winner as the league MVP for 1928–29.

"I often wonder what heights Worters might have reached had he had an outstanding club in front of him instead of the poor old Americans, the orphans of the storm," wrote Red Dutton in a letter to the Hockey Hall of Fame that supported Worters's induction.

There are countless stories of his toughness, like continuing to play after getting hit in the windpipe and only being able to eat mushed food, the 200 stitches in his face, or playing with a fractured hand in a cast, with his stick and glove taped to his body. A January 1937 hernia operation forced him to give hockey a rest, and he moved into business, first as a salesman for a Toronto brewery and then as the owner of a couple of hotels near Toronto's airport, including the Conroy Hotel with old teammate Charlie Conacher.

While these names dominate talk of the early days of organized hockey, others who came before them have been forgotten. Here's a reminder of some of them, a few who even pre-date the NHL.

FORGOTTEN FORERUNNERS

RILEY HERN *(1878–1929)* Following early success in his hometown of St. Marys, Ontario, and nearby Stratford, Hern turned pro with the Western Pennsylvania Hockey League's Pittsburgh Keystones in 1901–02. After a couple more seasons with the International Hockey League's Houghton-Portage Lakes, Hern jumped out of his contract with Portage Lake (IHL) to sign with the Montreal Wanderers (Eastern Canada Amateur Hockey Association) in 1906. In Montreal, he would win three Stanley Cups (1907, 1908, 1910).

"Hern played in the days before the big ten-inch pads, when a goaler wore the shin guards for personal protection and counted on stopping pucks by his skill and agility. In his peak years with Wanderers, he was one of the best goaltenders of his time," wrote D.A.L. MacDonald in a flashback column in the *Montreal Gazette*.

During his career, Hern operated a Montreal clothing store, and post-hockey he became a Montreal businessman specializing in boating, as well as a great booster of the local baseball team. He retired from hockey in 1911, taking up as referee and goal judge and was inducted into the Hall in 1962.

BOUSE HUTTON *(1877–1962)* How good of an athlete was

Hutton? He claimed Minto Cups before and during his hockey career for his play in net as a lacrosse goaltender; in 1902, he was a fullback on the Ottawa Rough Riders team that won the Canadian football championship; and there are his two Stanley Cups with the Ottawa Silver Seven (1903, 1904). "Hutton has it on any custodian in Canada as a fielder behind his nets," reads a *Toronto Star* story about his lacrosse skills. His obituary called him a "flashy" goalie. The Hall tabbed him for induction in 1963.

"PEERLESS" PERCY LESUEUR *(1881–1962)*

Inducted in 1961, LeSueur was handling the puck with a deft touch 40 years before Jacques Plante popularized the strategy. No doubt it helped that he was originally a right winger. While playing for a senior team in Smiths Falls, Ontario, he was called upon to play net. Smiths Falls challenged unsuccessfully against Ottawa for the Stanley Cup in early March 1906, with LeSueur protecting the cage. Shortly thereafter, he joined the Ottawa squad and played there for eight seasons, followed by stints with the Toronto Shamrocks (1914–15) and the Toronto Blueshirts (1915–16).

"Percy LeSueur is one of the greatest students of hockey. He is always trying to learn some new wrinkles and also always trying to teach others what he knows of the game. He very seldom has a bad night and can be depended upon to hold a wobbly defence together," reads a 1912 *Calgary Herald* story. After he retired from his netminding duties, he kept involved with the game as a referee and columnist for the *Hamilton Spectator* and by managing arenas, coaching, and offering his opinion—he was an original member of *Hockey Night in Canada*'s Hot Stove Lounge panel. LeSueur was also involved in an ownership group that bought the Detroit Cougars (now the Red Wings) and wrote and published a booklet called *How to Play Hockey* in 1909. The net that was popularly used from 1912 to 1925 was designed by LeSueur.

PADDY MORAN *(1877–1966)* Moran stayed home in Quebec City for the bulk of his career (with the exception of a short stay with the National Hockey Association's Haileybury squad) and jealously protected his crease, going so far as to use his stick like a hatchet.

"Some nights Paddy was so good that he was unbeatable," remarked Russell Bowie in a 1934 *Montreal Gazette* article, adding, "Then I knew I had to get his goat to score on him." Sometimes, Bowie would get Moran so worked up that Moran would chase him to the other end of the rink.

Backstopping the Quebec Bulldogs in various leagues, Moran claimed two Stanley Cup titles, in 1912 and 1913. A 1912 rating of goalies in the *Calgary Herald* puts him tops: "Paddy at times was backed up by a team of indifferent merit, but his work did not suffer as a consequence, and many a victory for the ancient city's team can be credited to his prowess in the nets." Moran, a customs house employee in Quebec after his hockey career, was inducted into the Hockey Hall of Fame in 1958.

A number of keepers overlap eras, including those profiled here.

CROSSOVER KEEPERS

FRANK "MR. ZERO" BRIMSEK *(1915–1998)* Brimsek

was playing for a beer company in Baltimore when he was discovered and brought up to the Pittsburgh Yellow Jackets of the Eastern Amateur Hockey League. After a couple of seasons there, he went east to the International-American Hockey League's Providence Reds, where Providence indeed smiled down on him, as he was called up to Boston early in the 1938–39 season. With the Bruins, Brimsek became the first goalie to win both the Calder and Vezina Trophies in the same year.

Harold Kaese described him as "an acrobat and magician, dancing Cossack, target for tonight—Brimsek is all of these and more. He is also a fire-eater, a sword swallower, and a human pincushion. For him, as for every other goalie, a hockey game is a physical and mental ordeal."

He'd play in Beantown until 1949, minus war-time service, including protecting the net for the U.S. Coast Guard Cutters. He wasn't the same player afterward, though, and even the rules had changed, including the addition of the red line. "I kind of lost my enthusiasm," Brimsek said. He'd also always had difficulty with his health. "Any time Brimmy said he felt good, we knew we were in for a bad night," said Bruins captain Milt Schmidt in *Without Fear*.

"The Goose-Egg Kid" played one last season, 1949–50 in Chicago, and walked away from the game, giving his equipment to Red Hamill's 12-year-old son. He worked as an engineer on the Canadian National Railway post-hockey.

BILL DURNAN *(1916–1972)* In the *Boston Traveler* news-

paper, just a few months before Durnan retired, the legendary Art Ross said that the Montreal Canadiens goalie was the best of the modern age. "While you can't compare the old game with the

Bill Durnan and Turk Broda shake hands following Toronto's win in Game 6 of the Stanley Cup Final on April 19, 1947, at Maple Leaf Gardens. (Imperial Oil – Turofsky/Hockey Hall of Fame)

present one, it may be that he's the greatest of them all. The more I see of Durnan, the greater he gets. He can do everything and he's at the very peak of his game despite his age," Ross said.

But Durnan quit after that 1949–50 season, taking a job with Canadian Breweries, Ltd. "I'd had enough. At 35, at the peak of my career, I felt it was time to move on elsewhere," Durnan told the *Globe and Mail* not long before his death in 1972. So after seven NHL seasons and six Vezina Trophies (1944, 1945, 1946, 1947, 1949, 1950), Durnan, the ambidextrous goalie from Toronto who also excelled at softball, was done.

After his early years on Toronto teams, he went to the Kirkland Lake Blue Devils of the Northern Ontario Senior League for four seasons and then the Montreal Royals of Quebec's circuit for three more. It was there that Montreal GM Tommy Irvin decided he was the Habs goalie; Durnan played hard to get, arguing he was making good money as an amateur, and sat out training camp in 1943.

"Opening night in Montreal arrived and Gorman still did not have Durnan's signature. Ten minutes before the faceoff, Gorman finally mentioned the figures for which Durnan would play. He signed the contract, rushed down the hall, and got into his uniform. Practically without a warm-up, he held [the] Boston Bruins to a 2-2 draw in his first game as a big leaguer," wrote *Toronto Star* sports editor Milt Dunnell after Durnan's death in 1972, six years after his HHOF induction.

An exceedingly modest man, Durnan was always quick to credit his teammates or good fortune for his success. In 1948, Durnan told *The Hockey News*, "Goaling has a certain amount of luck to it. Often a guy will flop down on a puck. It looks like a great save and he draws an ovation from the crowd. Actually the puck just comes to him and he falls on it, it's just a simple rolling puck and an easy save."

WALTER "TURK" BRODA (1914–1972) The fact that

Broda was the first NHL goalie to play 100 playoff games, with a 1-0 Maple Leafs loss to Detroit on March 27, 1952, speaks to the quality of his work and the excellence of the teams in front of him. A star keeper out of Brandon, Manitoba, he was signed by the Red Wings in 1935 and led the team's International Hockey League franchise, the Detroit Olympics, to the title in 1935–36. The Leafs took notice and bought Broda for $8,000; in turn, he brought them five Stanley Cup championships (1942, 1947, 1948, 1949, 1951) and two Vezina Trophies (1941, 1948).

Through his tenure in Toronto, which ended in 1952, Broda was always a good sport. In 1949, owner Conn Smythe launched a fat purge targeted at Turk's bulging waistline. "That was a development which he accepted with typical joviality, posing in steam boxes, in towels and being deluged with phone calls from well-meaning people who heaped diet suggestions on his willing ears. When the Royal Couple visited the Gardens, for instance, to watch a 15 minute exhibition game between the Leafs and the Black Hawks, Walter's entrance to play half of the game drew almost as much applause from the gallery of kids as did the arrival of the Royal Visitors themselves," wrote Toronto columnist Bob Hesketh, attesting to Broda's popularity.

After hanging up the pads, he started a long career as a coach, including for the Weston Dukes of Toronto's Junior B league; the Ottawa Senators of the Quebec Hockey League; the Ontario Hockey Association's Toronto Marlboros for seven seasons, including two Memorial Cups; the Eastern Hockey League's Charlotte Checkers; the OHA's London Nationals; and the American Hockey League's Quebec Aces. Ken Broderick was one of Broda's goalies with the Marlies, and he shared Turk's lesson: "He always said, 'Stay on your feet. If you're going to fall to your knees, that puck had better be underneath you.' That was his philosophy." Broda was inducted into the Hall in 1967 and died two weeks before his great rival, Bill Durnan.

NOTABLE OTHERS

BILL BEVERIDGE (1909–1995) Mired on far too many poor teams (he was in net for the final NHL games for two doomed clubs, the Montreal Maroons and St. Louis Eagles), Beveridge never got a lot of respect during his playing career, bouncing from team to team on loans or trades, though his career was extended by the need for players while World War II raged. "There's very little difference between goalies once they get into the NHL," he said in a 1965 Ottawa newspaper story, when he was working in real estate. When the Ottawa Senators returned to the NHL in 1992, he was one of the few in town (where he had been a city councillor and a hockey coach at Carleton University) who dated back to the original team, and he was on hand to see the puck dropped for the new version.

LORNE CHABOT *(1900–1946)*

When old-time names are mentioned as deserving induction into the Hockey Hall of Fame, Chabot's name comes up the most. Famed scribe Jim Coleman made his case in 1991 for the keeper who played for the Rangers, Maple Leafs, Canadiens, Black Hawks, and Maroons: "Lorne Chabot was an unjustly ignored man. Never has he been elected to the Hall of Fame; despite his all-star selection, his Vezina Trophy, and his two Stanley Cup championships. In 11 NHL seasons, he yielded an average of only 2.12 goals per game. In nine years of Stanley Cup playoffs, he yielded an average of only 1.73 goals

LORNE CHABOT

per game. He had a total of 78 shutouts. His story is one of hockey's tragedies. After a long illness, he died in a Toronto hospital at the age of 46. He was broke." Coleman left off the Allan Cups during Chabot's time in Port Arthur (now Thunder Bay), Ontario, and the laughable ordeal of his New York debut, where the press was told his full name was Chabotsky to attract more Jewish clientele to Madison Square Garden. And really, as far as comedic lines describing goaltenders go, few beat his response to why he shaved before games: "Because I stitch better when my skin is smooth."

VERNON "JAKE" FORBES *(1897–1985)* One of the

first high-profile players to stand up against management, today "Jumpin' Jackie" Forbes is known as much for sitting out a season in a contract dispute (1921–22, with the Toronto St. Pats) and leading a team-wide rebellion (with the Hamilton Tigers, which resulted in the team becoming the New York Americans) as for his excellent skills as a keeper.

He explained the rebellion in Hamilton in 1969: "In those days we were not paid for playoffs, so all the Hamilton players decided to strike. The club suspended all of us and Montreal won by default. The Hamilton team folded that year and five of us were sold to a new team, New York Americans, for $85,000."

He played 210 NHL games (but just two more in the playoffs) during his 20-year pro career on some pretty weak teams. In the 1969 story, he also said he only ever got 11 stitches in his face and only broke one finger.

"MIRACLE" MIKE KARAKAS (1910–1992) A native of Aurora, Minnesota, Karakas was the first U.S.-born star goalie and was a surprise star on a desperate Chicago team in 1936. Signed as a free agent after toiling on American Hockey Association teams in St. Louis and Tulsa, he was the rookie of the year in '36.

"Miracle Mike was a blindfold grab-bag choice made by Manager Clem Loughlin when Lorne Chabot, voted the best goalie in the league last year, decided that it was not worthwhile working for what the Hawks were offering him," quipped John Kieran in his "Sports of the Times" column in the *New York Times*, adding, "When Clem draped the heavy upholstery on Rookie Karakas and pushed him out on ice to face the big league sharpshooters, it looked as though the only thing that could save the Hawks this year was the Federal Migratory Bird Law."

From there, though, there were real ups—a Cup in 1938, when Chicago had finished the regular season with a losing record, and Karakas played with a broken toe—and downs. In December 1940, he was sent to the Providence Reds but refused to report. While sitting around in Chicago, he was borrowed by the Canadiens, who needed a goalie for five games. When he reported to the American Hockey League team, he helped them win the Calder Cup. For six seasons, "Iron Mike" appeared in every one of Chicago's games.

Post-hockey, he was a sales executive outside of Boston. Though not in the Hockey Hall of Fame, he was in the initial class of 1973 for the United States Hockey Hall of Fame.

DAVE KERR *(1909–1979)* Until his own death in 2007, newspaperman David Kerr campaigned constantly for his father's induction into the Hockey Hall of Fame; after all, Dave Kerr is the only goalie to ever appear on the cover of *Time* magazine (March 14, 1938). In the files at the Hall, there's a letter solicited by the younger Kerr from General John Reed Kilpatrick, the former president of the New York Rangers and Madison Square Garden, calling the goalie "an unspectacular workman. Always a source of confidence to his teammates. He worked hard at the hard job of goaltending." Notable writers like Baz O'Meara and Dink Carroll have made their pitches as well. Kerr's best year was 1940, when he was an NHL First-Team All-Star, took the Vezina Trophy with a 1.54 GAA, and won the Stanley Cup with the New York Rangers. His NHL totals were 203-148-75 with 51 shutouts. Post-hockey, Kerr ran a motel in Belleville, Ontario. Upon his death, teammate Muzz Patrick recalled Kerr as "a very low-key type of man, very polite, and didn't swear like the rest of us athletes. He was a great guy and a great goaltender."

ALFIE MOORE *(1904–1984)* Moore played a decade in minor leagues before he cracked an NHL roster, recording a shutout in his debut, with the New York Americans against the Montreal Canadiens on January 30, 1937. Up until that point, the Toronto native had a good knowledge of geography, playing at home as a junior and senior for the Toronto Aura Lee and then the London Ravens before he finally got a chance at the pros, with the American Hockey Association's Chicago Cardinals, in January 1927. There were the Kitchener Millionaires/Dutchmen in the Can-Pro Hockey League, the International Hockey

League's Cleveland Indians, and in the Canadian-American Hockey League, the Springfield Indians, New Haven Eagles, Philadelphia Arrows, Providence Reds, and Boston Cubs.

After his NHL debut, it took two more years for another crack at the bigs. Moore is a classic example of a goalie who couldn't establish himself as one of the best in the world. His NHL totals are only 21 games (7-14-0, one shutout), but he played 580 pro games over the years in various leagues. The most famous game for Moore, however, was a playoff game. In the 1938 Stanley Cup playoffs, Chicago Black Hawks starter Mike Karakas broke his big toe in the last game of the semifinal. When the Hawks' plea to use Dave Kerr of the Rangers as an emergency backup was denied, legend has it that they found Moore in a neighbourhood bar. He led the Hawks to an upset of the Maple Leafs, 3-1, but was declared ineligible for the second game of the Stanley Cup Final.

JOHN ROSS ROACH (1900–1973) He was an All-Star goalie for the Detroit Red Wings and retired after the 1934–35 season having played a then–NHL record of 491 games, with 56 shutouts and a 2.54 goals-against average. But he is not in hockey's hallowed Hall. Born in Port Perry, Ontario, Roach started his pro career in Toronto in 1921–22, backstopping the Toronto St. Pats to a Stanley Cup in his debut season.

The diminutive Roach—just 5-foot-5—was a popular figure, the St. Pats' captain for 1925–26, and known for his acrobatics. Toronto traded him to the New York Rangers for Lorne Chabot and $10,000 in October 1928. A playoff flameout resulted in a fire sale to Detroit, where he finished out his career. The newspaper in Trois-Rivières, Quebec, the *St. Maurice Valley Chronicle*, assessed the end of Roach's career in 1935, saying that he was "never afraid to face the worst barrage of rubber that opponents could throw, an eye like a hawk's, and an agility that amazed incoming forwards."

CHAPTER 2

THE ORIGINAL SIX ERA

THE ERA FROM 1942–43 until the NHL expansion in 1967 is called the Original Six, in reference to the six teams that made up the league. To many, this was the golden era of the NHL. As far as goaltending is concerned, there were six jobs in the big league, and that was it—only the elite made it.

The greatest of the greats come from this era, and three in particular continue to define goaltending: Hall, Sawchuk, and Plante.

Their stories, each the subject of wonderful biographies, tell the tale of the evolution of the position.

With Glenn Hall, the outstanding keeper from Humboldt, Saskatchewan, it was all about endurance and the butterfly style. Surely no one will ever top his NHL-record streak of 502 consecutive games played in net, plus another 50 in the playoffs. Hall, however, insists his streak was actually much longer.

"Prior to that, I had played seven or eight years without missing a game, but that doesn't show up. For example, when I was in Edmonton, I went to Detroit and played a few games in a couple of seasons. So my record in Edmonton looks as though I missed some games there. That was because I was playing in Detroit. I was never hurt. I was lucky when it came to injuries," Hall said in *In the Crease: Goaltenders Look at Life in the NHL.*

Hall took the 1956 Calder Trophy as the NHL's top rookie, usurped Terry Sawchuk as starter in Detroit, won or shared in three Vezina Trophies, was an NHL All-Star 13 times, and claimed the 1961 Stanley Cup with the Black Hawks. In 1968, he was the playoff MVP on the losing St. Louis Blues squad.

There was a timeless element to Glenn "Mr. Goalie" Hall, who would serve as a goalie coach here and there in retirement. "I think you can play forever. [Johnny] Bower played forever and so did Gump [Worsley], as did myself. Expansion gave us, well, because they all seemed to want an old goalkeeper in expansion, it gave us extra years. Even when I retired, I think I was 40, and they still were offering me a contract and wanting me to play. It wasn't as if somebody had taken your place. I had played long enough," Hall said from his farm outside Edmonton.

Hall's influence continued far past his playing days.

The Pittsburgh Penguins hosted the fathers of the players one year, and ex-goalies Bob Johnson (father of Penguin backup Brent), goalie coach Gilles Meloche, and former general manager Eddie Johnston found themselves together at a table on the cruise around the city's harbour.

Brent, knowing his father's favourite, asked the table, "If you had to pick, who was the greatest goaltender that you saw play in your whole life?"

The response? "It was simultaneous 'Glenn Hall,'" said Bob Johnson. "Glenn Hall, to me, he changed the game. Even though he was a stand-up, he started the butterfly. He was phenomenal. He was a precursor to goaltenders today."

Terry Sawchuk, who was great on his feet, always square to the puck, and deep in his crouch, got a lot of praise from the shooters of the day. "If he was on, you couldn't get a pea by him. His positioning was terrific. He was very quick, he was like a cat. He's the

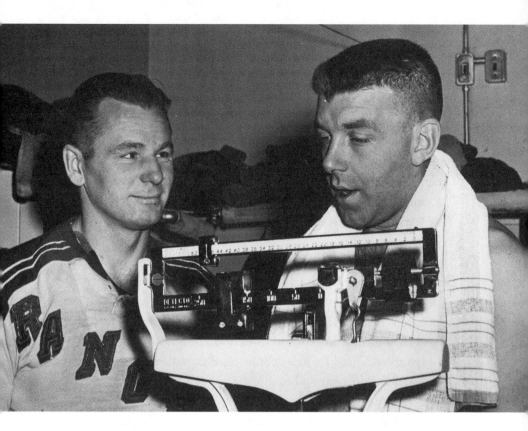

Johnny Bower and Lorne Worsley stand at the weigh scale during New York Rangers' Hockey School in Saskatoon in September 1955. (Photograph B-15312 by Leonard A. Hillyard, courtesy Saskatoon Public Library—Local History Room)

best goaltender I saw," said Don McKenney, a Boston centre in the 1950s who briefly counted Sawchuk as a teammate when he was traded to Beantown.

Hall himself called Sawchuk the greatest goalie he ever got to watch, and Sawchuk's Red Wings teammate Johnny Wilson said the Wings learned to live with Sawchuk's mood swings and lousy practice habits, as they felt lucky to have him stopping pucks. "None of us, even the ones who weren't all that crazy about Terry, would have traded him for any other goalie in hockey," Wilson said in *Shutout: The Legend of Terry Sawchuk.*

But Sawchuk's amazing accomplishments—21 seasons on five teams, 103 career shutouts, four Vezina Trophies, four Stanley Cups, Rookie of the Year honours in three leagues (the U.S. League, American Hockey League, and NHL)—sometimes get overshadowed by his assortment of crippling injuries and personal woes. He seemed to be a magnet for injuries; long before anyone even knew of him, he'd incurred an injury that would haunt him the rest of his life. While playing football at the age of 12, he hurt his right elbow, which caused him continual problems, leading to three surgeries over his lifetime, which removed 60 bone chips and left his right arm two inches shorter than his left. He incurred plenty more damage as a pro, including 400 stitches in his face, a busted nose, ruptured discs, a blocked intestine, a ruptured spleen, severed hand tendons, a broken instep, and punctured lungs.

Troubled by fears, anxiety, injuries, marital woes—his wife filed for divorce four times—heavy drinking, and so much more, it's a miracle he persevered.

"On balance, most people were willing to forgive him for being irritable. Life seemed to be an ordeal for him," explained the *Toronto Star*'s Jim Proudfoot.

However, it's not only his combination of natural athletic talent and misfortune that should be his legacy, but also his ability to overcome and endure. His life *was* an ordeal and ended in tragedy in 1970. As the story goes, Sawchuk got into a fight with Rangers teammate Ron Stewart and fell—some reports said it was onto a barbecue, others Stewart's knee—and was rushed to hospital. Sawchuk's gall bladder was taken out and doctors performed another operation to remove blood from his lacerated liver. Though he did regain consciousness following surgery for a short period of time, he didn't make it. The cause of death, according to the coroner, was a blood clot that entered a pulmonary artery.

"In my books, it'll never change, to me, he's the best goaltender I've ever seen," said Sawchuk's coach in New York, Emile Francis, himself a former netminder. "He could have played another couple of years, but he got in that little brawl with Ron Stewart. It's too bad." According to Sawchuk biographer David Dupuis:

It is really difficult to separate the man, his life from his stats. His tragic life is what fueled the inner rage and determination to take whatever life had to throw at him, to be the best, to hate to get scored on as much as he did! His life does make his accomplishments bigger than life. He had to overcome so much and still he was the best. There is no doubt that Glenn Hall may have been better than Terry—and very much healthier—but in the last few years of his life, Hall didn't have to play through the myriad of injuries that befell Terry. Just the herniated discs alone would have stopped any athlete.

As for Jacques Plante, he had the good fortune of playing on a dynasty, the Canadiens of the 1950s. He got his mitts on six Stanley Cups in Montreal. Like Hall, he would play into his 40s, putting in time with the Rangers, Blues, Maple Leafs, and Bruins as well as the WHA's Edmonton Oilers. He claimed seven Vezina Trophies and was named league MVP in 1961–62.

His decision to wear a mask on November 2, 1959, and his refusal to return to the ice after getting hit by an Andy Bathgate blast without it, changed hockey. But he wasn't the first to wear a mask in a game—that distinction belongs to Clint Benedict, who wore a mask in a couple of contests in early 1930. Not long after Plante proved a goalie's effectiveness wouldn't be diminished by facial protection, all goaltenders would be masked. Detroit trainer Ross "Lefty" Wilson originated the "Sawchuk-style" mask of the 1960s, using five sheets of fibreglass over a facial mould, a design favoured by other goalies, like Cesare Maniago, Roy Edwards, and Gilles Meloche. It took a decade for just about every goalie to wear facial protection. (The final holdout would be Pittsburgh's Andy

Brown, becoming the last NHL goalie to play without a mask on April 7, 1974. "Fearless" Brown would remain maskless in his last seasons in the WHA too.)

But Plante's influence goes far beyond his popularizing and developing improvements to the goalie mask, according to Todd Denault, author of *Jacques Plante: The Man Who Changed the Face of Hockey*:

> Before Jacques Plante, the position of goaltender was usually tendered by a player who remained anchored to the confines of his net with the sole purpose of stopping the opposition's oncoming pucks. Plante was able to transform the position of goaltender. Goalies had traditionally allowed the puck to come to them; Plante was the first to actively go after the puck. Thanks to an inquisitive mind and an unshakeable belief in himself, Plante was able to widen the boundaries of the goaltending position like no other. Amongst his many innovations, Plante was the first goaltender to play the puck, pass it up to his teammates, communicate with his defensemen, signal for icing, and, most famously, popularize the wearing of a protective mask. And while many of these ideas were roundly scorned at the time, Plante's continued and constant success validated his ideas, to the point that many of his innovations have over time became standard practice amongst all goaltenders.
>
> Every time we watch a game, whether it be the Stanley Cup Finals or a house league peewee game at our local rink, we see the influence of Jacques Plante. Today, it is standard operating procedure for any goalie to communicate with his defenseman, to play the puck, to be able to pass the puck up, and of course, they all have to wear the mask. It was Plante who popularized these techniques, and paved the way for them to become what they are today.

As an astute student of the game, Plante was called upon as a television analyst and as a goalie coach with the Oakland Seals, Philadelphia Flyers, Montreal Canadiens, St. Louis Blues, and even

HC Sierre in Switzerland; as well, goalies in Holland, Austria, and Germany benefited from his teachings. He was also head coach and general manager for the Quebec Nordiques of the WHA for a season.

On Goaltending, his exploration of the position, was published in 1972. "All the young goalies had that book. That's the first reference that we had," said Bob Sauvé.

The influence Plante had on the likes of Bernie Parent and Pete Peeters was more direct and hands-on. "Jacques was Bernie's mentor when Bernie was playing. He helped us. He really helped, Pete believed in him a lot. For me, as a veteran, I had never had anyone tell me what to do. And Jacques was great," said Phil Myre of his days with Plante and the Philadelphia Flyers.

Rick St. Croix, now the goalie coach in Toronto, respectfully listened to Plante in Philly too, even if the advice was suspect for that time. "He was pretty rigid. He'd ask us not to go down once in practice. Think about that—this was mid-'70s, not your '50s or '60s. Not to go down? But we were doing it, because Jacques said do it. That's pretty amazing. You wouldn't say that to a kid in today's world," said St. Croix.

Plante, Sawchuk, and Hall, of course, weren't the only stars of the Original Six era. Though some of their seasons pre-date the Original Six timeframe, Hall of Famers from that time include Gump Worsley, Harry "Apple Cheeks" Lumley, Johnny "the China Wall" Bower, Chuck "Bonnie Prince Charlie" Rayner, Walter "Turk" Broda, Frank "Mr. Zero" Brimsek, and Bill Durnan.

One name gave way to another, or names were exchanged for each other, the general managers eager to try out a new model. There were a myriad of minor leagues that serviced cities big and small. A keeper never knew when the break would come. For Brimsek, who was toiling in the International-American Hockey League, it was when Tiny Thompson had an infected eye. "It was a tough league and a lot of good goalies were just waiting for one of the Big Six to break down," Brimsek said to the *Globe and Mail* in 1986.

But what about some of the names that fought and clawed their way into the NHL? For a time, they were one of the six best goal-tenders in the world, even if their careers were short or anchored in the minor leagues.

Stars like Gerry Cheevers, Bernie Parent, Roger Crozier, Eddie Johnston, and Cesare Maniago are considered 1970s goalies, but all did their apprenticeships during the Original Six era. (It was during the final two seasons of this time that teams began to be forced to carry two goaltenders.)

The profiles that follow chronicle a few netminders who repre-sent the challenges of goaltending in the era, the patience needed to finally get a crack at playing net in the Original Six era—and the difficulty of staying in the big league for any length of time.

FRANK MCCOOL Ninety-four-year-old Wally Stanowski's
mind drifts back to the 1945 Stanley Cup playoffs. With so many players fighting for their country during World War II, the ragtag squad of Toronto Maple Leafs had made the playoffs in third place and faced the mighty Montreal Canadiens in the semifinals. The team's goalie was a rookie from Calgary, Frank McCool, who turned in a decent campaign, 24-22-4, with a league-leading four shutouts and was named the Rookie of the Year.

What was Frank McCool like? "He was cool," cracked Stanowski, recalling the stunning upset of the Habs, a squad that finished 28 points better than Toronto. He added, "We shouldn't have beaten Montreal, but Frank McCool was great. . . . He saved us, really, because Montreal still had a bunch of their originals playing. They should have beaten us badly. All the games were close, though." Not exactly, as the Canadiens won the fifth game 10-3, but the rest were.

McCool was only getting warmed up. In the final against the Detroit Red Wings, he threw three consecutive shutouts in the first three games (1-0, 2-0, 1-0). The Wings battled back, Harry Lumley notching two shutouts of his own, and tied the series. In Game 7, McCool and the Leafs prevailed 2-1.

Herbie Cain of the Bruins takes a shot on Leafs goalie Frank McCool during the
1944–45 season. (IHA/Icon SMI)

And then, poof, he was gone.

But not quietly.

Using the media as a bargaining tool, McCool talked about how
owner Conn Smythe and general manager Hap Day wouldn't budge
on his $4,500 contract. He wanted a $500 raise.

"If I were the type of fellow who could play hockey and not
worry, I wouldn't be leaving for home tomorrow night. As it is, I'm
washed up. All through. I shook hands with Smythe and Day at
noon. What are my future plans? I don't know except that they will
have nothing to do with hockey. Deep down in my heart, I don't
want to play hockey. I thought the Leafs should have been willing
to give me $5,000. But that's secondary, I guess, to an inner feeling

against playing," McCool told the *Toronto Star*'s Andy Lytle in October 1945.

The "inner feeling" was also a constant battle McCool had waged against ulcers. He'd actually taken the 1943–44 season off from playing to try to set his body right, having played two previous years while stationed in Calgary, Alberta, with the Canadian army.

Born in Calgary on October 27, 1918, to parents of Irish descent, one year McCool received a pair of skates as a gift. "They were old Automobile Ds. They had sharp points on the heels of the blades. I was from a poor family and couldn't afford pads, so every time I fell down or went to my knees to stop a shot, I was pricked by the points. It didn't take too long for me to learn a goalie must try to stay on his feet, and that's the style I developed," he said in 1963.

The 6-foot McCool excelled with his high school team in nearby Bowness before making Calgary's junior squad, which competed for the Memorial Cup in 1938. Rather than go to the pros, he chose Gonzaga College in Spokane, Washington, where he was loved by the Bulldogs supporters.

"Frank 'Cool' McCool, the nerveless goalie who covered himself with glory in front of Gonzaga's net last season" is how *The Spokesman-Review* described him. The newspaper followed McCool at the Chicago Black Hawks training camp in Hibbing, Minnesota, in the fall of 1939, reporting that Hawks coach Paul Thompson was "impressed by Frank's work in front of the net" as he competed with Mike Karakas for the spot.

He didn't make it in Chicago, though, as World War II disrupted everything. McCool signed as a free agent with Toronto on October 25, 1944. What followed was a Calder Trophy–winning season as the top rookie, leading the league in minutes, with 3,000 in 50 games, and shutouts, with four. Tom Foley wrote in the *Lethbridge Herald* that "McCool won the goaltending job with the Maple Leafs a year ago when that organization was dickering with every goaltender of note in the business, and although a completely unknown rookie when he joined their forces, McCool became one of the top net-minders in the trade within one year."

But it's the four shutouts that "Ulcers" McCool threw in the playoffs, en route to the 1945 Stanley Cup, that most still talk about.

Despite his tough talk with Smythe, McCool did come back for the 1945–46 season, but he only played 22 games, sharing the duties with Turk Broda, who was back from the war. His NHL totals are 72 games plus 13 playoff contests. That's it.

Back in Calgary, where he had grown up and played his early hockey, McCool worked for a short while as a night watchman before going to work at the *Calgary Albertan* newspaper, where he had worked years before as a copy boy in the sports department. His mentor there was Max Bell, and they remained friends all through their lives, McCool even moving to a Montreal hotel when Bell battled brain cancer.

McCool was sports editor at the *Albertan* by 1949 and rose to be general manager and assistant publisher by the time of his death on May 20, 1973, from stomach cancer, no doubt complicated by his duodenal ulcer.

One of McCool's regrets was that the higher he rose in the news-paper's ranks, the less time he had to coach hockey. He was a key figure in the community—his obituary lists 10 different boards and service clubs he was involved with—and the city of Calgary has a park and arena named in his honour.

His family grew up knowing the legend. "He didn't talk about it much, but everybody else was oohing and aahing. He didn't talk much about it, and neither did Mom. With seven kids, you're sort of preoc-cupied," said Gordon McCool, the second oldest of McCool's children.

Through the years, McCool remained humble about his accom-plishments, wrote famed columnist Jim Coleman. "Although his four shutouts in the 1945 Stanley Cup playoffs equal the all-time professional record, he never mentioned his hockey feats after becoming a newspaperman. When I lauded him publicly at a Calgary banquet 17 years later he turned scarlet with embarrassment.

His embarrassment was absolutely genuine—there wasn't a single phony bone or corpuscle in his long, angular body," read Coleman's tribute following McCool's passing.

JOHN HENDERSON "Long" John Henderson is exhibit A for being stuck in the feudal system that was the NHL of the Original Six era. Teams had established territories whereby they could claim players based on geography. A native of Toronto's east end who found success with the Weston Dukes in Junior B, Henderson was the property of the Maple Leafs and remembers signing his "C Form" with the hometown squad for a $100 bonus. "That meant I was their property for life. You had no say. You did what they said. You were a piece of meat basically. You did what you were told," complained Henderson, who played four seasons with the Ontario Hockey Association's Toronto Marlboros.

Except that the long, lanky, 6-foot-5 Henderson *didn't* do what he was told, and that ended up being his ticket out of town and his only shot at the NHL. He was stuck behind Al Rollins in the depth chart, and then it was Harry Lumley, acquired in a trade with Chicago. Lumley liked to have a knob on his goalie stick to remind him not to crouch too deep in the net. Toronto management felt this was a great idea and instructed Henderson to follow suit. Being so tall, crouching was a necessity. "I was at training camp and I couldn't stop the puck using that method. I just broke the stick over the net and skated off the ice. I went in, cut the knob that they'd put on my stick off, went back out and went back to my old style—and starting playing well," said Henderson.

Hap Day, the Leafs general manager, called Long John over and asked who gave him permission to remove the knob. Henderson replied it was his own idea. "I came up through your organization this way, and you thought I was good enough for as far as I've progressed. Why change me now? I just can't do it," he recalled saying. "Two or three days later, I was traded to Boston."

It was a bit of a shot in the dark for the Bruins. "I don't think I had ever seen him play," related Boston's GM Lynn Patrick in *The Hockey News* in 1954. Patrick got Henderson on the advice of the team's chief scout, Harold "Baldy" Cotton. According to Patrick, "He said he was the best goaltender outside the National league in the business."

Henderson went from a classy junior team, the Marlies, to a sad-sack Boston squad, where goaltender "Sugar" Jim Henry was at the end of his career. Of his second year as a professional, Henderson said, "I was a kid playing with grown men now. I wasn't impressed with the way they were treated, the sweaters, the underwear, it just wasn't the same. It just wasn't as first class."

Immediately, Henderson helped the Bruins, posting five shutouts in 45 appearances, and the team made the playoffs, facing the mighty Montreal Canadiens, making him a witness—and participant—to one of the most famous incidents in hockey history.

On March 13, 1955, the Bruins hosted Montreal for a late-season tilt. Henderson found that he had the number of Maurice "The Rocket" Richard, No. 9. "I had beaten him twice on breakaways from the blue line in, and he was miffed—so the story goes, I heard this from some of the players that played there, that he was miffed that he couldn't score on a rookie goalie," said Henderson.

Behind the net, B's defenceman Hal Laycoe clipped Richard on the forehead and cut him. Richard went mad, and linesman Cliff Thompson tried to separate the two. The Rocket punched Thompson, bloodying him. Richard was subsequently suspended for the remaining three games of the regular season and for the entire post-season. Montreal fans rioted when NHL president Clarence Campbell appeared at the next Montreal home game, on March 17, against Detroit. In the playoffs, the Rocket-less Canadiens knocked off Boston in five games, before losing the Cup to Detroit.

The next year, the Bruins had traded for Terry Sawchuk, and Henderson played only a single game for Boston, which proved to be his last one in the NHL. Frustrated, he asked to be traded, knowing he could play at the top level, and was suspended for his insubordination.

"You trade me, or I pack it in—I'm quitting," threatened Henderson. "They said, 'Kid, we're not going to trade you, because we need someone in case he gets hurt.' That's the end of that story. They called my bluff and I quit. I went into the business world in Toronto."

It was hardly the end of Henderson's story, just the end of his NHL days.

While working at the Consumers Gas company, Henderson played for the Whitby Dunlops, helping the squad win Allan Cups as Canada's senior champions in 1956–57 and 1958–59. He was also the backup as the Dunlops won gold at the 1958 World Ice Hockey Championship.

"Well, you got paid, but it was under the table and it wasn't a hell of a lot. It was just something I truly enjoyed doing," Henderson said. A friendship from the Dunlops would pay off down the road, but first he played a season in the Eastern Professional Hockey League with the Kingston Frontenacs in 1960–61 and a single game with the American Hockey League's Cleveland Barons.

Having had enough, Henderson quit hockey altogether. For four years at least.

Charlie Burns, a buddy from Whitby, Ontario, asked him to come play in San Francisco with the Western Hockey League's Seals. Things worked out for Henderson: "I wonder if I did the right thing—quitting in the first place and whether I did the right thing going back. However, I went back, I met my wife, we got married, and when she became pregnant, I said, 'That's it, no more.' I was at the end of my career anyway, so I quit." That actual end came after two seasons in California, a brief stop in Oklahoma City, and four years playing for the Hershey Bears.

Like at every other stop, Henderson spoke his mind in Hershey. Jack McCarten, who played for the U.S. National Team that beat the Russians in the 1960 Winter Olympics, was getting playing time ahead of Long John. "They started playing him because he was an American and had a bit of a celebrity status to him. I went to them and they said, 'We're going to cut your salary by a thousand dollars,' because they were playing him more than me," said Henderson. Henderson threatened to quit, knowing he had a job in public relations at a bank awaiting him. He told GM Bud Poile, "I have a contract. I don't respect you as a man, and I won't be playing for you again." Poile buckled, and Henderson's salary was not slashed.

"He was one of those individuals that he felt confident enough in himself, and he got himself in trouble a couple of times because he said a little too much," said Charlie Burns.

There was an undeniable pattern to Henderson standing up for himself. "If I felt it was not right, I was not afraid to speak up," he said. Did it continue in business life, which included public relations work and running a company that made insulated panels and doors? "I think it was more that the hockey brought it out of me. However, I think that's what helped make me successful in business, that if I disagreed, you would hear it—maybe a little more diplomatically than when I was playing hockey."

STAND UP, OR ELSE

Eddie Shore, the famed defenceman turned dictator in Springfield, Massachusetts, had his own way of making his goalie do what he wanted. "These goalies now, they're always on their knees. Pucks are flying over them like crazy into the net. In our years, most of the goalies stood up," said Ed Kachur, a native of Fort William, Ontario, whose career in the NHL and the minors lasted from 1956 to 1972. "I remember one time we went into Springfield, when Eddie Shore owned it. This Bruce Gamble, he was from Thunder Bay, he had him tied up to the crossbars so he wouldn't fall—and the guys were shooting at him."

AL ROLLINS He was the third goaltender to win a Hart Trophy as the NHL's most valuable player, and, even more remarkably, he did it on a team that won just a dozen games. He also claimed

Al Rollins poses during the 1952–53 season. (IHA/Icon SMI)

a Vezina Trophy, a Stanley Cup, two Allan Cups (18 years apart), and became coach and general manager for a string of teams.

But Al Rollins is not in the Hockey Hall of Fame.

Over the years, there have been campaigns for some other over-looked netminders, like Lorne Chabot, Davey Kerr, Gerry McNeil, and Rogie Vachon, but Rollins's file at the Hockey Hall of Fame has no proof of anyone advocating for his induction.

"Hockey was his life," said his son, Jerry Rollins, who played in the rebel World Hockey Association, including a stint under his dad, who coached the Phoenix Roadrunners.

Following his death in 1996, *Toronto Star* columnist Jim Proudfoot summed up Al Rollins's greatest year: "As backstop for the last-place Chicago Black Hawks in 1954, Rollins was awarded the Hart Trophy as the most valuable player in the National Hockey League. Hard to imagine, isn't it? Those Black Hawks won just 12 games; four were Rollins shutouts." (The previous Hart winner from the nets was Roy "Shrimp" Worters in 1928–29, who suffered for the New York Americans.)

Even in Rollins's own time, famed hockey scribe Stan Fischler thought the keeper was overlooked. "Al Rollins, the forgotten man— perhaps the most underrated goalie in NHL history," he wrote in *The Hockey News* in 1960, as Rollins made a 10-game comeback after three years with Winnipeg in the Western League to join the New York Rangers, the very team that had told him to quit hockey altogether in 1943.

Born October 9, 1926, in tiny Vanguard, Saskatchewan, Al Ira Rollins moved to the bigger city of Moose Jaw at age five. He was a teen sports standout, winning track events, playing rugby, and taking medals in two- and three-mile races through the streets of Moose Jaw. He was only 16 years old when he was tending net for the Moose Jaw Canucks of Saskatchewan's junior circuit.

In 1943–44, Rollins played for the New York Rovers, a senior team in the Eastern Hockey League and a farm team of the Rangers. In a medical office at Madison Square Garden, he was told that he had a rheumatic heart and shouldn't play hockey. He was released outright.

The 6-foot-2 goalie went back west, playing with the New Westminster Cubs, Seattle Ironmen, and Vancouver Canucks in the Pacific Coast League, and he was the MVP in 1944–45. Some early hype from an Oakland, California, newspaper: "Raves are plenty for Seattle's tall goalie, Al Rollins, a young player who is quick and agile and very clever with his feet, kicking goals away by the dozen."

He backstopped the Edmonton Flyers as the team took the 1947–48 Allan Cup as the top amateur team in Canada. The Black Hawks put him on their negotiation list and stashed him with the United States

Hockey League's Kansas City Pla-Mors, but they dropped him when they added goalie "Sugar" Jim Henry to their depth chart.

Rollins was with the American Hockey League's Cleveland Barons when he was traded to the Toronto Maple Leafs in November 1949 for Bobby Dawes, $40,000, and future considerations, which ended up being three more players. The team was desperate for a quality goalie. Baz Bastien had been the projected replacement for the aging Turk Broda, but he was struck in the eye during training camp in Welland, Ontario, in September 1949; the eye had to be removed, ending his playing career. And Broda had gotten a little round around the midsection. Bill Tobin, president of the Chicago Black Hawks, told the *Globe and Mail* newspaper that Rollins was "one of the brightest prospects ever to come out of Western Canada" and that he "has a lot of fight and he keeps himself in perfect condition. I predict a good future for him."

For the remainder of the 1949–50 campaign, Rollins protected the net for the AHL's Pittsburgh Hornets and got into two games for the Leafs.

The following year would be his coming out party. Rollins played 40 games to Broda's 30, and his 1.77 GAA gave him the Vezina. Toronto won the Stanley Cup that spring too, beating the Bruins and then the Canadiens, with Rollins playing four of the 11 games during the two rounds.

In '51–52, Rollins played all 70 games, for a 29-24-16 record, with five shutouts and a 2.20 GAA (second to Terry Sawchuk for the Vezina).

But it wasn't enough to keep him in Toronto, and in September 1952, the Leafs shipped Rollins, Gus Mortson, Cal Gardner, and Ray Hannigan to Chicago for Harry Lumley, an ace goaltender they had long coveted.

Milt Dunnell, sports editor at the *Toronto Star*, theorized why Rollins was never seen as the team's long-term number one. "Rollins had the misfortune to be the upstart who was trying to steal the job from the aging Turkey, whose only sin was that he was beginning to show tonnage as a badge of his success," wrote Dunnell. According to Dunnell, despite his great numbers, "Rollins failed to influence people and round up friends. Maybe it was because he lacked the kind of colour that would have overcome fan resentment. . . . When he fanned on a shot, he looked like a bum and everyone said so. If Broda had done it, they'd have said, 'Tough luck, Turk.'"

From what Jerry Rollins learned through the years, part of the reason his father was traded to Chicago was because he had asked for a raise in Toronto. "My father could be a bit outspoken also. He was really involved in the union movement. I don't think that helped back in the day," said Jerry.

In a February 1953 story by Bud Booth of *The Hockey News*, Rollins was called "a guy deserving of more praise than any other Chicago goaltender since the days of the immortal Charlie Gardiner. Citing instances of his great play would be no problem for anyone who has seen the outstanding performances turned in by Al in virtually every Black Hawk game to date."

In the same story, Rollins talked about his time with the Leafs: "I was happy at Toronto too, but it was a different sort of content. I didn't have the feeling of security that I've got here in Chicago, and I was constantly reminded of the fact that I was replacing a fellow [Turk Broda] who'd been the favourite of the fans for 15 years. It wasn't easy, believe me!"

Toronto's loss was Chicago's gain, even if the Hawks were a perpetually horrible team. In his MVP season of 1953–54, Rollins played 66 games, won just 12, and lost a league-leading 47 with seven draws, leaving him with 210 goals against and a 3.18 GAA.

Pete Conacher, who was on that Chicago squad, said, "He was a competitor, and he wanted to win. We didn't have the best team. He saw a lot of shots. Actually, that was the year he won the most valuable player. I think they gave it to him because he made it through the winter."

THN's Booth raved about Rollins's ability with the mitt, praising "the lightning-like glove hand with which he has consistently beaten the NHL's most respected and feared snipers. It has apparently been forgotten in the rush of applause for his stick work with the other paw."

Rollins would play until the end of the '56–57 season, the defender of the cage for all 70 games for a Hawks team that finished 16-39-15.

Rollins bailed on the NHL and went to the Western Hockey League's Calgary Stampeders for a season. He then played two with the Winnipeg Warriors and briefly visited the Portland Buckaroos in 1961–62. His sojourn with the New York Rangers—technically he was loaned by Chicago, since they still owned his rights—at least introduced him to a new generation of fans. "Coming back was a big kick to me, because I proved to myself and to a lot of other people that I still could play big league hockey," Rollins told Fischler. Given that the Rangers had told him to quit hockey all those years ago, it made for great copy.

With a hotel supply business on the go, Rollins stepped back into the amateur ranks with Alberta's Drumheller Miners. He was initially supposed to be an emergency standby, but soon he was the first-stringer, and the Miners won the 1965–66 Allan Cup over the Sherbrooke Beavers.

As the first hockey coach at the University of Calgary, Rollins presided over 56 games from 1964–65 through 1967–68, going 2-54. "We were essentially an expansion team in a tough conference, but Al Rollins was the first coach," said Dinos historian Jack Neumann.

Rollins was one of the figures behind the Calgary Spurs senior club in 1965, and he took over as coach during the team's first season. Rollins obviously enjoyed the hockey business, as he was also the head coach for the Western International Hockey League Spokane Jets from 1968–69 to 1970–71, guiding the team to a league championship in his first year behind the bench and then to two Allan Cup Finals. When the Jets won in 1969–70, it was the first time that a non-Canadian team had ever won the 63-year-old trophy. They lost the following year. Up next for Rollins was the WHL's Salt Lake Gulls/Golden Eagles for three seasons.

With the WHA's Phoenix Roadrunners, Rollins was the director of player personnel from June 1974 until becoming the GM-coach for 1976–77. At the time, Phoenix president Brian O'Neill said, "We believe that Al Rollins has the experience and ability in both areas, as general manager and coach, to handle the job. Al also communicates well with the players and he believes in coaching fundamentals."

Jerry Rollins said it was strange being coached by his dad, especially after growing up apart. "It's not unlike going into the family business. Some people think you get treated better. The truth is you had to perform at a higher level than any of the other people just to get ice time," he said of his time in Phoenix (November 1976 until the end of the season).

The family wasn't especially close at the time, said Jerry, whose parents divorced when he was 12 years old. He grew up with his mother in Vancouver, as his father travelled from city to city with his second family. Al Rollins had three athletic children from his first union and two from his subsequent marriage.

Rollins was an early admirer of European hockey talent and held the Roadrunners' camp in Finland in the fall of 1976. But the team didn't finish the season, folding due to financial issues. "I thank you, hockey fans. Thank the players for the great job they did under such great odds. They deserve your praise," he said in a post-game ceremony on April 6, 1977.

His last two seasons were as GM-coach with the Houston Apollos of the Central Hockey League and then the Tulsa Oilers. In "retirement" he tried being a player agent—Bill Derlago was a notable client—but the lure of the hockey business was too strong, and Rollins worked with the Spokane Chiefs of the WIHL for a couple of years, until a major junior hockey team started in town.

Al Rollins defied a lot of naysayers throughout his career, including those New York Rangers doctors who had told him to quit the game. Truth is, he couldn't quit. Even through a heart attack and bypass surgery in his early 60s, he kept on keeping on. He even remarried Bertha, "Bert," two decades after their divorce. According to Jerry Rollins, "Al was the love of her life, she never went out with another man all the years they were apart. She also knew more about hockey than any woman alive and was upset her [Calgary] Flames had fallen on tough times. She loved skilled players and was quite perturbed at me for being a goon."

The last days for Al, who died peacefully in his sleep of heart failure on July 27, 1996, were in Calgary, where he and Bert doted on their grandchildren and hit the golf course when he could. His players in Spokane put a stone memorial in his honour at his favourite golf club.

Posthumously, Al Rollins was inducted into the Saskatchewan Sports Hall of Fame in June 1999. Given the amount he gave to hockey, hopefully it will not be his last honour.

CHARLIE HODGE His early career made up primarily of

waiting for Jacques Plante to relinquish the Montreal Canadiens net, Charlie Hodge considers his career highlight to be the 1964 Vezina Trophy, which at the time was awarded to the goaltender who let in the fewest goals during the season. Hodge recalled, "It was going right down to the wire, in the last game of the season. Glenn Hall and I were tied for it. I ended up having a better last game than he did!" Hall's Chicago squad beat the Bruins 4-3, but Hodge only allowed a single shot past him as the Habs defeated the Rangers 2-1.

"It was actually a fluke," said Hodge, dismissing his accomplishment—eight shutouts and a 2.26 GAA. It's something that Hodge does with regularity. In more recent stories about his days as a scout, he is affectionately labelled "cantankerous" and a "loveable, good-hearted grouch."

A three-time NHL All-Star (1964, 1965, 1967), his name is engraved on the Stanley Cup seven times, five times as a player and twice as a scout for the Pittsburgh Penguins, but it isn't something he dwells on: "My name's on there. That's the main thing. As long as it's on once, I don't care!" (In fact, it is on the sterling bands in four variations: C Hodge, CH Hodge, Charles Hodge, and Charlie Hodge.)

How he got to that point of grumpy adoration is a tale of perseverance.

Born July 28, 1933, in Lachine, Quebec, his early hockey efforts saw him take to the ice as a skater before finally settling into the net. "As things went on, I started to realize that I wasn't as good at forward or defence, so I played goal," he said. His father, who had lost an eye in an industrial accident, set to making a netminder out of his son, constructing a net out of potato sacks and, pushing the furniture out of the way, setting up a mini-rink in the house, where the junior Hodge could take shots throughout the year. Hodge does lament that his father didn't live to see their common dream come true: "The poor old bugger died in September, and I played my first game in the National League in October."

As a teen, Hodge tended the twine for Lachine High School and in the church league. In the fall of 1949, at age 16, he was invited to the training camp of the Memorial Cup champions, the Montreal Junior Royals. "The first time I went, I never even got out on the ice," he said. After one look at his 5-foot-6 frame, he was told he was too small and to go home.

Sam Pollock, coach of the Junior Canadiens, had no such qualms about Hodge's height and took him under his wing. While the Junior Canadiens made the Memorial Cup in Hodge's rookie season, they didn't win. The next two years, Hodge led the Quebec Junior Hockey League in GAA, 2.59 and 2.22, and the team captured the top junior prize in 1951–52, with Hodge going 9-2 in the playoffs and posting a 1.70 GAA. In his final season as a junior, Hodge led the league in wins, with 35, five shutouts, and a 2.27 GAA.

After graduating from the junior ranks, his tour of ice rinks near and far really began. The Canadiens seasoned their diminutive goalie with the Cincinnati Mohawks, Buffalo Bisons, Providence Reds, Montreal Royals, Seattle Americans, Shawinigan Cataracts, Rochester Americans, Hull-Ottawa Canadiens, and Quebec Aces.

In his biography of Jacques Plante, Todd Denault wrote, "Hodge had toiled in anonymity in various cities and leagues waiting for the phone to ring. The call did come a few times through the years. Hodge played 14 games for the Canadiens in 1954–55, 12 games in 1957–58, two games in 1958–59, and a single game in 1959–60."

Hodge said his relationship with Plante was not adversarial: "He helped me pretty good. He talked about angles and that, and that's basically how I had to play the game because of my size."

Hodge's Vezina-winning year was the first time that he got to be the primary goalie in Montreal, as the Habs had traded Plante to the Rangers. His 62 games in '63–64 dropped to 53 the following year, then 26 and 37, as he shared duties with Gump Worsley; they shared the Vezina in 1966, its scope having been adapted to team goaltending with the new rules requiring two keepers to dress. The 1965 Stanley Cup was the only series in which Hodge played in the final.

In June 1967, a new NHL expansion team, the California Golden Seals, claimed him. Naturally it was a rough go in net that first season, but Hodge kept the team in games, with 13 ties to go with 13 wins and a league-leading 29 losses. A change in management meant he played only 14 games the following season.

During Hodge's first year in Oakland, Bert Olmstead, an old teammate of his, was the coach. "He made it tough on the players that were playing for him. He was a strict coach. But I got along good with Bert and was playing a lot," said Hodge. The general manager, Frank Selke Jr., elected for a change and brought in Fred Glover, who Hodge didn't get along with, stemming from their days in the minors. Hodge warned his boss: "I told him, 'Well, Freddie will do a good job for you, but I'll tell you right now, I won't get to play that much.' The writing was on the wall." However, Hodge did lead the Seals' farm team, the Vancouver Canucks, to a Western Hockey League title in 1969.

After the 1969–70 season, while mainly riding the pine in Oakland, Hodge was claimed by Vancouver in the 1970 NHL expansion draft. He went 15-13-5 with a 3.42 goals-against average in 1970–71 in a three-way netminding rotation with Dunc Wilson and George Gardner.

Then it was decision time, and Hodge, having difficulty agreeing to terms for a new contract with GM Bud Poile, opted to retire. After 358 NHL games, plus 16 in the playoffs—over 18 pro seasons—Hodge was done.

He stayed in town and raised three sons. According to Hodge, "I only played the one year with Vancouver, and then it was a case of moving the furniture home [to Quebec], and it would have been on my dime," he said. "I looked at it and said, 'Well, I have $5,000 in the bank and it's going to cost me $5,000 to move my furniture back.' That was it. I ended up staying in Vancouver."

Partway through the 1971–72 season, Hodge was tapped to coach the Western Canada Hockey League's Vancouver Nats; the following year, he only lasted 27 games.

Instead of hockey, Hodge turned his attention to selling real estate in the Lower Mainland, an interest he had had since his early days in Montreal, and he hooked up with a developer. Enjoying the line of work, and encouraged by his business partner, Hodge made a home for himself.

"I physically built it too, outside of the electrical and the water and the plumbing," he said. But then he made the mistake of taking some clients back to his place after a few showings around town. "Have you seen anything you liked?" he asked. They did—his home. "That was a mistake; I shouldn't have sold it, but I did."

In 1979, ex-teammate John Ferguson, the GM of the Winnipeg Jets, asked Hodge to be a scout for the team. "I started part-time with him, and went to full-time, and went on from there," said Hodge, again understating things. He scouted for the Jets, Penguins, and Lightning until 2010. "The thing is, if you're doing it part-time, it's not too bad. I know when I was doing it full-time, it was a case where I'd go on the road 21 days at a time. It was hectic when you were doing it full-time," he said.

Hodge's one achievement that will probably stand the test of time is the All-Star Game in the fall of 1967, in which the defending Stanley Cup champion Canadiens, with Hodge and Garry Bauman in net, teamed to toss a 3-0 shutout against All-Stars from the other five Original Six teams, coached by Detroit's Sid Abel. Hodge played the first and third periods, stopping 25 shots, and Bauman kicked out 10 shots in the second.

Hodge claims to not really remember the game, and that it is only in his recent memory because of Bauman, who died in October 2006. "I read it in his obituary—it's a hell of a way to find out!"

DENIS DEJORDY All that time sitting in the stands, waiting for Glenn Hall of the Black Hawks to cede his spot in the net, was good preparation for Denis DeJordy's post-hockey job. For the last 30 years, he's run the nine-car ferry service in the little Quebec village of Saint-Charles-sur-Richelieu.

"Usually it's only one or two or three cars. It's a very easy retirement, actually. I only work two hours a day. I open in the morning, and then the employees take care of it the rest of the way," said DeJordy.

DeJordy had to be patient then and is patient and relaxed now, content to deal with the 40 horses on his farm, though they are really the passion of his wife and five daughters, who are into dressage.

Regardless of anything else he did in his 17 years as a professional hockey goaltender, Denis Emile DeJordy, born November 12, 1938, in St. Hyacinthe, Quebec, will always be the man who replaced "Mr. Goalie," an impossible job for anyone. Glenn Hall had an incredible Iron Man streak going, officially 502 consecutive games in the NHL, 552 if you include the playoffs.

Fifty years after DeJordy stepped into the Hawks net for the first time, on November 6, 1962, there is still a little awe in his voice over Hall's achievement.

"The night I replaced him, he even started the game. I think he played the first 10 minutes of the game, then he finally pulled out. At that time, we didn't dress. I was sitting in the stands. They dressed me for the rest of the game," said DeJordy.

Denis DeJordy and Johnny Bucyk keep their eyes on the puck in the corner during the 1966–67 season. (IHA/Icon SMI)

He was pretty used to watching by that point, as the Hawks were one of the first teams to regularly truck around a second goalie. "My first year I didn't dress, but I travelled with the team. I remember that I used to just hang around the dressing room and the press box," he said.

Fortunately, DeJordy found lots of work in Buffalo, home of the Hawks' farm team. He was outstanding with the Bisons, playing from 1960 to 1963 (and a couple in 1964–65), leading the league at various times in wins, minutes played, shutouts, and goals-against average.

Hall was supportive of DeJordy. In 1965, Hall said, "I get paid the same just for sitting and watching the games. I'm 33 and I'd love to retire, but I can't afford it. I want Denis to do well. He's a good goalie and got all the moves. Now that we're winning, he's getting the confidence too. I hope he doesn't get hurt, because if he does, I know I'll be back there."

A lot of DeJordy's confidence came from his early years in hockey. He started in net at age nine, taking home used goalie pads that his grammar school had thrown away and begging his mother to sew them up. Along with his brother, Roger, and some buddies, Denis attended a tryout for the Jonquière Marquis. "I didn't bring any equipment— I thought they supplied everything," he said. All four youngsters were invited back to the proper training camp, and Denis signed a contract, making him the property of the Chicago Black Hawks.

He backstopped the Dixie Beehives to the James T. Sutherland Cup—and himself to the MVP award—in Toronto's Metro Junior B league in the 1956–57 season, rooming with a French-Canadian family to help him adjust, and then he played two years with the Junior A St. Catharines Teepees, leading the league in wins. When Jacques Caron, the goalie for the Peterborough TPT Petes, went down to injury during the 1959 Eastern Canada Final, DeJordy got a call.

"They were allowed to put an extra guy on the list, and one goaltender got hurt, Caron. Scotty Bowman called me. I was already home. I finished the last two series with them," said DeJordy, who played in the third game of the semis against the Hull-Ottawa Canadiens and then the Memorial Cup against the Winnipeg Braves. "I'll never forget, they sent me a bonus when I got back home. My bonus was $10. I should have kept it until today and told them they forgot to put a few zeroes on it."

After some time with the Eastern Professional Hockey League's Sault Ste. Marie Thunderbirds, where he was rookie of the year in 1959–60, DeJordy started his apprenticeship in Buffalo. He collected trophies there in 1963—the Harry "Hap" Holmes Memorial Award for fewest goals against and the Les Cunningham Award as the league MVP. That was also the year that the Bisons won the Calder Cup as the AHL champs over the Hershey Bears.

Chico Maki played with DeJordy in the minors and then with the Hawks. "He worked hard. Dedicated. Boy, he was one of the most dedicated boys I've ever seen. He lived and breathed, ate, slept and drank, thought hockey, hockey, hockey," said Maki, who roomed with the goalie for a time.

It never seemed that Chicago management was happy with DeJordy; after all, he was not Glenn Hall. Having just shared the Vezina Trophy with Hall, DeJordy sat out early in 1967, protesting his salary; he wanted $35,000, and the Hawks offered $20,000. In comparison, Hall had made $42,000 the year before and was making $47,500 in St. Louis. He was dispatched to the minors on a moment's notice. "We hope Denis can work his way back. These things happen to all athletes and I guess you just call it a slump. But we can't take any chances. We have to do something," Hawks GM Tommy Ivan said in November 1962, after sending DeJordy to the Dallas squad in the CHL.

In 1969, Chicago coach Billy Reay condemned DeJordy's style: "With all our faults, we still would have made the playoffs this year if we'd had any consistent goaltending. DeJordy can be a lot better goalkeeper than you might think, if we could only get him to quit flopping around on the ice."

It was not a surprise when DeJordy got traded to the Los Angeles Kings in February 1970, heading west with Gilles Marotte and Jim Stanfield in exchange for Bill White, Bryan Campbell, and goalie Gerry Desjardins. In Chicago, he had worn a mask in practice but he began wearing one in games too in L.A.

DeJordy did his best in Hollywood, given the starring role finally for the 1970–71 season, starting 60 games and going 18-29-11 on a weak squad. In a lengthy interview in the *Los Angeles Times*, DeJordy shared a lot of his tendencies as a keeper:

When I'm going to have a good game, I'm nervous and edgy. The way I get myself going is to think about one of the toughest guys on the other team. Like for the Seals, I start getting stirred up just thinking about Carol Vadnais. When I'm playing well, I'm yelling at my teammates all the time. Most of it doesn't mean anything, they just know that I'm in the game. If I'm quiet, they know something's wrong.

When DeJordy played with Chicago, he kept a book that detailed the styles of the various shooters. After expansion, he stopped the writing. In 1970 he said:

There are far too many players now. In the old days, you would play the same team more than a dozen times and you would get to know every player's moves. Moreover, there would be only one rookie on each team. It's all changed now. There are always guys you've never seen before. Some guy comes in and makes an unusual shot, and I ask, "Who's that?" Not seeing the players nearly as many times has made it harder on the goalies. It used to be that it would take a perfect play to beat you, but now it's more wide open and you don't have time to study the individual players. There are a lot more 7-3 and 6-4 scores than there were before expansion.

DeJordy, along with Dale Hoganson, Noel Price, and Doug Robinson, was a part of the deal that brought Montreal's Rogie Vachon to L.A. in November 1971. He only suited up for seven games with the Canadiens and was traded to the New York Islanders in June 1972, but he never dressed for the team and was dispatched to Detroit in October.

DeJordy spent more time with the CHL's Fort Worth Wings and the AHL's Baltimore Clippers than the Red Wings. His last NHL game, on December 5, 1973, was a doozy. Up from Baltimore, he surrendered four goals to Chicago in the first period, with three of them within a span of 70 seconds. DeJordy was booed off the ice and replaced by rookie Doug Grant. "I took DeJordy out because everyone was hooting and jeering him whenever he made a save," said Alex Delvecchio, the Detroit coach. "That's bad for team morale."

Baltimore had defeated him; explained DeJordy, "I lost a little interest there. I knew it was my last year." Surprised by the call-up, he was not sharp; Dick Redmond scored on the first shot from the red line. DeJordy explained, "I think I'm the only goaltender where the owner pulled me out. Bruce Norris called down and said, 'Get him out of there.'"

In September 1974, the Wings announced DeJordy had retired and assumed a job as an assistant coach, "specifically to tutor their young goaltenders." Therefore, DeJordy is widely considered the first goaltending coach in the NHL, though it wasn't a full-time gig—he also ran a sporting goods store.

"I was at the end of my playing days and was asked if I'd be interested. I did it for two or three years," said DeJordy. The young netminders in the Wings system were Jim Rutherford, Doug Grant, and Terry Richardson.

CHAPTER 3

UNDER EVEN MORE PRESSURE

GOALIES WHO COACH

THROUGH THE YEARS, there have been bench bosses who were top-level netminders, but not many. The list of those who ran a team over an extended period is a short one.

Consider that, of all the men who have coached in the NHL between 1917 and 2013, only these names played net in the NHL: Percy LeSueur (coached the Hamilton Tigers for part of the 1923–24 season); Hugh Lehman (coached Chicago, 1927–28); Emile Francis (coached New York Rangers, 1965–75; St. Louis, 1976–77 and 1981–83); Eddie Johnston (coached Chicago, 1979–80; Pittsburgh, 1980–83 and 1993–97); Gerry Cheevers (coached Boston, 1980–85); Roger Crozier (coached Washington Capitals for one game in 1981–82); Rogie Vachon (coached Los Angeles, as an interim three times for a total of 10 games, 1983–84, 1987–88, and 1994–95); Ron Low (coached Edmonton, 1994–99; New York Rangers, 2000–02); Glen Hanlon (coached Washington, 2002–07); and Scott Gordon (coached New York Islanders, 2008–11). For the sake of argument, add Jacques Plante and Al Rollins, who both coached in the WHA. After eight years with the Quebec Remparts, including a 2006 Memorial Cup win, Patrick Roy is off to a great start in Colorado. He scored the Jack Adams Award in his first season while his Avs jumped from last in the West to third overall.

As well, there is the curious case of the 44-year-old Lester Patrick. A defenceman during his Hall of Fame career, he suited up as an emergency goaltender for the New York Rangers, whom he coached, in the 1928 Stanley Cup Final.

Therefore, the question has to be asked, if goaltenders make such great analysts on TV, and so many of them have successfully moved into management, then why aren't there more keepers turned head coach? Brian Hayward, who simultaneously worked as the goalie coach for Anaheim and a broadcaster for two seasons until he figured it was too much of a conflict of interest (and too much work) said:

> Isn't that strange? I don't understand why that is. I think it might be because there's still, I used to laugh and I won't name the current NHL coach who was a teammate of mine, but any time that I would say something in the locker room, he would say, "Shut up and stop the fucking puck!" There was that bias. . . . Goalies are different. They train differently, they do everything differently. I think there is a little bit of a bias that players will look at a goaltender versus an ex-player, forward, or defenceman, and say, "He didn't experience what I experienced."

Marty Turco compared being a goaltender to being a football kicker and punter, summing up a coach's mindset: "Oh, by the way, can you win us the game?"

As the general manager in Hartford/Carolina from 1994 to 2014, Jim Rutherford, a former goalie, has hired four different head coaches. None were former goalies. During the 2012–13 NHL lockout Rutherford said, "I have thought about that, actually. Certainly the goalie understands the game. Maybe goalies are more long-term planners than day-to-day planners that coaches have to be. I don't know really a good reason for it."

After her career ended following stints with the American National Team and three years playing with the men in the minors, Erin Hamlen got swept into college coaching, and she now runs the women's team at the University of New England. It's a numbers game, she pointed out: "A lot of it has to do with the fact that there's so many more players out there than goalies. By the nature of averages, you're going to get more players anyway, more skaters than goalies."

Continuing the football comparison, Glenn Resch brings up his own experience in Ottawa as an assistant coach, and not as a goaltending coach: "My interest was always working on individual skills, rather than the team concept approach. I think now it's really compartmentalized now, where the head coach—it's just like in football—the head coach oversees the big plan, the big picture, but he's got two or three coaches. That one guy's just in charge of the penalty killing, the power play, defence or offence. I think goalies like the more individual parts of the game rather than the whole component."

Not everyone wants to be a head coach either, said former collegiate netminder Keith Allain, who has been an assistant coach in the NHL and internationally as well as a goalie coach. "As a goalie coach, your focus is a lot more narrow, and I knew goalie coaches who would never want to be a coach. They liked just thinking about the goaltending and thinking about the game through the eyes of a goalie. To me, personally, I liked having a broader approach. I enjoyed being a coach. I liked seeing the game from a goalie's perspective, but I didn't like being that narrow-focused," said Allain, the coach of the 2013 NCAA Division I champion Yale Bulldogs.

Phil Myre feels he got pigeonholed into the goalie coach role and was never considered for a head coaching job because of it. "There is definitely a prejudice there, but it's up to the individual to fight that prejudice. I don't think that I spent enough time or energy to try to fight it, which I should have. You look back, and I don't know why there is a prejudice, because there's a lot of coaches that never played in the NHL. Scotty Bowman never played a pro game in his life, but he's the best coach in the history of the NHL," said Myre, who was part of the coaching teams in Los Angeles, Detroit, and Ottawa and later became a scout.

Kelly Hrudey believed his own lack of specific hockey knowledge would be a detriment as a head coach. "I couldn't, for example, tell a guy the proper way to get the puck off the boards. I've watched it a million times, but I don't really know the technique; I just know kind of what he's got to do," he said.

The flipside is the ignorance that coaches often have about the art of goaltending, and every goalie seems to have a story. Here's Allan Bester's. He played in the 1980s, as the stand-up philosophy was making way for the butterfly style. His coach on the Maple Leafs, Dan Maloney, didn't understand the new way. "Maloney went, 'Allan, you gotta stay on your feet, pull your stance in, you gotta stand up.' I'm trying it in practice, I'm trying it in a couple games, and it's not working for me," Bester said. So he appealed to Johnny Bower, the part-time goalie coach for the team. The retired great told him to stick with what got him to the NHL and play whatever way felt comfortable. The next game in Montreal, Bester led his team to victory. He said, "I went down on every single shot. I don't care if it came from the corner, if it came from the far end, wherever the shot came from, I went down on [it]. We win, and as I'm walking off the ice, Dan Maloney goes, 'Now that's the way to stand up, Allan!' From that point on, I knew coaches knew nothing about goaltending."

Glen Hanlon built an impressive resumé as a coach after his NHL career ended. He was a goalie coach and then an assistant coach in Vancouver, ran the American Hockey League's Portland Pirates, and was an assistant in Washington before ascending to the head role with the Capitals from 2003 to 2007. He would later coach the Slovakian National Team and squads in Finland and Russia. Goalie Brent Johnson played under Hanlon in Washington and thinks that a netminder's habit of internalizing thoughts does hurt their ability to interact with players when coaching. Hanlon was "very soft-spoken, didn't really let his feathers get ruffled—at least not in front of us," Johnson said of the lowly Capitals of that era; Hanlon finished with a 49-84-9-15 record. Johnson added, "I don't know if goalies lack that driving force to be a head coach, that almost sixth sense where you are able to reel guys in and talk to them so they know basically everything that's going on in your head. I don't think a lot of goaltenders put that out there," said Johnson.

But is there a difference between being a goalie in the NHL and having played goal along the way? Both Jacques Martin and Roger Neilson were goaltenders early in their careers.

Ken Broderick, who excelled as a goaltender for the Canadian National Team more than he ever did in 22 NHL games, played under Neilson as a pre-teen and then for Turk Broda, the Hall of Fame goalie, who coached the Toronto Marlboros for years.

Broderick explained, "[Neilson] took me as a 12-year-old and showed me how to play the angles and whatnot. By the time I was 16, 17, I had Turk Broda as a coach. He was the type of coach that would stand behind the net and not worry about the defencemen or the forwards and what they were doing; he was watching me from behind the net, on playing my angles. Turk, I'll tell you, he was a great goaltending coach, and he won two Memorial Cups, so he knew how to handle a team."

But Broda never coached in the NHL.

John Davidson went from tending net for the New York Rangers to a Hall of Fame career as a broadcaster, and then he went into management, first as the president of the St. Louis Blues and now in a similar role with the Columbus Blue Jackets.

He was stumped by the question of why there aren't more goaltenders turned head coach. "It's a good question, and I honestly haven't even thought about that one, and I don't know if I can answer it. Maybe they're too smart," he said.

VANCOUVER (MILLIONAIRES) HOCKEY TEAM

HUGHIE LEHMAN (GOAL)

ATTA BOY EAGLE EYE!

Hal 1919

(City of Vancouver Archives, CVA 99-777, photographer Stuart Thomson)

HUGH LEHMAN If there's such a thing as an accidental coach, Hugh Lehman fits the bill. In 21 seasons as a goaltender, 1906 to 1927, Lehman's teams challenged for the Stanley Cup eight times. His last stop was with the Chicago Black Hawks, for the full 1926–27

season (he led the league in minutes played) and then four games during the following season.

Retired from the game, he was helping the Hawks out in the office when he walked in on Major Frederic McLaughlin, the owner of the team, on his knees, diagramming a play on the floor for his players. He was illustrating what he thought was a sure-fire way to score a goal.

As the story goes, the major looked up, saw Lehman, and asked, "Hughie, what do you think of the play?"

"That is the damnedest bunch of junk I've ever seen in my life," replied Lehman, turning around and walking out of the office.

When summoned into McLaughlin's office the next day, Lehman figured he'd smart-mouthed himself out of a job. Instead, the major rose, put his hand on Lehman's shoulder, and stated, "Hughie, you are the new coach of the Black Hawks."

Lehman, who had been a player-coach with the Berlin Dutchmen in 1909–10, was stunned, but he took the gig, replacing Barney Stanley. In his 21 games behind the bench, Lehman's Hawks went 3-17-1, finishing fifth in the American Division of the NHL and 10th overall.

The only reason his venture behind the bench deserves a mention is that there wasn't another goaltender turned coach in the NHL until 1965–66, when Emile Francis took over the New York Rangers. Technically, Francis had been preceded by Percy LeSueur of the Hamilton Tigers for part of the 1923–24 season, but that was out of necessity, the team being in chaos.

The tale of "Old Eagle Eyes" Lehmann (the second "n" would later be dropped) begins October 27, 1885, in Pembroke, Ontario, and ends April 12, 1961, at Toronto General Hospital, where he passed away at age 75. In between was a Hall of Fame career (class of 1958).

The small (5-foot-8), thin, dark-complexioned keeper first made headlines when the Galt, Ontario, Pros challenged unsuccessfully for the Stanley Cup, losing a total-point series to Ottawa in 1910; he then switched teams to the Berlin (now Kitchener) Dutchmen and lost a sudden-death Cup game to the Montreal Wanderers, 7-3. In

Kitchener, he met the Patrick brothers and was invited to go west, where he took the Vancouver Millionaires into challenges for the Cup in 1915, 1921, 1922, 1923, and 1924, winning just once, in 1915. He is the Pacific Coast Hockey League's all-time leader in games (303), wins (160), losses (139), and shutouts (19). For the 1913–14 season, he served as player-manager for the New Westminster Royals

Lehman was known for being active in the net. "Not content with turning aside numerous shots that rained in on him, he frequently left his net and carried the loose puck and passed it out to his forwards," reads a *Winnipeg Free Press* story.

After all his years in the PCHA, Lehman only spent two seasons in the NHL, with Chicago—he'd been traded to the Windy City for cash in October 1926. After he resigned as coach on August 27, 1928, he took a similar job in Kitchener in the Can-Pro Hockey League and followed the squad to Toronto in the IHL, where he was fired in October 1930. Lehman also refereed in the International Hockey League for a season.

Away from the rink, he spent more than 50 years working in road construction, most notably as president of Warren Bituminous Paving Co. Ltd.

"Few players can match his nomadic exploits and, quite possibly, there never has been a goalkeeper who can match his iron-man career," wrote Jack Sullivan of the Canadian Press upon Lehman's passing.

Sullivan tracked the old goalie down for an interview years before, only to be turned away. "I'd just as soon forget it. You don't want to talk to an old gaffer from the past," was Lehman's explanation.

EMILE FRANCIS In all the years that Emile Francis served as an NHL coach or general manager in New York, St. Louis, and Hartford, he didn't believe in goalie coaches—he wanted to do it himself. Whether it was hands on, showing the goalies what to do on the ice, arranging a practice around giving a keeper a workout, or

sending a message down to the coach from above, he was involved. "I worked with them all the time," said "the Cat."

Francis's best-known protégé is Ed Giacomin, who entered the Hockey Hall of Fame in 1987, five years after Francis was inducted in the Builders category.

Giacomin explained:

> He knew how hard to work me. He knew if I needed the work; I don't know how he knew it, but it seemed like he realized in order for me to play, I had to work hard every day and every game. There would be times that I'd get peeved at him a little bit and we probably wouldn't talk for a couple of days. He would throw me in the net and decide to do a shooting drill when I knew he was pissed off at me. He'd have them shoot an awful lot of shots, and from different angles, especially if I let a goal in that I shouldn't have let in. He proved it to me that way with the drills, "You know you can stop them." He just had a different air about himself, how to work with players.

The key word for Francis was always "work."

"What the Cat does best is work, checking into his office at dawn's early light and going home at midnight," wrote Neil Campbell in the *Globe and Mail* in 1983, calling the effervescent 5-foot-6, 135-pound Francis "a perpetual-motion bantamweight."

In the same article, Vic Hadfield of the Rangers said, "The players knew he worked so hard and, seeing that, they couldn't help working hard for him."

It was a lesson Francis learned early on. Born September 13, 1926, in North Battleford, Saskatchewan, he grew up in the Depression, when even a nickel hockey puck was out of financial reach. Ingenuity ruled, and frozen horse or cow manure served as projectiles. His father died when Emile was eight years old, so he spent oodles of time with his uncle, who was a defenceman on the North Battleford Beavers senior team and later coached his nephew. Sneaking into

Emile Francis in the net for the Saskatoon Quakers in October 1955. (Saskatoon Star-Phoenix, courtesy Saskatchewan Archives Board)

games when he could, a passion for hockey developed, and he fantasized about the players he heard on the radio from Foster Hewitt on *Hockey Night in Canada*. Playing net meant that he stayed on the ice for the whole game, a welcome challenge.

He loves to recall an early premonition: "I was 13 years old, and I woke up in the middle of the night, and here I am playing for the Chicago Black Hawks. I got up and said, 'Geez, I can't play for Chicago. I've got to play for Toronto!' Guess what—I turned pro with Chicago!" Not only that, but one of his heroes, Charlie Conacher, ended up being his coach with the Hawks.

But first he battled his way up from the North Battleford Beavers in the North Saskatchewan Junior League to the Eastern Amateur Hockey League's Philadelphia Falcons and Washington Lions. After serving in the reserve army as a non-commissioned officer just as World War II was ending, he was back in his native province, taking the Moose Jaw Canucks into Memorial Cup play. The following season, with the Regina Capitals, he created an advancement in goaltending equipment, something for which his peers owe him a debt of gratitude.

Francis's other passion was baseball, and he played shortstop in the summer and managed the team of semi-pro players—Canadian broadcasting icon Johnny Esau was the team's announcer, since he couldn't crack the lineup. At another player's suggestion, Francis adapted his Rawlings-manufactured George McQuinn model base-ball glove into a goaltending trapper mitt, adding an oversized cuff of leather to cover the lower arm as well. When he made the NHL, Francis perfected the model with the trainer from the Chicago Black Hawks. In the minors, it was not an issue, but when he debuted it in the big league, other teams protested, and he was invited to make a pitch to NHL president Clarence Campbell. Francis made his case about the increased protection for his hand, and Campbell okayed the trapper.

The Hawks were not a strong club. "Unless you're playing for a team that's competitive, you may not be around too long," he said of those days. Over two years, Francis's record was 24-43-6 through 73 games.

He struggled in his sophomore season and sought out advice—from the opposition. "My strong point was always my glove, because I earned my living playing baseball in the summer and hockey in the winter. I was a shortstop, so I had good hands. But all of a sudden now, it's halfway through my second year, geez, I started to get beat on my glove hand, and just missing. I was wondering, 'What the hell is going on here?' because I couldn't believe it," Francis said.

One night in the Boston Garden, he braved the $100 fine for talking to the opposition and asked Frank Brimsek if they could meet up; Brimsek told him which bar he'd be at. In a back-corner booth, the Cat told Mr. Zero about the problems he was having catching. Brimsek surmised that Francis was playing goal like he played shortstop. "You're coming out too fast. Then as a shooter's coming toward you, because you're out so far, you've got to back up a little. If you're in the right place, you should straddle the goal crease with one foot on either side of the goal crease. I think that you'll find that you'll have no problem again," Brimsek advised, adding that a greater lie stick might help too.

"Well, the next day at practice, shit, just like he said exactly—I was coming out too fast. I never had that problem again. But he knew, being down the other end, he knew what I was talking about right away," said Francis.

When he was shipped to the New York Rangers with Alex Kaleta in exchange for goalie "Sugar" Jim Henry, Les Russell summed up Francis's stay in the Windy City in *The Hockey News*: "Emile Francis worked his heart out with the Black Hawks, but it was a losing cause. Never one to back up from any shot or opponent, the load was too much for the youngster to carry. He moves exceptionally fast. His swan dives and splits are something to see. The feet that he jumps around with speed is responsible for his nickname 'the Cat.'"

But even a cat can get caught. Ivan Irwin played with Francis in a few cities and remembered one chilly incident: "He got hit in the face and knocked out a few more of his teeth. It was a cold night and he came out again and was in the nets. All you had to do was take a breath through those and your teeth are broken off, and you couldn't feel them."

In the Big Apple, Francis spent more time in the minors than in the Madison Square Garden net, putting in time with the American Hockey League's New Haven Ramblers and, when the Rangers switched allegiances, the Cincinnati Mohawks; he'd later play for the AHL Cleveland Barons too. All told, over four seasons, he got into 22 Ranger games, for a 7-9-5 record.

Francis always saw himself as a future coach. He said,

87

I used to work with all the forwards. If a guy was in a slump, you'd stay after practice and help him regain his touch. Hell, I think I did more coaching when I played goal than the coaches did, because you're on the ice 60 minutes a game, you can see everything that's going on. You've got to direct all the traffic in your own end. You can really help out your defencemen by handling the puck or by letting him know there's a guy on his tail, or a guy waiting for him on the other side of the net. You've got to be out there talking all the time, every time that puck is coming in your end. So you're like another coach out there, really.

In May 1960, after six seasons in the Western Hockey League, including 1952–53, when he was the circuit's top goaltender and MVP, Francis hung up the pads, hampered by a bum shoulder. "I've been playing pro hockey for 14 years. It has been a long hard struggle and I'm not getting any younger," Francis said at the time.

That fall, he took over the Ranger-sponsored squad in Guelph, Ontario, in the Ontario Hockey Association; New York had to arrange for his rights first from Spokane of the WHL. Frank Orr, a Hockey Hall of Fame writer, said, "He's a gregarious man. I met him first when I was working at the *Guelph Mercury* in 1960, when he retired as a player and the Rangers put him in there as a coach with Rod Gilbert and Jean Ratelle." Orr went on to surmise that all those years running the semi-pro baseball team in Saskatchewan had prepared Francis well to run hockey teams: "He was a smart little guy. He probably has better baseball stories than hockey stories."

The Rangers asked Francis to act as assistant general manager. His familiarity with the youngsters in the organization helped—Ratelle and Gilbert had moved up with him—and in 1965, Francis was named GM. All told, "The Little General" spent 18 years with the Rangers in management and as coach off and on. There were multiple occasions when he turfed the coach and stepped into the void himself.

Francis preached defensive responsibility—"I live by three D's: depth, desire, and determination"—and bringing down the goals-against numbers, hence his desire to work with the goalies so closely.

"The most important thing for a coach," said perennial Rangers All-Star Harry Howell in 1969, "is to get a team ready for a game, mentally and physically. Nobody I've seen here ever came close to Francis. The Cat is a fundamentalist and a psychologist. He stresses the things that win and lose, and he never stops reminding you. He has a way of building up players instead of tearing them down."

In the media capital of New York, however, it was impossible to please everyone, and Francis came under fire for never winning—the closest his team came was 1972, when they lost in the Stanley Cup Final to Boston—and for being reluctant to swing the big trade with first-line players. He weathered the challenges of the first expansion in 1967, and then the encroachment of the World Hockey Association. Francis told the *Saskatoon Star-Phoenix* in 2002,

The whole complexion of the game changed. The years from 1972 to 1979 became extremely tough. We had two leagues competing against each other, the product lost some quality, and teams were offering minor leaguers money they didn't deserve. Then in 1979, we took in the best four franchises from the WHA into our league. With the continued expansion, and the age-old law of supply and demand, we had fewer star players but there were million-dollar salaries. There were guys in the league who should have been paying their way through the gate.

The St. Louis Blues franchise—"New York West"—was a frequent trading partner over the years, in part because Francis had suggested Lynn Patrick as general manager to Blues owner Sid Salomon. In 1976, the Blues offered Francis 10 per cent ownership, and at various times, he was president, governor, general manager, and, when he let the coach go, once again he stepped behind the bench. He took a team facing rough times and made them competitive again. "To me, it was just another challenge. I always felt confident that we could put something together," Francis said in 1981. (He also served as general manager of the Central Hockey League's Kansas City Blues in 1976–77.)

A bigger challenge turned out to be finding an owner for the Blues. The Salomon family was in financial peril, and so were the Blues. By Christmas of 1977, the team was broke, and he began laying off employees and clamped down on expenses, even keeping hockey sticks under lock and key. "Every day, there'd be new writs coming in. I'd tell them, just put them on the pile. They came and took our credit cards; we had nothing left," Francis said in 1983.

Francis convinced a local pet food company, Ralston Purina, to buy the team as a "civic responsibility." They ponied up $200,000 before the deal was even complete just so the team could hold a training camp. The deal went through on July 27, 1977, and the new owners bought the Blues, the Checkerdome Arena, and assumed $8.8 million in debt. When management changed atop Ralston Purina, the team was put up for sale.

A group led by Bill Hunter, who had started the WHA and had been an owner of the Edmonton Oilers, had a deal to buy the team and move it to Saskatoon, Saskatchewan. Despite the ties to his home province, Francis bailed and, on May 2, 1983, asked for and was granted release from his contract. (Meanwhile, the NHL vetoed the team's move out of St. Louis, and after much chaos and court time, Harry Ornest bought the Blues to keep them in town.)

Hartford quickly snatched up Francis, as the Whalers had only made the playoffs once since entering the NHL four years earlier. At the introductory press conference, owner Howard Baldwin said, "Experience is something this organization has lacked, and it is something that Emile Francis brings us. I can state with total conviction that we've added a man with the highest credentials."

Francis rescued a number of Blues players from the chaos: "I took a bunch of guys with me to Hartford from St. Louis. Christ, when I took over Hartford, we evaluated the team. We'd meet every day after practice. After the first 10 days, we thought there's only three guys on the team that could play in the National League. So we had to reverse draft. Just before the season opened, shit, I drafted seven guys from other teams, and they had to fly in and meet us in Buffalo to open the season. They didn't even get a chance to practice with us."

During his time as GM of the Whalers, from 1983 to 1989, Francis built a competitive team, and, after the squad nearly knocked off the Montreal Canadiens in the 1985–86 Adams Division final, losing in seven, Francis was named NHL Executive of the Year by both *The Hockey News* and *The Sporting News*. The next season, the Whalers won the division. After the 1988–89 season, Francis was named president of the Whalers, a position he retired from in 1993.

"He had a very good way about him," said Rick Ley, the former Whalers captain turned coach—and Francis was a part of the committee that hired him.

After 47 years in hockey, Francis didn't exactly give it up cold turkey—he still worked a little with the Rangers and served on the Hockey Hall of Fame's Selection Committee for 18 years. "The Cat" was awarded the Lester Patrick Trophy in 1982 for his contributions to hockey in the United States, the same year the Hockey Hall of Fame recognized him; in 2002, he was honoured by the Saskatchewan Sports Hall of Fame. His son, Bob Francis, briefly made the NHL as a centre and later followed his father into coaching, in the International Hockey League, AHL, and the NHL, with the Phoenix Coyotes.

His labours finished, Emile Francis gave his new home some consideration. "I was working 12 months a year, so I thought, 'When I retire, I'm going somewhere where if I want to play golf I can play,'" he said, having settled on Florida. "You can't play golf in Saskatchewan for about eight months of the year."

EDDIE JOHNSTON

Eddie Johnston revelled in an onerous workload. The last goalie to play a full season—70 games in 1963–64 with the Bruins—Johnston knew from experience that it was hard to crack the NHL and equally difficult to get time in

The eyes of Eddie Johnston and Bobby Orr of the Bruins and Peter Mahovlich of the Canadiens are all on the puck during the 1969–70 season. (IHA/Icon SMI)

net. Over 16 NHL seasons, from 1962 to 1978, he got into 592 regular season games and 18 playoff games.

"You'll never hear me complain about playing every game. Heck, it has taken me too long to get to the NHL for me to want any vacations during the season. I want to play every game and I like playing every game," said Johnston in *The Hockey News* in January 1964.

He continued that workload after his on-ice career was done—14 seasons after the uncut campaign—coaching, scouting, and managing. Ironically, the die was cast in that direction during his time in Boston with the advent of the two-goalie requirement. Not having to play every game, he found that he had a lot to give back, and he learned from watching the other sports tenants of the "Gahden" or, more accurately, hanging out with them in the bar.

"I got a lot from basketball, from the picks. Tommy Heinsohn used to play for the Celtics and they used to run the picks. I brought them into Boston and when I coached in Chicago, I broke the record for power play goals, and I broke my own record here twice in Pittsburgh," said Johnston.

Picks are not illegal in hockey, he said—at least not when he was coaching: "You establish a position so if the guy ran into you, it would help." One less player standing would result in an open man.

It's a good example of how Johnston's brain was always working, always analyzing, always thinking about hockey. When he "retired" from his position as senior adviser to Pittsburgh Penguins general manager Ray Shero after the team's Stanley Cup victory in 2009 (the third time his name got etched on the Cup), the *Pittsburgh Post-Gazette* ran a lengthy feature on him entitled, appropriately, "Eddie Johnston: A Hockey Life."

That life began on November 24, 1935, in Montreal, Quebec, and it was tough from the get-go. In Montreal's west end, Johnston, under an assumed name, would take on tough guys and even prisoners from the local jail in boxing fights that might net him $7. He delivered newspapers, worked in a bowling alley at night, hung wallpaper, all to make a buck.

Hockey was another challenge, and it was his six siblings who introduced him to goaltending. "I had a couple of older brothers, and they were looking for a dummy, so they put me in there," he said. A teammate on the Montreal Junior Royals was Scotty Bowman. Johnston left home at 14 to pursue hockey, would tend net for five different squads in the Quebec junior league (Jonquière Marquis, Trois-Rivières Reds, Chicoutimi Sagueneens, Shawinigan Cataracts, and, the crème de la crème, the Montreal Junior Canadiens). He helped the Junior Canadiens into the Memorial Cup tournament, but they lost to the Toronto Marlboros, 1-0, in the Eastern Canadian championship. "I think I stopped 40 or 45 shots," said Johnston.

He is particularly proud of his titles in the minors and reminisces about the Thomas O'Connell Memorial Trophy with the 1957–58 Shawinigan Cataracts in the Quebec Hockey League, the Eastern Hockey League win with the Johnstown Jets over the New Haven Blades in 1959–60, and knocking off the Sault Ste. Marie Thunderbirds while playing with the 1960–61 Hull-Ottawa Canadiens in the Eastern Ontario (Senior) Hockey League.

There were jaunts into senior leagues in Ontario (Chatham Maroons) and out east (Moncton Hawks), and he spent full seasons with the Western Hockey League's Winnipeg Warriors and Edmonton Flyers. Have pads, will travel.

As a Montrealer he was the property of the Canadiens, but the Habs had a pretty good goalie tending net in the 1950s in Jacques Plante. Legendary sportswriter Red Fisher spotted Johnston at a camp in Victoria, BC. "In those years, players made the team based on their performances at training camp, and Johnston was by far the better of the two goalies in exhibition games. In a perfect world, Johnston would have remained with the team, but you don't replace a goalie whose team had won the Stanley Cup a record five years in a row," wrote Fisher in the *Montreal Gazette* in 2009.

Instead, Johnston was traded to Chicago for cash in September 1959, but a fellow named Glenn Hall was in the nets there. On the road again, Johnston played in the EHL with the Johnstown Jets, the Hull-Ottawa Canadiens of the EOHL, and went back west for a year with the Spokane Comets of the WHL. His big break was being claimed by Boston from Spokane in the Inter-League Draft of June 1962.

Sharing the net with Bob Perreault, Johnston got into 50 games for the Bruins in his "rookie" season at the ripe old age of 27. After his unabridged year, Johnston seemed a little snake bit, with injuries hitting him again and again. Besides the usual cuts, breaks, and bruises—"I was black and blue from training camp on. Our armpads were nothing"—there were more serious issues, like getting hit in the head in October 1968 in Detroit and spending 18 days in the hospital as a blood clot threatened his life. He returned to action gingerly, having lost 25 pounds from his 6-foot, 190-pound frame. "It's the nature of the position," said Johnston.

Boston teammate Ed Westfall recalled Johnston's unique solution to facing Bobby Hull of the Hawks and his wicked slap shot: "Eddie used to say, 'I closed my eyes and hoped to hell he didn't hit me.' He could tell by the sound if the puck was in the net, had whacked into the boards, or if it had banged into the glass. 'Whooosh' meant it was in."

During his run in Boston, from 1962 to 1973, Johnston also mentored many future stars, none bigger than Bobby Orr, who joined the Bruins in 1966, at age 18. Doug Orr asked Johnston to look after his son, and the young protégé moved in with the veteran—and soon became his chauffeur, picking up the fun-loving Johnston at bars or after movies, even wearing the gift of a chauffeur's hat.

"His dad asked me if Bobby could stay with me. I said to his dad, 'Are you sure you've got the right guy?'" said Johnston, adding, "I was used to going downtown and having a couple of beverages. Bobby stayed with me for a couple of years. He never took a drop of drink until he was 21. I put him under wraps."

The Bruins won the Stanley Cup in 1970 and 1972, with Johnston the solid backup. "It's a special thing in your life. When you're growing up as a kid, your ultimate goal is to play in the National League, but to win a Cup is very, very special. That name never comes off, and it stays on the Cup forever," he said.

Johnston was chosen to be a part of the 1972 Summit Series, but he never saw any action behind Ken Dryden and Tony Esposito. It peeved him off that his own coach, Harry Sinden, wouldn't play him. That, in part, prompted a trade to Toronto—but it wasn't a simple transaction.

Jacques Plante ended up in Boston, and Toronto was owed compensation. The Leafs submitted a list of players they were interested in, and Boston returned it with fewer names. At the same time, the New England Whalers owned Johnston's WHA rights and were wooing him, even though he had a year left on his NHL contract.

With an investment in a nightclub and business endorsements in Boston, Hartford was the more alluring destination.

Two months after the deal was consummated, his wife, Diane Johnston, said, "It's a funny thing, but for most of his years in Boston, Eddie wasn't married and the Bruins didn't send him any place. Now he's married, he has children—little Edward was just born three weeks ago—and a house, and he gets traded."

Leafs GM Jim Gregory inked Johnston to a three-year deal and thrust him into an awkward three-man goalie crew with Dunc Wilson and Doug Favell. "It was a little different, but it worked out pretty good. We all got along, which is very important. I was the experienced guy, the guy that had been there," said Johnston. Still, he absorbed lessons from coach Red Kelly, always with the idea of coaching in his mind.

When he was traded to St. Louis for Gary Sabourin in May 1974, a big part of his job was mentoring, another step toward coaching.

In his four seasons in St. Louis, he played 118 games. For a period, his coach was ex-Bruins teammate Leo Boivin. "I'm not going to change goalies while I'm winning," Boivin said in February 1976. "If Eddie needs rest, I'll give it to him, but he doesn't want the rest." Banged up, Johnston would soak his swollen fingers after every game. At the time, Johnston said, "Age means nothing. I want to play as much as I can."

Blues GM Emile Francis sold Johnston to Chicago in January 1978, and he finished out his career with four games there. Turns out Francis was the one who encouraged the Hawks to consider E.J. as a coach. "I recommended him to Chicago, and he started by coaching their farm team," said Francis, himself a former goalie turned coach.

Immediately after hanging up the pads, Johnston was given the chance to run the AHL's New Brunswick Hawks in Moncton. On one memorable night, the team faced Maine, who were coached by Pat Quinn. Johnston was forced to fight back after Quinn climbed the divider between the benches to get at him. Quinn and Johnston tussled, falling over the boards and onto the ice. After the team went

41-29-10, losing in the second round of the playoffs, he was called up to the bigs—a hell of a lot quicker than he'd gotten there as a goaltender.

"He talked about coaching for quite a while. He was always coming home from games with solutions, and pretty soon we were hearing that important people were saying they wanted him to be their coach," said Diane Johnston in a *Chicago Tribune* story.

The Leafs had asked about Johnston's availability as a coach, but Hawks GM Bob Pulford said, "There was never any question of his coaching here or not coaching here . . . I told Eddie in March that he would be coaching here this year, and no one in this organization varied from that."

In the 1980 *Tribune* article, writer Skip Myslenski contrasted the cold, calculating Pulford to Johnston, "a rollicking rogue, an open and open-faced Irishman who played on Bruin teams that were characterized by jeans, irreverence, and more than an occasional hangover. 'I've seen every part of it,' he says. 'I broke curfews. I snuck out. They're not going to fool me. I know it all.'"

Though the Hawks won the Smythe Division with a 34-27-19 record, improving by 14 points and losing in the second round to the Sabres, Johnston was out. He'd had enough of Pulford.

With a scathing exit interview with the *Trib*'s Bob Verdi, Johnston could have signed his own death warrant for future employment, except it turned out that the rest of the league detested Pulford too.

After being announced as the new coach in Pittsburgh, Johnston told Verdi:

I feel like I'm getting out of jail. I heard from several places that after I said what I thought when they fired me, Mr. Bob Pulford told everybody that I'd never get another job in the National Hockey League. What's amazing is that Mr. Pulford keeps a job. He's completely incompetent. The Black Hawks think they have solved their problems by getting rid of me, but the real problem is still here. Mr. Pulford. He's got no business being a general manager. The rest of the general managers in the league just laugh at him.

At the root of the problem, apparently, was Johnston's old friend Robert Gordon Orr. When Orr's knees finally gave up the ghost while playing in Chicago, he was hired as an assistant coach. That didn't last long, and he too took his shots at Pulford. After Johnston visited his friend—best man at his wedding, godfather to his children—Pulford got wind of it. "The bottom line is that I got gassed because I was a friend of Orr's and because Pulford knows Orr thinks he's a fool. That's a pretty sick way to run a hockey team. Well, Pulford was jealous of Orr too, and he figured Bobby was influencing the way I coach the hockey club," Johnston told Verdi.

Today, Johnston is still puzzled by his time in Chicago: "We went from last place to first place, and we won a playoff series. [Owner] Bill Wirtz said, 'We'll get you a lifetime contract.' I go in there on the Wednesday, in Montreal, and to this day, nobody's ever told me I was fired."

In Pittsburgh, aside from a three-year stint in Hartford (partly orchestrated by Emile Francis), Johnston found a true home, though not without its hiccups. He coached the franchise from 1980 to 1983 and then from 1993 to 1997. As well, Johnston served as the general manager and, for one season, as an assistant GM to Tony Esposito after a demotion for not making the playoffs.

Johnston never forgot his goaltending roots, said Paul Harrison, who played for him in Pittsburgh: "With Eddie, every practice was built around goalie development and working on skills. And, of course, you couldn't fool him. If you let a bad goal in, he knew it. You could BS your way out of some of the goals with some of the coaches, but not Eddie. Eddie was a taskmaster. You worked hard in practice for him and he was a great guy to play for."

Johnston's three years in Hartford as GM, starting in 1989, are notable for his being required to dismantle a club, with the owners wanting high-priced talent like goalie Mike Liut, Ron Francis, and Ulf Samuelson out. "They were the heart of the team. We lasted with a lot until the trade deadline," said Rick Ley, Johnston's choice as Whalers coach. Ley and Johnston were friends back to their days with the Leafs: "E.J., we had a very good relationship. We played quite a bit of golf together. He would occasionally come down to me and mention something about the goalie."

Johnston's legacy with the Penguins is huge. He drafted Mario Lemieux. He acquired Paul Coffey. And, if you want to consider how deep his Pittsburgh blood runs, consider that he gifted Ron Francis to the Pens, setting up the 1991 and 1992 Stanley Cup teams. "That was such a great trade for the Penguins that they probably should have given me a small ring or something," Johnston said in Ron Cook's lengthy celebration of his life in the *Post-Gazette*.

Brought back to coach the Pens in 1993, he has never left, serving as a sounding board for management, even as it evolves. He's at team functions, golf tournaments, and helps out where he can. "If they ask me anything, if they need something, community stuff or whatever, I make sure I'm available. I go down after every game, and if they ask me what I see, I'll tell them," he said.

Johnston, after all, is everybody's buddy, just as he was in 1980, when the Pens first hired him: "There are a lot of qualified candidates available. But we got our man. As I asked around about Eddie, I couldn't believe all the friends he had in hockey," said Paul Martha, VP of the Pens.

How come you have so many loyal buddies, E.J.? "It cost me a lot of money!" he said. "I got that from my dad. He always told me, 'It's nice to be nice, it doesn't cost you any money.'"

SCOTT GORDON
When New York Islanders head coach Scott Gordon was pressed by reporter Cory Wolfe about what he knew, as a former goalie, about running a power play, Gordon quipped: "Well, I can honestly say that I've seen a lot of power plays score on me. It's just from a different vantage point."

Like his long road to the NHL, where he was the first East Coast Hockey League player to make the jump, the coaching career of Scott Gordon was a long and twisty trail. His journey did take him through

Quebec City twice, playing net for 23 games for the Nordiques from 1989 to 1991 and then again as an assistant coach with the International Hockey League's Quebec Rafales. In his first go-round in the provincial capital, he met fellow goalie Garth Snow, who would hire him to coach the youngsters on Long Island on August 12, 2008.

"We went through a rigorous interview process, and Scott stood out among the other candidates as being a great communicator and providing structure to his team, accountability in the locker-room and disciplined play. Scott has been one of the top up-and-coming coaches in hockey and with good reason," Snow said after hiring Gordon.

A native of Brockton, Massachusetts, he joined the NCAA's Boston College Eagles for the 1982–83 season, getting into six games; he was the club's starter for three years, making the Division I tournament each season, getting as far as the semifinals in 1985 before losing to Providence College 4-3 in triple overtime.

Gordon's minor-league odyssey began when he signed as a free agent by Quebec in October 1986. He suited up for the American Hockey League's Fredericton Express, Baltimore Skipjacks, and Halifax Citadels, as well as the East Coast Hockey League's Johnstown Chiefs (yes, of *Slap Shot* fame). The Nords needed goalies, using a record-tying six keepers in the 1989–90 season, when Gordon got into 10 games. In a good example of the more wide-open hockey of the era, the Bruins peppered Gordon with 52 shots—26 in the first period alone—in a 3-2 victory over Quebec; it was Gordon's third game. At the other end of the rink was Réjean Lemelin, who earned his 200th career win and said afterward, "He [Gordon] played very well. Young players who come up from the minors have a tendency to play on their knees but he stood up."

He even got to suit up for the U.S., playing in the World Championship in 1991 in Finland and the 1992 Olympics in Albertville.

Back in the minors, he played with the AHL's New Haven Nighthawks and then the Halifax Citadels again, then the Nashville Knights and the Knoxville Cherokees in the ECHL, and finally the Atlanta Knights of the IHL. It was in Georgia that his career turned, and he was offered an assistant coaching position. When the NHL's Thrashers came to town, the IHL team moved to Quebec City but folded after two seasons.

Gordon's first head coaching gig was with the ECHL Roanoke Express, from 1998 to 2000; though he led the team to 38-22-10 and 44-20-6 records, his contract was not renewed. Back as an assistant in the AHL, with Bill Armstrong's Providence Bruins, he started to get noticed for his ability to work with young players.

"Scott is an unbelievable coach," said former Kitchener Rangers blueliner Matt Lashoff to the *Waterloo Record*, adding, "I was fortunate to spend most of the year with him. He's an unbelievable player's coach and people person. The way he breaks down the game helped me out so much."

When Armstrong was replaced with Mike Sullivan, Gordon was retained, and when Sullivan left to work with the NHL Bruins, Gordon was tabbed to be the farm club's honcho. Gordon's Bruins made the post-season each year, and he notched a 221-141-20-27 record, won 55 games in his final season, and was named AHL Coach of the Year.

The initial meeting between Snow and Gordon at Nassau Coliseum lasted seven hours. At the introductory press conference, Gordon admitted to jitters before his crack at the NHL: "I've built a quiet confidence within myself where the most nerve-racking part was this right here—the press conference. And that more than anything was just because we didn't have that [in the AHL]."

With the Isles, Gordon took over a bottom-rung club from coach Ted Nolan and improved it by 18 points by his second year. "He's a good coach to play for. He won't jerk you around. If you're doing a good job, he'll tell you, but if you're doing poorly, he'll correct it," said right winger Kyle Okposo in the *New York Times*.

With young stars like John Tavares and Josh Bailey on the rise, Gordon advised fans to be patient in *The Hockey News*: "This wasn't supposed to happen overnight and it certainly hasn't happened overnight. But the process is hopefully going to be very rewarding to everybody."

But with a myriad of injuries—like the unlucky goalie Rick DiPietro—Gordon's team went into a tailspin. "Injuries are something that you can't control. But I've tried to keep an open mind to realize that we haven't been given a full deck and to identify when players are giving their best effort and when they're not and what their abilities are," he told the *New York Times* in March 2009.

Following a 10-game losing streak early in his third season, on November 15, 2010, Gordon was relieved of his coaching duties but retained as a special adviser to the general manager. On the way out, Gordon said the right things. "Whenever you're in a situation that we were in—not having won 10 games—you can very easily expect the unexpected. I enjoyed working with Garth and Charles [Wang, the owner]—they've been great to me. I'm always going to remember that as my first opportunity. As someone who had no NHL head coaching experience, I'll forever be appreciative of that," Gordon told *Newsday*.

Gordon's duties as an assistant coach with the American National Team, at the 2009 IIHF World Championship held in Switzerland and the 2010 Olympics in Vancouver, as well as head coach for the 2011 IIHF World Championship in Slovakia, brought him to the attention of Brian Burke, the GM of the Toronto Maple Leafs. Feeling that Ron Wilson's assistants, Tim Hunter and Keith Acton, had gone "stale" Burke hired Gordon and another New Englander, Greg Cronin, as assistants.

Speaking to the Canadian Press shortly after debuting in his new job in Toronto, Gordon said, "I think every coach has some philosophies and beliefs. You've got to try to find what works for you that works for the group. You can't jam everything home that you believe in to make yourself happy—everything's got to kind of work together."

Gordon lasted in Toronto until May 2014, when he was fired along with fellow assistants Cronin and Dave Farrish.

CHAPTER 4

EXPANSION AND THE WHA

TALK ABOUT GETTING a new lease on life. From the constraints of the Original Six era burst expansion in 1967, doubling the number of teams from six to a dozen, which were spread across the continent.

Each of the expansion teams was allowed to pick 18 skaters and two goaltenders from the existing clubs, and each of the existing clubs was allowed to create a protected list, which would exclude a netminder and 11 other skaters. Players in the junior leagues or of junior age were also excluded, as were players in the Western Hockey League and the Central Hockey League. During the first two rounds of that Expansion Draft, only goaltenders were chosen.

The NHL expanded again in 1970, with the addition of Buffalo and Vancouver, creating a total of 28 full-time NHL jobs for goaltenders. (Worth noting is that the Western Hockey League, a professional league that was home to many NHL stars on their way up and down over the years, ceased operations in 1974.)

Then in 1972, well, everything exploded with the arrival of the World Hockey Association, and then two more NHL teams appeared in 1974 (Kansas City and Washington). There were more places to play and, more importantly, there was more money up for grabs.

There is a stigma attached to players who went to the WHA, said goaltender Ernie Wakely. "There was always that thing by the NHL that they weren't going to recognize the WHA. They don't really give us any credit for the players that went, except if you're Bobby Hull and a few of the other players. For most of the other players, that was their chance to play and show that they were capable— although I had already proven that I could play in the NHL," he said.

When the WHA eventually folded in 1979, four more teams— Edmonton, Hartford, Quebec City, and Winnipeg—were admitted into the NHL, bringing the total to 21.

It was a wild and rewarding time to be a hockey player, an era that will never be duplicated.

JACK NORRIS   GOALIE
L.A. KINGS

JACK NORRIS It sounds like a Hardy Boys mystery, *Jack Norris and the Case of the Missing Equipment.*

Twenty-two years old and called up to the Boston Bruins, Norris arrived in Toronto and left his hockey gear with the porter at the Royal York Hotel. When it came time to go to Maple Leaf Gardens on January 30, 1965, it was gone. Unable to play, Norris missed his NHL debut, while an ill Eddie Johnston was forced into the nets.

Missing equipment or not, Norris was forced back into duty in Beantown, as Johnston, already battling flu, got his knuckles broken by a Leafs slash. "We went to Boston the next day and played against the Rangers, and I had to use all Eddie's equipment— his jock and his skates, everything. Of course, everything didn't fit that good, but, you know what? You've got to do what you've got to do. That was my start in the NHL," said Norris. Norris and the Bruins lost 4-2, beginning a rough stretch of his NHL career, during which he allowed 40 goals in his first nine games.

The *Globe and Mail*'s D. Kenneth McKee described Norris's style, "Norris . . . plays high shots much like a prize fighter ducking invisible blows, employs his catching glove on almost all plays, preferring a backhanded stab to use of his stick."

It was only later that Norris found out what had happened to his gear, which had served him well with the Western Hockey League's Los Angeles Blades. A woman with her kids had instructed a porter to put all hockey equipment into her trunk, and off it went to Sudbury, Ontario.

The mishap is rather an appropriate metaphor for the hockey career of Jack Norris, who grew up on a Saskatchewan farm and made it to the NHL and the WHA, with multiple stops in the minors along the way.

Playing local hockey, Norris was a defenceman, and one of the better players in his area to boot. But then the local goalie moved away, and Norris made a life-altering decision. "I put the pads on and started playing goal. I was pretty good and just never came out," he said. The Estevan Bruins of the Saskatchewan junior league brought him up when he was 16 years old; coach-GM Moe George had to go pick him up on the farm, as Norris had no car or money.

Designated as Bruins property, Norris was invited to training camp along with a half-dozen other rookie goalies. All were called to the office early in camp, and Norris was presented with a three-way contract, with his pay changing based on the league he found himself playing in: NHL ($7,000); American Hockey League ($4,500); Western League or Central League ($3,500).

"I said, 'Well, haven't I got any say on this contract? I think I should make more than this.' They said, 'If you don't want to sign it, I'm sure one of those other five guys will want to. So if you want to play, you'd better sign.' So I signed it."

Struggling in Estevan, Norris wrote to his hero, Glenn Hall, who was playing with the Black Hawks. To his surprise, "Mr. Goalie" wrote back within a week, a six-page missive that Norris still cherishes. Norris would eventually face Hall in NHL action, and he sought him out post-game. "I said to him, 'You know, I wrote you a letter when I was 18 years old and you answered it,'" he said, then changing the tenor of his voice to mimic Hall's high-pitched voice, "He says, 'I remember that letter, I do! Well that's good, you've made it.' I said, 'Well, I'm here anyway. I don't know if I've made it or not, but I'm here.'" Closing the circle, in the WHA with Edmonton, Norris's goalie coach was, you guessed it, Glenn Hall.

Norris apprenticed in Los Angeles and with the Minneapolis Bruins of the Central Professional Hockey League before being called up; as a result of Johnston's cut hand, Norris got in 23 NHL games that season and spent the next two in the minors.

Perhaps his most memorable moment with the Bruins was the time Bobby Hull nearly killed him. It occurred in an exhibition game in London, Ontario, against the Black Hawks. The kinks were still being worked out of the new arena, and everything fogged up. Norris admitted that by the second period, "I couldn't even see my blue line it was so foggy. I'm down really low, and I can remember seeing feet." The rest of the story is, well, a little foggy. Bobby Hull took a pass and fired a shot through the mist, cracking Norris in the skull. Knocked out, Norris came to in the dressing room. "I woke up and I'm laying there, and I see this guy at my feet, holding his stick, straight up and down. It's Bobby Hull standing there. He thought he had killed me. That's the first time I ever met Bobby Hull," said Norris.

On May 15, 1967, Norris was a part of one of the biggest trades in NHL history. He was shipped to Chicago with Gilles Marotte and Pit Martin for Phil Esposito, Ken Hodge, and Fred Stanfield. He played only seven games with the big club, enjoying most of his success with the Central Hockey League's Dallas Black Hawks, including a championship. On June 11, 1969, he moved again. Norris recounted, "When I went to Chicago, they protected me going into the draft, me and Dave Dryden. Then their turn came up to pick, and Montreal had Tony Esposito, and they dropped him, so Chicago took Tony Esposito and dropped me. Then Montreal took me. It was like a trade, so I was actually traded for both Espositos."

In the Montreal organization, Norris was stuck in the AHL with the Montreal Voyageurs. Then the L.A. Kings came calling in May 1970, and he was traded there. He has fond memories of living in an apartment building close to the Hollywood Racetrack and within walking distance of the Forum. The backup behind Denis DeJordy, Norris got into 25 games before being claimed by Seattle of the Western Hockey League in June 1971's Reverse Draft. Off Norris went to the Pacific Northwest, and a handful of games with the AHL's Springfield Kings followed.

Having bounced around so much, the arrival of the WHA in 1972 was a godsend for Norris. It was a no-brainer to join the new league. He said, "I can explain it in one word: money. I was making $16,000 in the NHL in those days with L.A. That was my top salary. I went to WHA and made $45,000."

As in his NHL days, Norris bounced around. He was selected by the Calgary Broncos/Cleveland Crusaders in the February draft and traded to the Alberta Oilers for cash in June. Edmonton marked the first time he was the main guy—he played 64 games in 1972–73 and led the league in minutes, with 3,705. In June 1974, he was sent to Indianapolis but never suited up, and then he was traded to the Phoenix Roadrunners, where he finished out his career after a couple of seasons.

John Migneault, a defenceman, was a teammate in Phoenix. He said, "Jack was a straight stand-up guy, stay square to the puck and challenge the shooter. He made the shooter hit him. I know he embarrassed me a lot in practices, because we used to have a little side bet going. He was hard to beat."

Norris was one of the first to use a curved goalie stick, and all those skills he learned as a defenceman came in handy. "I'd just stop it, and with the curve on my stick, I could get it up high, and I would just whip it right back out. Plus, I had a lot more control around the net. It wasn't that big of a curve; I could still backhand," he said.

Early in his career, Norris had bought a 4,000-acre grain farm in Saskatchewan, and he worked it with his father and brother all through his hockey days. Norris sold the farm a couple of years ago, moving to Delisle, but he continues to help out friends on their land. "The only reason I'm working now is that I'm afraid that if I ever quit I'll die," he joked.

No regrets, as they say. "I had an amazing career, just the way it turned out. A lot of guys had way more talent than I had, but I worked harder. That's where the difference came in. I wasn't a natural. I just tell kids all the time when I go to speaking things—'The harder you work, the luckier you get.' That's exactly how it turned out for me. I worked hard and I got lucky," concluded Norris.

AL SMITH

Al Smith had a lot to prove after he abruptly left the Buffalo Sabres bench before the start of a game on February 13, 1977, waving goodbye to the crowd and owner Seymour Knox and skating off into the sunset. The veteran was frustrated by his lack of playing time, and the final straw had come earlier that day, when it was dictated to coach Floyd Smith by GM Punch Imlach that rookie Don Edwards, an emergency call-up from Hershey, was to be in net against the North Stars.

With Gerry Desjardins injured, Smith had told Al that he would start. Floyd Smith recalled:

> That was an unfortunate situation. Punch comes down and says, "You've got to play Edwards." I said, "I can't. I've got to play Al. I told him." He said, "No, it's only a couple of days before the deadline. We have to figure out if this kid can play or not." He was right, Imlach was right, no question. We had tried all week getting Al ready to play. When I told him, he didn't say too much. After the

Al Smith of the Penguins braces for a shot in the 1970–71 season. (IHA/Icon SMI)

warm-up, we went to start the game. He came out on the bench and just turned around and skated off.

I never saw him after that.

Al Smith was hardly done with hockey, however. Ignoring the year left on his Sabres contract, he went back to the WHA's New England Whalers, where he had backstopped the team to the 1973 Avco Cup. Smith was named the Ben Hatskin Trophy winner as the league's top goalie, with 30 wins (tops in the WHA), 20 losses, and three ties to go with a league-leading GAA of 3.22.

Rick Ley was the captain of that Whalers team, and he bonded with Smith, living close by and driving to the rink with him. Ley's wife, Ellen, is the godmother to one of Smith's children. Ley saw Smith as two different people. "He was all business when he was at the rink, but when the game was over, he was a fun-lovin' guy that cared for his teammates and played for his teammates. There were just a couple of guys, they found out that we were hockey players and they thought they were going to show us up. It didn't work out well for them," Ley said, chuckling at a brouhaha he and Smitty got into in a Hartford bar.

Born in Toronto on November 10, 1945, Allan Robert Smith played his youth hockey around Toronto, graduating to the Ontario Hockey Association's Marlboros for a few games in the 1964–65 season. The next year he got into 22 Marlies games and two for the parent club, the Maple Leafs. Setting the precedent for what was to come, though, he walked away from the game in December 1966. Dispatched as a fill-in to the Tulsa Oilers but never seeing action, Smith returned to Toronto and found Bob Whidden entrenched in the net with the Marlies. "Combined with the fact that I was playing badly, it was too much. I just quit. I didn't think I had any future," Smith said in 1968. He went from part-time to full-time at a hospital supply firm and ignored hockey for a month.

Jim McKenny and Jim Keon, Dave's younger brother, were the Marlboros who convinced Smith to return. He had to swallow his pride and ask management for another chance. Within two months, he was on the bench for the Leafs, eventually pressed into action when all three goalies ahead of him, Johnny Bower, Terry Sawchuk, and Gary Smith (no relation), were on the shelf.

Seasoning afield came in Victoria, BC, with the Western Hockey League's Maple Leafs, and then the Central Professional Hockey League's Tulsa Oilers. The GM of that Tulsa club, which would win the Jack Adams Cup, was Ray Miron. It was a pretty fun team, admitted Miron, laughing at the memory of Smitty throwing hotel furniture into the swimming pool. Smith was just one of the characters on the squad. "We had a few others that liked to have fun," Miron said. Of Smith he said, "He was tough too. I remember we played in Oklahoma City and we had to show our stuff that day, because we were going to meet them in the playoffs. We had a brawl with them and Smitty was right in the middle of it."

At 6-foot-1 and 196 pounds, Smith was nicknamed "the Bear" and knew how to throw his weight around. From 1969 to 1971, while with Pittsburgh, he got five majors for fighting.

He was pretty wild away from the rink too, said Sabres broadcaster Rick Jeanneret, who went with Smith and a bunch of other guys on a fishing trip to northern Ontario. Smith's long, greasy hair drew attention in the bar. According to Jeanneret, "There were a couple of local yokels that thought they would take on this guy with long hair and were giving him a hard time. The whole thing spilled out into the parking lot. My favourite moment was when Al Smith had a hold of one guy by the ears and was banging his head against a panel truck, and the panel truck drove away and he was really upset because he didn't have anything to bang the head against anymore. He was a beauty."

Floyd Smith actually played a season alongside Al Smith in Toronto, when the goalies were Al Smith and Bruce Gamble. "Al was a very intense guy, a very aggressive goaltender. He might have been the toughest guy we had on the team!" said Floyd of the 1968–69 Leafs.

In a 1971 article in *The Hockey News*, Smith addressed his penchant for getting involved: "I can't fight. I expect to get hammered one of these nights. But I'm the biggest guy on the team, so there's no reason I shouldn't. All I do is grab an extra man or help out if our guy is getting beat."

Never really getting into more than seven games in Toronto (plus the 1968 All-Star Game), Al Smith was claimed by Pittsburgh in the June 1969 Intra-League Draft. He became a fan favourite with the Penguins, a workhorse—finally—on some rotten teams. Any frustrations could be worked out with a tussle, and he had 41 penalty minutes for the Pens in 1970–71.

The 1968 All-Star classic was also home to a notable first: because Toronto goaltender Johnny Bower was injured and couldn't play, he was replaced with Al Smith, their starting minor league goaltender, making Smith the first to play in an All-Star Game despite not having dressed for the Leafs the previous year. Two years later, Detroit took him in the Intra-League Draft, and he split the duties with Joe Daley.

The WHA changed the landscape for Smith. The Whalers took him in the draft, and he took them to the title.

But Smith wanted another crack at the NHL, and after the Wings traded his rights to the Sabres, he gave it a whirl, knowing that Hartford was in financial difficulty and his $125,000 a year contract was a burden. Smith got caught behind a hot Gerry Desjardins. "I played in 37 straight games. I think that's still a record for the Sabres," said Desjardins, who suffered an eye injury that ended his career after the streak. He noted, "Smitty should have gotten a chance. He worked hard. He was on the bench for all those 37 games."

Back in Hartford for 1977–78, Smith delivered his Hatskin-winning season, but it really was the beginning of the end. The following season, he only managed to go 17-17-5. He stayed on as the Whalers joined the NHL, playing a third of the season, sharing with John Garrett.

His old boss, Ray Miron, took a chance on him in Colorado, buying him from Hartford in September 1980. "We were having goaltender problems there in Colorado. We never did have a real good goaltender there in the five years I was there. I brought him in. I thought he'd help us, but he was past his prime. . . . He played well, but probably not as well as I thought he might," said Miron.

After 37 games with the Rockies, Smith was done and headed to Vancouver to sell cars. He also worked the BC interior picking fruit. Back in Toronto, he took to driving a cab and dove deeply into a passion for writing.

"The thing about goaltending is that it's debilitating. You leave with less than you came. But what fantasy is more debilitating than this? It hasn't been fun. It's obsessive, compulsive," Smith told the Canadian Press in 1998, before the debut of his autobiographical play, *Confessions to Anne Sexton*. Smitty financed the play with his pension settlement from the NHL. It was all or nothing, and it turned out to be nothing, with the play drawing extremely poorly.

Writer Robert Everett-Green described the goalie in the swan song of his life: "At 52, Smith has a big belly, a ruddy complexion and little of the hair that used to hang over his New England Whalers jersey. He talks with the optimism of the perpetual gamer, and the despair of the guy on tired legs who knows a breakaway is next to impossible."

Four years later Smith was dead, passing away at St. Joseph's Health Centre in Toronto's west end on August 7, 2002.

DOUG FAVELL Forget being oil rich, in 1965, the Boston
Bruins farm team in Oklahoma City was goalie rich. The four keepers in the system were Gerry Cheevers, Eddie Johnston, Bernie Parent, and Doug Favell. All but Favell would win Stanley Cups, and Cheevers and Parent are in the Hockey Hall of Fame; in total, the foursome would play 1,991 NHL games, plus another 198 playoff games.

Fortunately, Favell is not one of those bitter men who look back on what could have been. Today, he's a lot like he was during his playing days—a guy who likes to laugh and keeps the dressing room loose. He can drift back to the memories of being shelled in Colorado or suffering through a three-goalie system in Toronto with a chuckle and a story. Billy Libby of *The Hockey News* once praised Favell as a "charming, emotional and enthusiastic youngster. When he grins, good will beams through the gaps left by missing teeth. He is honest, outspoken, irreverent, and funny."

All told, Favell was an NHL goalie for 14 years, so long, in fact, that he was the *only* player chosen in both the 1967 and 1979 expansion drafts. To what does he attribute the longevity?

Doug Favell makes an acrobatic save for the Leafs in 1973–74. (IHA/Icon SMI)

"It certainly wasn't skill!" he said, adding, "It must have just been luck. I don't know, you hear a lot of detrimental things, and then you hear a lot of nice things about you. You see something, 'He was one of the most underrated goaltenders.' Then you see stuff, 'Well, he wasn't that good.' You're going to hear that stuff, that's sports, that's what it is. You just can't take it, you've got to let it roll and just keep going."

And roll Favell did.

He was born in St. Catharines, Ontario, where his father, Doug Sr., was one of Canada's finest lacrosse players—a goaltender to boot. Naturally Junior played lacrosse too, and he credits the hand-eye coordination he developed as a forward as a boon to his hockey goaltending skills. It was his hockey coach/father who suggested that an eight-year-old Doug Jr., a bigger-than-average kid, try being a goalie if he wanted to play in the competitive 8- to 12-year-old group. "If I wanted to play, I had to play goal," Doug Jr. said simply.

Harry Lumley was his hero, and Favell was fortunate to meet him; it turns out that Doug Sr. had played lacrosse with Lumley in Owen Sound. "As much as I may have liked him, his style, I ended up having more of a Glenn Hall–style," said Favell.

Given the geography of the Original Six, Favell was claimed by the Bruins and assigned to the Ontario Hockey Association's Niagara Falls Flyers. There he met Bernie Parent, and the two goaltenders' careers and lives would be intertwined from then on. "Our styles were so divergent that we didn't help each other a lot at that point. Of course, Bernie didn't speak a lot of English, but we were still friends," said Favell. The Flyers won the 1965 Memorial Cup.

Parent and Favell played together in three cities—Niagara Falls, Oklahoma City, and Philadelphia. They were both drafted by the Philadelphia Flyers in the 1967 expansion draft, and they were traded for each other, Toronto to Philadelphia, in a complicated transaction that resulted from Parent's return to the NHL from the WHA.

"We were competitive, but I think what it did is that it made us both better. We pushed each other to be better. I think it probably helped me more than it helped him, with my style so totally different," said Favell.

Together, Parent and Favell formed a solid nucleus for an improving Flyers squad that would win the Stanley Cup in 1974 and 1975—without Favell. "I think Dougie is a hell of a goalie, one of the best five in the world," said coach Fred Shero in 1973.

By that point, Parent had played in Toronto, bolted for the WHA, bailed on his team during the playoffs, and returned to the Flyers. Favell, whom the Flyers had kept over Parent a couple of years earlier, was deemed expendable and was claimed by the Leafs.

Leaving the Flyers when they were on their way up and then watching them win was painful. Favell explained, "You knew they were right on the verge. It was a tough thing to do, spend six years going through all the crap we had to, and then end up right when you're on the brink—of course, you didn't know they were going to win the next year, but we knew we were close to being on the brink. Then having to go somewhere else and start over, because the Leafs were on the bottom then."

While Toronto was close to home, the three-goalie system run by coach Red Kelly was a little unorthodox. One of Bruce Gamble, Eddie Johnston, or Favell would be in the stands. "That was not a lot of fun. It varied on injuries, it varied on what guy was playing well, and it varied on Red Kelly, who you never knew what he was thinking," said Favell.

The Leafs traded him to the Colorado Rockies for cash in September 1976. "Once again, it was almost the same thing . . . The Leafs start getting better, and we're going a couple of places and then all of a sudden, I'm back on an expansion team again," said Favell, though the Rockies were only new to the city, having suffered for two seasons in Kansas City as the Scouts. Favell helped build the team in Denver, aided by stars like Wilf Paiement and Barry Beck. The team made the playoffs in 1977–78 but fell to the Flyers in two straight.

"I just fell in love with Colorado. It's a beautiful place, especially when you lived in mountains," said Favell, who retired after the 1978–79 season and a short while later was hired as an assistant coach at Denver University. He also did commentary for Calgary's farm team in Denver and coached his son's hockey team. In 1985, Favell returned to St. Catharines and took over the Junior B team in Thorold, and he coached at Brock University with Paul Jackson. He also brought with him a used car wholesale brokerage business that he still runs to this day, International Gallery of Cars.

The Buffalo Sabres hired him in 1987 as the team's goalie coach, and he worked with the likes of Tom Barrasso, Darren Puppa, Clint

Malarchuk, Jacques Cloutier, and Darcy Wakaluk. Cloutier said, "Doug was great. He let you play, but he was really helpful, not only on the ice, but he was really helping you mentally."

In 1991, Favell saw the writing on the wall, and knowing that he didn't want to be a full-time goalie coach throughout the year, he left hockey. He said, "I was tired of being a goaltender [coach]. I wanted to do more than that, because I had coached. I wasn't just a goaltender coach at Denver or Brock. I ran my own team in Thorold. I wanted to do more."

When he isn't running his car business, Favell winters in Florida and loves to golf.

The other legacy that Favell leaves behind is the painted mask—he was the first one to do it, following shortly thereafter by his partner, Bobby "the Chief" Taylor.

It started on a whim on Halloween night in 1971, for a game against Los Angeles. A Flyers' trainer, Frank Lewis, was the painter, and Favell claims the idea: "I said, 'Geez, Frank, it's Halloween. Why don't we paint my mask orange tonight?' So he took the mask home and painted it, and that night I wore it. We won . . . I think if we'd lost, I'd probably have painted it white again." (Favell had the blue and white of the Maple Leafs painted over the orange when he was traded to Toronto.)

Taylor wants to make sure Favell's story gets told in its entirety, including the kind of humour that Favell appreciates.

"He was a really fun guy. I went to our trainer, Frank Lewis: 'Frank, you can't leave me with just a white mask!' So what he did, he painted a starburst design. Well, he called it a starburst. But what it looked like was a dartboard, with the bullseye right on my nose. I said, 'Way to go, Frank! Now I've got a target on my head,'" said the Chief.

LES BINKLEY If, as they say, the eyes have it, then Les

Binkley didn't. What he did have was contact lenses and a major issue trying to convince the hockey hierarchy of the 1960s that his ocular enhancement was not indicative of a disability.

"The sad part of it is, I look back on it now, I could have been in the NHL years before," said Binkley, who finally cracked the bigs in 1967. A native of Owen Sound, Ontario, and born on June 6, 1936, he sought out Harry Lumley of the Red Wings, who lived in town, for advice. "When Lumley came back home at the end of the season, I used to corner him and ask a lot of questions about goaltending and he'd tell me as much as he could," Binkley said in 1977.

Binkley became the property of the Chicago Black Hawks, and he played in Galt until the team learned that he wore contacts. He was set adrift, and a correspondence course would result in his big break.

There was a stop with Kitchener's Senior A team, Intermediate B at Walkerton, Ontario, a season in Baltimore, two years with the Eastern Hockey League's Charlotte, North Carolina, squad, and another two with Toledo, Ohio, in the International Hockey League. Out of the blue in 1961, the American Hockey League's Cleveland Barons found themselves in desperate need of a goaltender; injuries had decimated their regulars, and a backup was fogged in at the Toronto airport. Toledo was just a two-hour drive away.

"I went up and played quite well, so [Cleveland general manager Jim Heady] asked me if I would be interested in coming back the following year as a spare goalie and trainer. I said, 'I don't know a thing about training,'" said Binkley. So began one of the more interesting routes to the NHL.

Armed with a trusty pair of scissors, Binkley would help the players tape up before practices and games and organize whatever needed organizing. "At practice I missed all the skating at the beginning, and then I missed all the hard skating at the end," he said.

The trainer learned how to play the players. Sometimes a skater would blame his skates for his poor play and beg Binkley to sharpen them. "I'd walk around the rink and bring them back. Not sharpening, naturally. I'd hand them to him, and maybe he gets a goal or two, and he says, 'Jesus, that was a good sharpening! Can you

Penguins defencemen Bryan Watson and Duane Rupp (#2) clear the front of the net for Les Binkley during the 1970–71 season. (IHA/Icon SMI)

do them exactly the same?' I said, 'Sure, sure. I can do them for the next game,'" explained Binkley. For that just-off-the-sharpener heat, he'd use a match or a lighter on the blade.

At the end of Binkley's first season in the dual role, starting goalie Gil Mayer got hurt, and Binkley played the last eight games of the season. He was a regular from then on. Coach Fred Glover gets credit for working a lot with Binkley.

"Fred would come out on the ice after practice with me and force me to improve my leg work. 'Play the puck with your skates,' he'd say. So I'd be doing the splits, yet staying on my skates, making sure not to fall down. Then he'd take my stick away from me and slide the pucks along the ice so I'd have no choice but to use my skates to block the shots," Binkley told writer Stan Fischler in 1977.

While Binkley was the AHL Rookie of the Year in 1962, an All-Star in 1964 and again in 1966, and took the Hap Holmes Memorial Award in 1966 (awarded for the fewest goals against), there wasn't a spot for him in the NHL until expansion.

After 12 long years in the minors, the new Pittsburgh Penguins bought his contract from Cleveland. His initial contract paid him $12,500 and contained a laughable clause for an expansion team—$500 if he won the Vezina Trophy as the league's top goaltender. Still, Binkley did his best with the Pens, counting six shutouts in 54 games and helping the team get to within two points of a playoff berth; they might have made it too, if not for the broken fingers that forced Binkley to sit for a spell near the end of the season.

In all, Binkley, a master of the kick save, played five seasons in Pittsburgh and was inducted into the Penguins' Hall of Fame in 2003 and is on the Ring of Honor mural in the Mellon Arena.

Given his years toiling away in obscurity, it should not be a surprise that Binkley was among the first to jump to the WHA, thereby doubling his salary. After one season with the Ottawa Nationals, the team packed up the U-Haul trailers for a move to Toronto as the rechristened Toros.

Binkley saw less and less action in Toronto, from 27 to 17 to seven games in his three seasons. But millions saw him on the network broadcast showdown against daredevil Evel Knievel. The penalty-shot publicity stunt from Maple Leaf Gardens in March 1975 was supposed to be four attempts to score on goalie Gilles Gratton. Frank Gifford called the action for ABC's Wide World of Sports.

But of course there was more to it than that. Toros owner John Bassett handed his credit card and a limo to players Jim Dorey and Larry Mavety to take the stuntman out on the town, in an attempt to mess him up before the big show. But Knievel showed up, and Gratton didn't. Binkley went in net and stopped only two of the four shots. It was reported that Knievel got $5,000 for each goal.

In an interview in the *Milwaukee Journal*, Knievel debunked the news that he had a hockey background. He chortled, "Man, that goalie, that Kinky or Blankey or whatever his name was, was really a stooge. You know what I think? I think he believed like all those people who watched on TV that I really had played hockey before. He was actually nervous, like I really knew what I was doing out there. Hell, the last time I saw that much ice was the night I had 20 scotches on the rocks in Red Lodge, Montana." Knievel went on to claim that he used figure skates, not hockey skates, and that his ankles were taped so tight that he thought his "toenails were gonna pop off."

That publicity stunt with Knievel was probably the highlight of his WHA stay—unless you count a similar Toros intermission gimmick, during which he stoned a 12-year-old from Brantford, Ontario, on a breakaway. "The kid came in and tried to deke me. When I moved across the crease, his eyes lit up at the space between my pads. He couldn't resist it, and when he shot, my skate flashed across to make the save. And I don't think to this day that Wayne Gretzky can believe he didn't score on that one," Binkley told the *Montreal Gazette*.

Binkley's knees gave him trouble, his left kneecap eventually being removed, so he gave up the on-ice game in 1976, but he certainly didn't leave hockey.

John Ferguson, whom he'd played with in Cleveland, looked out for his old buddy and brought him into New York to help the Rangers. Being a goalie coach in the late 1970s is different than being one today. His main charge was John Davidson. "We went and had lunch and a couple of beers. We just talked. They just want somebody to relate, that has played and understands the different feelings that a goalie has," said Binkley.

When Ferguson moved to Winnipeg to head the Jets, Binkley followed. It wasn't a regular gig. According to Binkley, "Fergie would phone me saying, 'This guy isn't playing very good. Can you come in and help him?' So I'd be in there 10 days, two weeks at practice, just going over the basics again to try to get him some confidence again."

As a scout for the Jets and the Penguins, Binkley mainly looked after southern Ontario and many American colleges. He would make a point of talking to people in the arena, from the maintenance guys to the Zamboni driver. Binkley explained, "They know the players that are playing in that building. We would ask them different things about a player—what is he like? 'Well,' he says, 'let me tell you, as soon as that whistle blows, if you're in front of that doorway, you're apt to get hurt. He wants to get off the ice.' Whereas some other guy, he says, 'He's out here before practice and stays out after and works on different things.'"

After 23 years as a scout, Binkley retired. "I turned 65 and I said, 'I'm out of here.' I'd been at it for, hmm, 49 years."

JOE DALEY The World Hockey Association helped extend the lives of aging NHL stars while making the careers of fresh young talent, journeymen, and players at crossroads.

For Joe Daley, the WHA gave a goalie who'd bounced around the minors and NHL a chance to shine and make his mark.

Born February 20, 1943, in East Kildonan, a community in Winnipeg, Manitoba, Daley was the first player selected by the Pittsburgh Penguins in the 1967 expansion draft. By then, he was already something of a young veteran of the minor-pro circuit, having tended goal for a number of clubs, including the Eastern Hockey League's Johnstown Jets, the Memphis Wings of the Central Professional Hockey League, and the American Hockey League's Pittsburgh Hornets.

When the Buffalo Sabres joined the NHL, Daley achieved another first, becoming the team's first-ever player when GM Punch Imlach selected him in the 1970 Intra-League Draft. Daley split duties with Roger Crozier for a season before finding himself in Detroit. Detroit had originally owned Daley's NHL rights, as they sponsored his junior club, the Weyburn Red Wings.

With Detroit, he'd reacquaint himself with Al Smith, whose

A young girl from Winnipeg's Crestview School takes on Joe Daley in March 1975. (Winnipeg Tribune fonds, University of Manitoba Archives & Special Collections)

arrival in Pittsburgh when Daley was a Penguin had actually made him expendable. With both now in Detroit and sharing playing time, they bonded—as members of the union will—much to the chagrin of management.

"Al Smith and I were criticized for being too close as teammates in Detroit. I guess they wanted us to compete more against each other to play. But we supported each other," Daley said.

The situation in Detroit wasn't ideal, and the "so-so" pay and disagreements with management made it even easier for him to decide to leave when the Winnipeg Jets came calling. The Jets chose

Daley in the WHA's inaugural draft in 1972 and offered him a longer contract and double his NHL pay.

"Being able to come home was great, and the fact that Bobby [Hull] was coming was a nice bonus. But to think we were going to build a team that was going to be competitive worldwide was something that I never would have thought was going to be possible. It was a move that I never, ever regretted," said Daley.

Daley played a support role in the Jets' first season behind Ernie Wakely, but he would thereafter take over as the club's number one. The Jets produced one of the most deadly scoring lines in professional hockey, with Hull, Anders Hedberg, and Ulf Nilsson forming the Hot Line. With numerous talented European skaters making up the nucleus of the team's offence, the Jets revolutionized the way hockey is played in North America.

Daley and the Jets captured three league championships, the Avco Cup, and even got the best of the finest international squads. The Jets became the first North American regular squad to beat the touring Soviet National Team, scoring five in a row in a January 1978 contest at the Winnipeg Arena to take the Soviets 6-4. That would be the same Soviet team that squashed the NHL All-Stars 6-0 in the deciding match of the 1979 Challenge Cup.

The NHL took notice of the Jets, and New York Rangers GM John Ferguson would sign away two-thirds of the Hot Line, Hedberg and Nilsson. Upon arriving in the New York dressing room, the Rangers bragged to the twosome that they were joining a heck of a team. According to Daley, Hedberg replied, "You should have seen the one we left."

The Jets were so good that even Montreal Canadiens bench boss Scotty Bowman was wary about his powerhouse club facing them. In a story related at a dinner years later, Daley said Bowman explained he'd been in Winnipeg to scout Jets defenceman Lars-Erik Sjöberg. After seeing the club in action, Bowman told his boss Sammy Pollock that if the Jets ever challenged the Habs to an exhibition contest, the Canadiens should think twice before accepting.

And for those looking for the inspiration of the freewheeling Edmonton Oilers of the 1980s, Daley rhetorically asked, "How many times have you heard Glen Sather when he was in Edmonton say he tried to replicate the way the Jets were built and played?"

While the Jets were making waves with a style fresh to North American rinks, Daley held fast to the tradition of barefaced goaltenders. He only started wearing his mask in the last five years of his career.

Daley explained, "It was just a case of not finding one that was comfortable. I tried various ones. Lefty Wilson made me one when I was in Detroit that I hated. I never really got comfortable with one until I had resolved myself to the fact I was going to give it a good effort, so I started practicing with it on until I got comfortable."

Strangely, it wasn't facing Hull's booming slapshots in practice that convinced him to finally don the mask, but his backup Wakely's advice. Of taking Hull's shots, Daley said, "I was never scared of Bobby. He hit me a number of times, not in the face, but in spots where I didn't have much equipment, so I know what it was like. It's just part of the job."

Daley and the Jets finished the final WHA season, 1978–79, as Avco Cup champions, defeating Wayne Gretzky and the Oilers. It would be Daley's last year as a professional as the Jets only offered him a tryout for the team's inaugural NHL season. He said,

I had gone through expansion with Pittsburgh and Buffalo, my year in Detroit was during a time they were transitioning . . . and I knew the struggles the Winnipeg Jets were going to go through in the NHL. John Ferguson didn't offer me a contract to come to training camp to try to make the NHL Jets, so I thought, "My game is slipping a little bit, I'm tiring of the travel," I was 36 at the time . . . I think the timing was perfect. I didn't want to go into a situation where you struggled every night just to compete, never mind win, and I knew that that was going to be the problem for a few years. I thought the opportunity to walk away from the game a champion was worth it.

Nicknamed the "Holy Goalie" by *Winnipeg Tribune* sports editor Jack Matheson, Daley was the only Jet to spend all seven WHA seasons with the team, and only one of six WHA players to finish with the same club they started with in the league's first season. His 167 wins also ranked first among all WHA goalies.

Daley and Ferguson didn't part on good terms, and Ferguson even blocked Daley's wish to become a colour commentator on Jets broadcasts. Daley would eventually move to British Columbia, running a restaurant and working in sales.

But he'd return to Winnipeg again and open a sports memorabilia store with his son Travis, Joe Daley's Sports Cards. That market, however, crashed after the Jets moved to Phoenix in 1996, which nearly wiped out the store.

Daley remembered, "After the Jets left, business declined and it was a struggle. We've had some great times and we've had some tough times. . . . There were times when it wasn't fun. Days were long and business was poor and you'd wonder, 'Am I going to continue to do this?' But for some reason I did, and now it's back to being enjoyable again."

Business has picked up since Winnipeg once again landed an NHL franchise, and old WHA Jets and Daley boosters still drop in for a visit.

While being interviewed in his shop, several customers arrived to browse or say hi, including a former Winnipegger now living in Toronto. As a boy, the ex-pat had watched Daley defend the Jets nets, and he was over the moon to be meeting his old hero, introducing him to his son. When he asked if Daley had any memorabilia of his old Jets days, Daley went into the back and returned with two hockey cards of himself, which he signed and then presented to his fan—*gratis*, mind you—refusing to accept his insistent offers to pay. A few minutes after he left, the fan returned, this time with his wife in tow (she'd been waiting in the car), to have her snap a photo of him standing next to Daley. For Daley, kibitzing with the fans is the highlight of his days behind the counter.

FORCING MANAGEMENT'S HAND

Recovering from injury, Curt Ridley had been banished to Dallas by the Vancouver Canucks' new GM, Jake Milford. It was supposed to be just a rehab assignment, but Ridley soon realized that he didn't fit into Milford's plans: "I thought, 'Enough, he's bullshitted me.' So I flew back to Vancouver and basically hid out. They didn't know where I was. Well, he found out where I was, and I called him. I said, 'Listen, let me make my own deal. You don't want me here, plain and simple,'" said Ridley.

Ridley called an old teammate, Glen Sather, the general manager-coach of the Edmonton Oilers. "Slats" agreed to take on his old buddy, but he would have to go to the minors. "They had great goaltenders, and I didn't have a problem. Obviously, Milford got wind of this, and the next day I know, I got a phone call. 'You've been bought by Toronto,'" said Ridley. There is a silver lining to the original assignment though: Ridley met his wife in Dallas and still lives there. "Thanks, Milford!"

GERRY DESJARDINS "That's the price of the game," Gerry Desjardins can say now. But back on February 10, 1977, it was a different story. Tending the net for the Buffalo Sabres, Desjardins dropped to his knees to catch a shot by Gary Doak, and his Bruins' teammate Peter McNab deflected the puck.

"It came right up and caught me in the eye. It was just the one angle where the puck was able to touch my eye and it did," he said. The face-fitting mask that Desjardins was wearing—his famous blue mask with crossing swords—actually caused most of the damage, but without it, he would have lost his eye. "Call it a fluke or whatever, or somebody telling me, 'You've got to go on and do something else with your life,'" said Desjardins.

Of course he didn't, at least not right away. His vision hazy, "Desi" tried to play in practice wearing a cage-type mask, a forerunner to what today's goaltenders use. He had surgery to remove a cataract that had formed, but the blurry vision never went away.

"What I see out of that eye is like looking through binoculars that are completely out of focus," he said.

Desjardins returned to the Sabres for training camp and tried to play in a couple of regular season games. "The last game I played was in Washington. I just played one period, they scored three goals on me in the first period. I was having trouble seeing the puck, especially from long range," he said, explaining his troubles as a lack of depth perception.

A native of Sudbury, Ontario, Desjardins got a late start, but he was a goaltender from his second game on, when he was 12 years old; his first game in an indoor arena didn't occur until two years later. He bookended two seasons with the Toronto Marlboros with a season with the London (Ontario) Nationals, a new team that had a new arena to show off.

As a junior with the Marlies, Desjardins found a mentor in his coach, Turk Broda, a goaltending legend with the Maple Leafs. He said, "He made me better. I'll give you an example. One day, he was so frustrated with me, he says, 'Gimme those damn gloves!' I gave him my gloves and he stands in the net, no pads, no nothing, and he was daring my teammates to shoot the puck at him. 'This is how you do it!'"

When the Leafs played at Maple Leaf Gardens, Desjardins was paid $10 a game to sit in the stands, just in case either team needed a replacement goalie. "One night, one guy did get hurt and I was almost crapping my pants. Roger Crozier got a slap shot right in the forehead from Frank Mahovlich. They took Roger off the ice and I thought I was going to get the call. After 15 minutes, Roger came back all stitched up," said Desjardins.

The Canadiens took advantage of a clerical error by the Leafs— the team had failed to spend $100 to protect him—and signed him to a contract in a parking lot. Instead of getting to play in Montreal, however, Desjardins played from 1965 to 1967 with the Houston Apollos of the Central Hockey League; during his second season there, he was shelved after surgery for torn ligaments in his right

Gerry Desjardins goes deep into a crouch. (Courtesy Gerry Desjardins)

knee. He thought he'd get a break with NHL expansion, but he spent the season in the American Hockey League in Cleveland, where he was named the league's top rookie.

His NHL debut finally happened in 1968, as the Los Angeles Kings acquired him in a trade for draft picks. The Kings already had a pretty decent goalie though—Terry Sawchuk. The notoriously moody veteran didn't share a lot of goaltending counsel. "He would just give me some advice on how to conduct myself, and especially what to do with my money," said Desjardins.

Then Sawchuk was traded. "That was my break, my big break. I figured, 'I'm in now, number two,'" said Desjardins. Ahead of him was Wayne Rutledge, but he got injured a couple of games into the season, and Desjardins was finally a number one NHL netminder. Late in his second season, the Kings traded him to Chicago, where he backed up Tony Esposito and Gary Smith. In total, he got in just 33 games in three years with the Black Hawks, broken up with a month as a Golden Seal.

It's a story that deserves exploration.

In February 1971, Desjardins broke his arm, and even he admitted it wasn't healing properly. Regardless, Hawks GM Tommy Ivan traded him to California on September 9th, with Kerry Bond and Gerry Pinder for Gary Smith.

Desjardins, who sat in on a conference call with NHL president Clarence Campbell and the teams, said, "I went to training camp in Oshawa with the Golden Seals and the arm hadn't healed, so [Seals owner] Charlie Finley went through the roof. To make a long story short, that's why I went back to Chicago. Finley figured the Hawks had dealt damaged goods and he was right. I couldn't play." The Seals sent him back to Chicago on October 18 for Paul Shmyr and Gilles Meloche.

If it was action he craved, Desjardins got it in spades after being claimed by the Islanders in the expansion draft.

"Being with the Islanders was probably the worst time of my life because it was a new team and we had a bad team that first year," said Desjardins, referring to the squad's 12-60-6 record. His partner in crime was Billy Smith. According to Desjardins, "We faced a lot of shots with the Islanders; 40 shots or less were a rarity."

Desjardins jumped to the WHA in 1974, to the Michigan Stags. He said, "It was like going to the unknown. I just figured I had to get away from the Island. I just had enough. I just wanted to go to a winning team, but that didn't turn out. Well, it turned out eventually because I ended up being with the Sabres in a roundabout way. I didn't spend a full year with the WHA."

The Stags went broke and were on the move to Baltimore. There was a clause in Desjardins' contract that made him a free agent if the team moved. "It was the first time I had ever hired an agent to represent me. He put that in my contract, and I'm happy he did," said Desjardins. Buffalo Sabres GM Punch Imlach heard about the clause—Desjardins doesn't know how, but he was old friends with Imlach from his days with the Marlies—and brought the keeper to town.

The nightmare became a dream as Desjardins went 6-2-1, with a 2.78 goals-against average to end the season. He paired with Roger Crozier to get the Sabres to the Stanley Cup Final, where they lost in six games to the Philadelphia Flyers.

The loss in the final was a "downer." Desjardins prefers to dwell on the final game of the semifinals, where the Sabres survived a late flurry by the Montreal Canadiens—"Punch was behind the bench, and he just grabbed his fedora and pulled it down around his ears"— to win the series. "We pulled it out and I had one hell of a game. Cournoyer had about three breakaways that game and I stoned him three times. That was the highlight. I couldn't believe it, coming back on the chartered plane. At the airport, there had to be over 10,000 people, fans, Buffalo fans, waiting for us," said Desjardins.

In general, Crozier and Desjardins switched off during the playoffs. In Game 3 of the Cup Final, in Buffalo, the fog rolled in, making Desjardins' stay in net even more stressful. Imlach wanted to go with Desjardins in the decisive Game 6, but Gerry said no. "I just felt like I couldn't do it. But Roger went in and played very well, only one goal against really, right down to the last minute, minute and a half. I'm sure I couldn't have done better than that," said Desjardins, referring to the Flyers 2-0 win. "I know for a fact I couldn't have done better than that, but I was just a basket case."

There were two more seasons for Desjardins before the eye injury, and then his couple of attempts afterwards. Post-hockey, he had a mortgage business and worked with Pat Stapleton with a nation-wide hockey program, sponsored by Pepsi and Canadian Tire, called Fundamentals in Action.

"It was geared to the minor hockey associations right across Canada. "That lasted for a number of years. When Pepsi pulled their sponsorship out of the company, the company kind of soured after that," he said.

Next, Desjardins distributed steel, catering to machine shops, fabricators, and the auto industry, with four warehouses in southern Ontario. "My life turned out alright. I was lucky enough to get into some sort of business, and was fairly successful, have a good family. My wife and I are both retired now, so now we can travel," he said.

PHIL MYRE When the Atlanta Flames started out in 1972, the team selected two goaltenders in the expansion draft from the same province, two years apart in age: Phil Myre and Dan Bouchard. They would play together on the new squad for six seasons, uniquely different in their styles yet strong enough in their abilities to get the team to the playoffs in just its second year of existence.

"Danny was a different character, and we came from the same town in LaSalle, where I moved to when I was 12. He was younger, playing at a lower level. But we knew each other," said Myre, who was born in Ste-Anne-de-Bellevue.

Growing up, Myre would throw a ball against the wall and pretend to be Jacques Plante or Terry Sawchuk, but he didn't play organized hockey until moving to LaSalle. He was at a bus stop when he saw someone from his new school going by with hockey equipment. A "tryout" was a new concept for Myre, but the team was short on goalies, and it turns out he was long on talent. Two years later, he was in the Bruins system, playing in Victoriaville, using equipment borrowed from the local parish. "I often wonder what would have happened to my life if I hadn't been at that bus stop that one day. I probably wouldn't have played hockey that year," he said.

Starting so young, Myre actually got five years of junior hockey in, though the first year was sitting on the bench and learning. That paid off, and the next four years, Myre's teams made the Memorial Cup—the Victoriaville Bruins made it twice, in 1964 and 1965, and, after the team had moved to Shawinigan, again in 1966. The Montreal Canadiens drafted Myre from the Bruins, but they allowed him to go to Boston's junior squad, the Niagara Falls Flyers, in the Ontario Hockey Association, instead of the Montreal Junior Canadiens. The team in Niagara Falls was stacked, and included top scorers like Derek Sanderson and Jim Lorenz, but didn't get far. The following year, the Flyers were expected to miss the playoffs without their stars, but instead they won the Memorial Cup under coach Hap Emms. "We were kind of a Cinderella team that year," said Myre.

Rick Ley was the captain of those Flyers teams, and he recalled Myre's heroics: "He was awesome. There was one team that was better than us, the Kitchener Rangers, and he single-handedly won that series for us. After that, we kind of breezed through."

The Habs assigned him to the Central Hockey League's Houston Apollos for the 1968–69 season, and he responded with the Terry Sawchuk Trophy as the league's top goalie and a Second-Team All-Star berth. The next year, he was supposed to mature with the American Hockey League's Montreal Voyageurs. Instead, Gump Worsley retired in December 1969 and threw the plan into chaos. Myre said,

> I went up there and played with the big team a little too early. I went up and only played 10 games that year with the Canadiens. I think it would have been more beneficial to play on the Voyageurs team for the whole year, but that's the way it was.
>
> Being a Montreal boy and a French-Canadian, playing for the Montreal Canadiens, there was added pressure. Playing for the Canadiens was a great experience from the standpoint that you watched Jean Béliveau, Cournoyer, J.C. Tremblay, all these guys that I had idolized when I was a kid, and all of a sudden I'm in the dressing room making jokes with these guys. It was quite an experience.

Initially, Myre was stuck behind Rogie Vachon. The coach, Claude Ruel, would send the trainer into the dressing room with a puck just before warm-up and hand it to the starter. "You never knew if you were going to play. I guess that he wanted both of us ready to play. From a psychological standpoint, it was really tough. To make matters worse, the trainer would go back and forth and tease us," said Myre.

Then came along a tall, thoughtful phenomenon to take over the Habs net—Ken Dryden. "He came in with just a few games left in the season and played really well. They started him in the play-offs and he won the Conn Smythe. He was just outstanding," raved Myre. "The next year, Rogie went and asked to be traded, and I was stuck there. I only played maybe a dozen games that year. It was tough to get in the nets. He was almost perfect every night, this guy." Myre rode the backup role to a Stanley Cup ring in those magical 1971 playoffs.

When the expansion draft came along, Myre welcomed the chance to finally show his worth.

In Atlanta, Myre and Bouchard were partners, but they diverged when it came to their personalities and goaltending styles. Myre explained,

The players, the defencemen, had to change what they did on the ice depending on who was in the net. Danny loved to handle the puck and I didn't. I always told the defencemen, "I'm going to go back there, stop it, and I'm going to leave it for you. It's your puck." I did as little as I could with the puck, because I knew I was limited in what I could do. We'd work out some plays to make it easier. I wanted to handle it as little as possible, and Danny was the opposite. He'd go back there and shoot it around the boards or he'd try to make a breakaway pass. So that was different. I played an aggressive style with angles, positioning, and Danny played pretty deep in his net. So we were really different. I used my feet a lot, but he used his hands a lot—he had great hands and I had great feet. We were very different personalities. I'm more quiet and Danny is vocal.

Bouchard and Myre split the season almost down the middle, year after year. They found that there were teams that they performed better against—Bouchard in Detroit, Myre in Philadelphia or Minnesota—and that often determined the assignments.

Flames defenceman Noel Price said, "I think the guys liked to play in front of Phil more. Danny was, I guess the easiest term is outspoken. Some of the things he said didn't sit well with some of the players. Phil Myre was a really quiet, unassuming guy, and he went in and worked his butt off. That's the kind of goalie you want to play in front of, because you know that every time a puck comes toward him, he's going to do whatever he can do to stop the goddamned thing. We liked him better. Danny probably had more natural talent."

The platoon system is difficult to continue long-term, and after six years, Bouchard's demands for more playing time resulted in a change. "I guess Danny went to the press and said he wanted to be traded or play more. That started the ball rolling," said Myre, who was dispatched to St. Louis in a big trade in December 1977, along with Curt Bennett and Barry Gibbs for Yves Belanger, Dick Redmond, Bob MacMillan, and St. Louis' second-round draft choice (Mike Perovich) in the 1979 entry draft.

There was confusion in St. Louis, with the Salomons in the process of selling the team to Ralston Purina. Draft picks weren't signed, and players jumped to the WHA. "It wasn't pretty. We did have a few good players, but no depth," said Myre, who played 83 games in St. Louis over two years. He added, "I didn't win a lot, but I played a lot, which is what you want as a goalie, as an athlete, you want to play a lot. I remember I was Player of the Week once and I had played three games, gave up three goals, but never won a game." (He got a 14-inch TV for the honour.)

After suffering through some rough times, his trade to Philadelphia in June 1979 (for Blake Dunlop and Rick Lapointe) had Myre flying, playing under coach Pat Quinn, who'd been a teammate in Atlanta. "I felt that I was getting to be in my 30s now, and I felt that maybe I could win a Cup here. We came close, went to the finals in '79–80, and lost to the Islanders. Then we had the 35-game unbeaten streak. That was amazing. What a run that was. We lost our second game that year, and then never lost until January 7th," said Myre, who was in net for 18 games during the streak.

By that point in his career, Myre recognized that part of his job was to mentor the young goalies in the Flyers system—Pete Peeters, Rick St. Croix, and Pelle Lindbergh. There was also still room for him to learn, and he absorbed lessons from the Flyers' goalie coach, Jacques Plante: "What Jacques did, he gave you a pattern to follow, a system. It was great. I picked his brain for two years when I was in Philly. I wish I had had him when I was 21 and not 31."

Myre didn't know it at the time, but he was on the way to a career in coaching and scouting. However, he had a couple more stops along the way first.

The Flyers sold him to the Colorado Rockies at the trade dead-line in February 1981. Myre remembers his time in Denver more for the circumstances than the ice time: "My wife had a baby the day that I was traded, by C-section. I pleaded with them to stay for a couple of days so that I could take care of my wife. They said, 'No, we need you. You've got to play. We're fighting for a playoff spot.' So I left the next day. It was tough to leave my wife and my baby back home. I never came home for six or seven weeks." The Rockies missed the playoffs.

Myre signed with the Buffalo Sabres as a free agent, though a nagging ankle injury kept him from being very effective—on the ice. He had also studied to get his coaching certification from the Canadian Amateur Hockey Association, the first active NHLer to do so. Therefore, his deal was actually structured whereby he was an assistant coach as well as a goaltender when he was in the AHL with the Rochester Americans. Turns out he was with the team a lot.

Americans coach Mike Keenan didn't play favourites with his aide/goalie, and Myre suffered through some torturous practices just like the rest of the team. Most of Myre's time in the net came mid-season for the Amerks, and he did spot duty in Buffalo after

Jacques Cloutier was sent down. He learned a ton from Keenan. "He was a tough coach, but he was really good to me. I'd go into his office before practice every day and he'd give me the game plan for that day. There were a few times he said, 'I'm going to cut this guy a new asshole, but here's what I want you to tell him after.' It was a good cop–bad cop thing," said Myre.

The Los Angeles Kings hired him as an assistant coach in 1984, and he moved to Detroit in 1988. Starting in 1993, he was director of player development and a goalie coach with the Blackhawks, and he also helped with pro scouting. The Ottawa Senators hired Myre in 1995 as a pro scout and goalie coach. Until recently, he was a scout in Montreal.

Through it all, Myre has been a little frustrated that the chance to be a head coach was never presented. He said, "For some reason I ended up being tagged as a goalie coach. I probably let it happen too long. I should have come out of that and done more from a team coaching standpoint, because once you get tagged with something . . ."

GUMP'S ADVICE

Pete LoPresti was used to clueless coaches telling him, "I don't care how you stop it, just stop it. I'd rather you look bad stopping it than good letting it in." To his surprise, when he arrived as a young kid at training camp to play with the Minnesota North Stars, veteran cager turned pseudo-goalie guru Gump Worsley told him essentially the same thing. "I remember after two days of practice he finally comes down to the bench," began LoPresti. "He leans over and says, 'You're working too hard with this. Just stand there. They'll hit you. They're not that smart. The net's only four feet by six feet. You just have to outthink 'em. They're not that smart. I did it for 30 years!' And it never hit me until after I was done, but he was absolutely correct. I would say that if Gump was alive today, he would look at all the movement that these guys do, he would have a heart attack."

GILLES MELOCHE No one would blame Gilles Meloche

if he still woke up in the night, caked with sweat, nightmares of being a human target etched upon his psyche. But that's not the case. Instead, he takes a lot of pride in what he accomplished in the NHL, even if he did find himself on some *really* bad teams.

"I played five years in California, two years in Cleveland, and seven years in Minnesota. So I played in three different cities, but I never got traded. I think somehow they must have been happy with my work, even though we were on shitty teams and had a lot of long nights. I just enjoyed the game. From day one, I was the first one on the ice and the last one off. I played 60 games a year. I just loved the game," Meloche related.

It's not all that different today for Meloche, who stepped down as the goalie coach for the Pittsburgh Penguins at the end of the 2012–13 season. He had been charged from day one with keeping the team's number one pick overall from the Cape Breton Screaming Eagles, Marc-André Fleury, at his best.

Meloche would not be the most famous graduate of the Ville-Émard Hurricanes minor hockey program—that would be his future boss in Pittsburgh, Mario Lemieux—but he was the first from the city to make it to the NHL. After becoming a goalie at age 12, his first stops were around Verdun and then with the Quebec Remparts, who claimed the 1971 Memorial Cup over the Edmonton Oil Kings at home in le Colisée.

The 5-foot-9, 185-pound goaltender was drafted by the Chicago Black Hawks 70th overall at the 1970 amateur draft. After a pair of games in the Windy City, Meloche was peddled with Paul Schmyr to the California Golden Seals on October 18, 1971, for goalie Gerry Desjardins. Schmyr convinced Meloche that they should drive out to California, so Meloche and his wife followed Schmyr and his family on a cross-country jaunt. Alas, they forgot to tell the Seals of their journey, and the club sent out search parties.

Soon enough, Meloche was recognized as one of the young stars of the NHL, albeit on a terrible team. Consider that in the 1972–73 season, he led the league in minutes (3,473) and goals against (235) in 59 appearances (12 wins, 32 losses, and 14 ties).

Jim Rutherford, then of the Detroit Red Wings, said, "I remember the first game that I saw Gilles play. He came into the Olympia. I remember our players saying before the game, 'Ah, they've got some young kid in there. Just shoot the puck!' I think we had 50 shots and we lost 3-2, or 2-1. He stopped two two-man advantages. He was stopping pucks from everywhere. We quickly found out who Gilles Meloche was."

He was an anomaly. "I was 21 years old playing in the National League, and there were no 21-year-old goalies at that time. When you got through the system, usually you were 27, 28. The press kept me mentally up, because everywhere I went, my write-ups were, 'Playing on such a bad team, playing game in and game out,'" he said.

Marshall Johnston was a teammate and Meloche's coach in Oakland. He said of the youngster, "Realistically, he was the only star of the team. He literally gave you a chance to win every night. That's how good he was."

Sometimes his efforts came with fringe benefits. Johnston recalled a game in the old Boston Garden during which the Seals were horribly out shot. They should have lost 15-1 but instead won 2-1, thanks to Meloche. The owner was grateful. "Charlie Finley owned the team, and the next day, we're in New York and Charlie marches everybody into the Gucci store and bought everybody a pair of shoes," said Johnston.

Remarkably, Meloche barely spent any time at all on the injured reserve: "I think I got lucky. I was injury-free for 18 years. I missed six weeks at one time, just a freak accident in practice. I lost my blocker and Reggie Leach skated over my hand and cut the tendon."

Meloche considered himself a "scramble" goalie, with his hero, Glenn Hall, in mind: "I would butterfly, but up the wing, rushes, I would stand up, try to come out and cut the angles, so you're just using reflexes."

Meloche's greatest showcase came in Minnesota via Cleveland. The Golden Seals became the Cleveland Barons in 1976; when the Barons were dispersed in June 1978, Minnesota, which inherited much of the team, kept him.

In the 1980 playoffs, the Canadiens were up three games to two against the North Stars. Meloche stood on his head to tie the series in Game 6 and then performed a masterly classic in an incredible 3-2 win in Game 7 in Montreal.

After being eliminated, Montreal's Rod Langway said, "I don't care what anyone says, Meloche was the difference in the series and is the backbone of that team. Everyone worked extremely hard on both teams, but it was Meloche who made save after save and kept them in there. Even in the two games we won in Minnesota, he didn't play badly."

The next year, the North Stars made it to the Stanley Cup Final, losing in five games to the New York Islanders. Meloche also made the NHL All-Star Game twice during his stay in Minnesota.

Dennis Maruk played with Meloche during the Seals/Barons years and again years later in Minnesota. He'd matured, said Maruk: "He got stronger. As players got faster and strong too, with their shooting and everything, he just continued playing. I think he was able to excel at his position because of his work ethic and knowing the game extremely well. That's why he had a successful career."

In May 1985, the North Stars traded Meloche to Edmonton, and the Oilers subsequently flipped him to Pittsburgh. From 1985 to 1988, he played 34, 43, and 27 games for the Pens and then called it quits.

He said, "I was 38 years old. I knew it was time. It's just a transition. They changed the general manager. It was getting tough at the end, so I knew the end was near."

He opened a Dilallo Burger franchise in the St. Henri part of Montreal with his brothers, Denis and Robert, that is still in operation 30 years later.

In 1989, Pittsburgh hired Meloche as a scout, and he has been there ever since and is also a strong part of the team's alumni association.

"Scouting is not an art. You make some mistakes and you make some good moves. It's just being around the game, knowing the game," he said.

Meloche first scouted Fleury as a 15-year-old in Cape Breton. "He was an exceptionable athlete. We needed a goalie bad, and we were lucky to get a hold of him," he said.

For Meloche, being a goalie coach is about knowing when to step in and when not to. He said, "I've been around the game my whole life. I played 18 years. You go back to when you were playing. When you were playing good, you see the puck like a basketball. But you will be struggling once in a while, so that's when you step in and get back to the basics. I always say, 'If you're in the National League, you have the talent to be there.' Ninety-five per cent of it is the mental part of it."

His son, Eric Meloche, made the NHL as a forward for a couple of seasons and played pro hockey around the world for a dozen years. Dad said, "I'm proud of him. He had the right frame of mind. He played hard, he played tough."

After his own 40 years in professional hockey, Gilles Meloche is content: "There were a few highs and a lot of lows. I just enjoyed the game. In my life, I consider myself lucky that I never worked a day in my life."

GILLES GRATTON
Traditionally the domain of the strange and wonderful, the mercurial and temperamental, the Goaltenders' Union never included anyone quite like Gilles Gratton, before or since.

While many ambitious young players might consider spearing their grandmothers just for a chance of turning pro, Gratton never much cared for hockey and sort of fell into a playing career rather than pursuing it.

Born July 28, 1952, in LaSalle, Quebec, Gratton started out as a forward, playing on the third line of his peewee team while his older brother, Norm—who would also make the NHL—skated on the first. But when the team's goaltender, Dan Bouchard, who also made the pros, decided to play bantam, the club needed someone to fill the breach, and Gratton donned the pads. It didn't prove to be one of those eureka moments that many goaltenders experience, and, in fact, he didn't even enjoy it very much.

"Not much, no," he said. Was he at least good at it? "I guess I was okay."

He didn't see much of a future in it, and two concussions would limit his Junior B career to only a handful of games. "I didn't think I was going to play anymore," he admitted.

Enter Chuck Cato, a scout for the Boston Bruins. He'd checked out Gratton and his LaSalle team, the best team in bantam and midget, and offered him a contract to play for the Ontario Hockey Association's Oshawa Generals.

"I didn't know what to do because I didn't like school, so I thought I might as well go, learn English. So I went over and played three years," said Gratton.

His play blossomed with the Generals, and in his final season, he earned an All-Star selection. It was enough to get him drafted by Buffalo. The Sabres took him in the fifth round of the 1972 NHL Amateur Draft, 69th overall. Gratton, however, was far from thrilled by the Sabres' offer of $5,000 to sign, $8,000 his first year, $10,000 the second, and a free ticket to the Central Hockey League. Fortunately for him, players at the time had good options to play elsewhere in North America, specifically the World Hockey Association. The Ottawa Nationals came up with a far more lucrative deal—$20,000 to sign, $25,000 and $30,000 in the first and second years, respectively—and Gratton turned pro.

"If the World Hockey Association is not created, I'm not playing anymore. I'm not going to the Central League," sniffed Gratton. "[The WHA] offered me $75,000 for two years. I'm 20 years old, I have no money and now I'm going to go to work? So I decided to go," he said.

He played a season in Ottawa and then followed the club to Toronto when it moved and became the Toros. Besides the financial incentives, the WHA also allowed Gratton to avoid Punch Imlach, who was running the Sabres. One of the players who realized Gratton dodged a bullet was fellow Toro and ex-Leafs star defenceman Carl Brewer, who butted heads with Imlach back in the '60s. "He told me a lot of stories about Punch Imlach, so I don't think I would have liked to have played for him," admitted Gratton.

The feeling more than likely would have been mutual, seeing as Imlach held Johnny Bower, who probably couldn't be more unlike Gratton, as perhaps his favourite player. Gratton's antics also wouldn't have been good for Imlach's notoriously bad heart. Who knows what he would have made of Gratton streaking during a practice at the George Bell Arena, wearing nothing but his skates and goalie mask. At the time, Gratton called the prank payment for sticks he took from team trainer Larry Ashley.

"I came out naked after practice and skated around. I did that a lot. To tell you the truth, it felt good. . . . Hockey is boring, which is why I quit, and skating around like that is not boring," Gratton said.

It was incidents like that, doing upside-down push-ups in full gear, and his natural piano playing abilities that grew the Gratton legend. So too did his antics in net.

Backup Toro netminder Les Binkley said, "He was just in another world. He would fall down and the trainer would run out. The trainer would come back, and I said, 'Well, what did he say?' He says, 'Lupus is going to collide with Jupiter, I don't know.' He was a good teammate, but he was just a little strange."

Gratton would also make pretending to be hurt a high art form. Toros teammate Mike Amodeo told the *Toronto Star*, "He called it his 'dead fish' routine. If he felt we needed to regroup, he'd flop to the ice and lie perfectly still, stopping play. After a lot of twitching and spasms, he'd then make a miraculous recovery and the game would resume."

It was one of those flops that first got Toro Gavin Kirk's attention, especially Gratton's interaction with the trainer who went out to check on him.

"Gilles said, 'I got the puck right here in my ribs, in behind my padding, and it hit the same spot where in my earlier life somebody hit me with a sword when I was a Spaniard.' The doctor, who was an orthopedic surgeon, said, 'Gilley, I think you've got the wrong type of doctor here. You need one with a couch,'" Kirk said at the time.

Not everyone was amused. For *The Big M*, Paul Henderson lamented to Ted Mahovlich about the team's troubles in net, "If you don't have goaltending you've got problems, and we had a fruitcake for a goaltender. I mean Gilles Gratton was out of control. He was a space cadet from another era."

As humorous as some of his antics could be, he could also be downright frustrating. He famously pulled himself out of a game against Houston and went back to the hotel after facing 45 shots in two periods while the Toros only managed 11. "I had done my job," he told Steve Dryden for a feature article in *Inside Hockey*. On another occasion, when he wasn't scheduled to start or backup a playoff game against San Diego, he decided to enjoy a beer at a pool hall instead of joining his teammates before the game.

But that's not to say Gratton had no abilities. In fact, hockey historian and journalist Stan Fischler saw a player with a great deal of talent: "I was doing WHA games and watched him with the Toros. Excellent stylist, fast and good hands. He was considered a sure thing in the NHL."

"I think he could have been one of the greats. He just seemed to be a natural at it. He didn't seem to have to work at stopping the puck," Toros teammate Tony Featherstone told *Inside Hockey*.

Gratton initially charmed Toros owner Johnny Bassett, so much so that Bassett invited him to live in his own home and indulged his musical hobby, allowing him full use of his grand piano. But even that relationship soured, when Gratton walked out on the team.

"I love the kid. He lived in my home for a while last year and my kids thought the world of him," said Bassett to the Canadian

Press, adding Gratton could be among the best NHL goaltenders if he played to his potential. "But he is not mature. He said he wasn't happy here last season, but I believe one of the reasons he didn't want to return was because he didn't want to face his teammates. He let them down and he knew it."

Gratton said, "I wasn't the right player for him but he was the right owner for me, that's for sure. He was a great guy, but I was screwed up. I'm the guy who left Toronto; I should have stayed. I had a five-year contract, but I left because I was pissed off because they fired Billy Harris, my coach. That was a mistake, because John Bassett was great to me."

By leaving the Toros, he wound up with the St. Louis Blues, who'd bought his rights from Buffalo. He found another admirer in fellow goaltender Ed Staniowski. "He was a roommate of mine, a very interesting character," said Staniowski, now a lieutenant colonel in the Canadian military. He added that he enjoyed Gratton's company and that Gratton was a "very good goaltender. There's no question, when he was on, he was as good as anybody who ever played the game."

Gratton, however, only played a handful of games for the Blues and walked out after feuding with coach Garry Young. "That was a mistake. I didn't like St. Louis, I didn't like the coach, I didn't like anything, and I left," Gratton said.

There was talk he'd return to the Toros, but the Blues weren't inclined to do him any favours and blocked his move, forcing him to spend the rest of the season under suspension.

"I thought that was it for me, I thought my career was over by then. But then the Rangers called me in the summer; John Ferguson wanted me on the team so I said okay, we'll try for another year, I guess," said Gratton.

At the time of his signing, coach and general manager Ferguson gushed at his new acquisition. "He has been a model student. He's a super goalie; he's intelligent, he hasn't bothered me at all. I've never seen a goaltender who worked so hard at practices as he does. He's just a very talented person. He can play the piano by ear like you've never heard before," Ferguson told the *Montreal Gazette*.

Rangers star forward Rod Gilbert also marvelled at Gratton, calling him the best goalie he shot against in practice, no small compliment considering he'd faced the likes of ex-teammates Gump Worsley, Ed Giacomin, and Terry Sawchuk.

But the honeymoon was brief. Fergie couldn't have known what he was getting himself into, even though he'd counted iconoclasts like Jacques Plante and Gump Worsley as teammates in his playing days in Montreal.

"One night I told the coach that my moon wasn't squared with my sun. He kind of looked at me, shook his head, and he just walked out of the room," Gratton said.

On another occasion, Gratton told Ferguson that a leg injury related to a wound he'd received while fighting in the Franco-Prussian War was still bothering him. "One night I told him I couldn't play because I had an injury from a past life," Gratton said, admitting, "I didn't feel like playing, I didn't feel well."

Fergie's patience eventually wore thin, and after a 6-3 loss to the Islanders, he told the press Gratton wasn't providing NHL goaltending. After appearing in 41 games and posting a bloated 4.21 GAA, Gratton was done as a big leaguer. He got sent down to the Rangers American Hockey League affiliate in New Haven, but he did little more there than collect his paycheque.

If Gratton's relationship with a no-nonsense warrior like Fergie wasn't ideal, Gratton blamed himself. Manhattan generally, and places like Studio 54 specifically, offered many less-than-ideal temptations for a professional athlete, and like Rangers teammates before him, Gratton found himself lured to them.

"[Fergie] was okay; he was nice to me. I'm the one that screwed up. When I was in New York, I was partying all the time, drinking and smoking, stuff like that," said Gratton, who believed he suffered from depression. He added, "That was why I smoked and drank and partied—you do these things when you don't feel well. . . . I think in life when you're in an environment that you don't appreciate, you just get like that. It just wasn't my thing to be in that environment. As soon as I left, I was okay. . . . I didn't enjoy playing."

He threw in the towel at only 25 years old after having suffered six concussions. Gratton explained, "And my back was bad, so I just decided to go, because I was hurt too much. But I didn't tell anyone. I just left, that was it."

As Fergie tells it, the signs of trouble ahead were clear early on and he should have spotted them sooner. When St. Louis booted him, they issued a press release stating Gratton had respectfully submitted his resignation as a member of the Blues to team owner Sid Salomon III.

"Gratton's version was different. He told me that he told Salomon . . . 'You can stick your team up your ass, I'm not coming back!'" Ferguson wrote in his memoir, *Thunder & Lightning*.

Although a gifted athlete, Gratton was far better known for his bizarre interviews with the press and erratic behaviour. "Brother, they didn't call him Grattoony the Loony for nothing," Ferguson wrote.

According to Ferguson, Gratton at various times claimed to be a 12th-century sailor, an Indian hobo in the 1300s, a Spanish landowner in the 17th century, a Spanish priest a hundred years later, and a Victorian-era British surgeon. Gratton at one point insisted his life as a goalie was his punishment for stoning peasants in a past life. But the reality was much less fantastic, and while the press and his peers labelled him a flake, he was really crazy as a fox. Although a believer in reincarnation, Gratton admitted he was more often than not pulling people's legs, inventing stories, and making jokes.

"It's not a belief—I remember. . . . I've done a lot of past life regressions, so I could talk about it all day. But I was just trying to have some fun when I talked about it. It wasn't serious. I could have just kept quiet, but it was just so the newspapermen would have something to talk about. . . . Astrology was used as an excuse not to play too, but it also wasn't true," Gratton said.

One of Gratton's lasting legacies to the game remains the lion mask he wore, which today resides at the Hockey Hall of Fame. At a time when protective gear was fairly plain, Gratton spent $300 to get a design that stood out, a painted fang-bearing lion.

"I am a Leo. This mask has become me. I'm a lion. That's no bull. I really feel stronger," he said at the time. The first Ranger to see the mask may have been Ferguson, and on Halloween night no less.

"My bell rang and there, standing in my doorway, was this guy wearing a goalie mask with a fierce-looking lion painted on it. 'TRICK OR TREAT!' he yelled. It was Gratoony the Loony," Ferguson wrote.

Over 30 years later, another Ranger, Martin Biron, would pay tribute to Gratton, getting a likeness of his iconic lion painted on his own mask for the 2011 Winter Classic. But far from feeling honoured by the gesture, Gratton was apathetic: "I heard about it. I don't really care."

When Gratton left the game, he left it behind for good. He travelled to India and spent three years in ashrams for meditation and prayer. In 2006, he started working for Classic Auctions, a historical hockey memorabilia auction house. But it had absolutely nothing to do with a resurgent interest in the game. It was simply a coincidence, Gratton having met company president Marc Juteau through a friend. He has zero contact with old pros or anybody else involved in the sport, and his son seems to have inherited his father's indifference for the game, even turning down Montreal Canadiens tickets from Gratton's boss.

According to Gratton, "It was on a Thursday night so I asked my son if he wants to go and he said, 'No, I have school tomorrow morning and I don't want to go to bed late.' That's how interested he is. He says if Marc wants to give us tickets, tell him to give us tickets for Saturday."

BERNIE WOLFE Bernie Wolfe has considered going back into hockey, perhaps as a general manager for an NHL team. Then he thinks about it further, and he concludes that he doesn't want to take a pay cut.

At the moment, he runs Bernard R. Wolfe & Associates, Inc., a financial planning firm based in Washington, DC, that manages $14 billion in assets. The entire NHL is valued at about $3 billion.

Wolfe said, "It wouldn't be all that different than what I do today. It would be strategizing, planning, contractual structuring. I do that all the time. Coaching, on the other hand, I'm not sure if I would have the patience. When I played, we were terrified of management. I think management is afraid of the players today."

Wolfe tended net for a relatively short period of time, 1975 to 1979, on some pretty poor Washington Capitals teams. In his 120 games, Wolfe got 20 wins, with one shutout, against 61 losses and 21 ties. His final goals-against average was 4.17.

He is proof positive that success can follow the most dismal of days.

"In the NHL, we weren't a very good team. I knew I was going to get 40 or 50 shots every game. I also knew that teams were going to change their styles when they played against the Washington Capitals. For example, when we played the Flyers, and they were winning their Stanley Cup in those days. Their defencemen would not be playing the points, but would be playing the tops of the circles. Everybody wanted to fatten their averages. I was used to winning. It was no fun losing," he said.

Born in Montreal on December 18, 1951, Wolfe was a peewee-aged sniper but was called to the net as a fill-in and never left. Though the Sorel Black Hawks of the Montreal Metropolitan Junior Hockey League came calling, he wanted an education—in English. Wolfe enrolled at Montreal's Sir George Williams University for a commerce degree and was a walk-on to the varsity hockey team. "No one had really heard of me," he said. It wasn't too long until they knew his name, however. Wolfe led the team to the Canadian collegiate final in 1974 and was named tournament MVP; he was also named top male athlete at the school.

The Los Angeles Kings sent him an invite to camp in Victoria, BC. "I was surprised. I guess somebody had told them about me," he said. Given the chance to report to the team's affiliate in Albuquerque, New Mexico, Wolfe chose to keep his amateur status and return to school for a final year.

Wolfe said, "I'm embarrassed about my thinking, but I said, 'New Mexico?' Here, I'm a kid from Montreal; I'd never been to many places in the United States at the time. I said it to myself, 'You can't drink the water in Mexico.' Little did I know that New Mexico is a beautiful state."

Billy Taylor of the Capitals scouted Wolfe during the university championships, and by the end of the first period, he'd made a deal to acquire him from L.A. In June 1974, Wolfe signed up for a reported $40,000 a year for two seasons, plus a $15,000 signing bonus.

It was rare for a player to go from the Canadian college ranks to the NHL. Wolfe recalled, "They teased me back then and called me, 'Joe College.'"

Equally rare was a player of Jewish descent.

Noted writer Leonard Shapiro of the *Washington Post* once did a story on Bernie's mom, Fay Wolfe. "When they start yelling 'Ber-nie, Ber-nie,' oh, what a wonderful thrill that is. But it's nerve-wracking for any mother to look at the game if your child is playing. I get very nervous, and when I see somebody go into him, I get very angry," she said.

Wolfe remembers the feature well, and fans still bring it up. "She was such a typical Jewish mother. She was disappointed I wasn't a lawyer or a doctor. I still get people coming up to me saying, 'That was the greatest article I've ever read,' because they were able to identify with it—not being a pro athlete but just with their own mothers," he said.

Then, abruptly in November 1979, Wolfe announced his retirement. He was 27 and planned to do financial consulting and some public relations work for the Capitals. "I had enough, to the point that my contract was a guaranteed deal and I retired with one year still to go," he said. "Not for any medical reasons. I just didn't enjoy it anymore."

Gary Inness was one of the other targets in the Caps net, and he reflected on his partner: "He had a good start, then he backed away from it. Bernie never really seemed to enjoy being a goaltender. Bernie was quite clear that he wanted to move on to other things."

Wolfe has said that it was a tough decision and that he had two children to think about: "I kept on asking my wife, 'What do you think I should do? What do you want me to do?' She wouldn't give any opinion. She said, 'You need to make this decision.' So the entire summer, I was going back and forth. Finally the day of training camp, I made my decision not to go. I'm happy to say that I've never looked back, I've never regretted that decision. I've never missed it either."

But he did go back. Sort of. In the summer of 1992, an expansion draft was in the works for the Lightning and Senators. The Capitals signed the 40-year-old Wolfe to a contract, in an effort to protect Don Beaupre, Jim Hrivnak, and Olaf Kölzig. League president John Ziegler vetoed the deal, and the Caps signed Steve Weekes instead.

It's just one more example of Wolfe getting some publicity for his company. He's still in attendance at many Capitals games and tries to keep up his visibility.

He said, "Hockey has helped me in a lot of ways. It's gotten me to the White House. Being in Washington, my business, and everything else, when people talk about our firm, they also say, 'He used to be the goaltender for the Washington Capitals.'"

OUT OF THE FRYING PAN AND INTO THE FIRE

For all the bellyaching, pain, and agony that come with being a goaltender, in the end, it is still just a game. There are real jobs far more intense than being a goalie.

Like firefighting, which also has a team atmosphere.

Terry Richardson, now a scout with the Washington Capitals, was a goalie in the 1970s and a firefighter in the 1980s. "There were some times a life was in your hands. It was a different kind of stress, but I would say more stressful for sure. There were a lot of down times, where you were just able to have a lot of fun too around the fire hall, but when the bell rang, everybody's face changed," said Richardson.

PAUL HARRISON When his hockey career wound down,

Paul Harrison wanted to be a fireman. They weren't hiring, but the police were. After 30 years on the beat and his retirement approaching, he could look back and appreciate how hockey had prepared him for what was to come—and helped him raise thousands of dollars.

Home is Timmins, a northeastern Ontario community on the Mattagami River with a mining-based economy. The mayor suggested the police force, but Harrison balked. "I never had any interest in that whatsoever," he said. The police chief sold him on it, especially the team aspect: "He made a lot of similarities to being on a hockey team." For the first dozen years, Harrison walked the beat.

His real calling, however, would come as there was an attempt to install the drug prevention program D.A.R.E. (Drug Abuse Resistance Education) into northern Ontario, but there was no money for it. Harrison ended up being tapped twice for the program, taking a course to be a teacher in the program in 1996; he has since travelled throughout North America and even to the Philippines to train others in the program, which resulted in a transfer to the Ontario Provincial Police.

While he was learning, Harrison was also raising money for the initiative. On the phone to his old buddies, Harrison has run the NHL Alumni Hockey Dream Draw since then, with the money going to local hockey systems and drug prevention programs.

"All the lessons I needed to learn in life I learned playing minor hockey. They've served me well," said Harrison, who was born in 1955 in Timmins and learned to be tough as "the runt in the neighbourhood." If he wanted to play with the big boys, he had to go in net. He explained, "It was a blessing because by the time I was playing organized hockey, I was accustomed to playing with kids that were three or four years older than me. So when I started playing structured hockey, the kids my own age, they couldn't score on me to save their life."

But it wasn't a smooth journey. Harrison said, "It wasn't just an easy ride from the outdoor rink to the NHL. I was cut three times from minor hockey teams growing up, peewee, bantam. I spent a whole season on the bench in midget, never got on the ice. It was like, 'What the heck?' But the lessons I learned from that were beneficial later on."

Harrison was a late bloomer, an overage draft pick for the Ontario Hockey League's Oshawa Generals in June 1973, out of the Timmins Kinsmen juvenile squad. Though his numbers were never great (GAAs of 4.10 and 4.20), he was drafted in the 1975 amateur draft by the Minnesota North Stars (third round, 40th overall) and the WHA's Cincinnati Stingers (fifth round, 61st overall).

In Oshawa he played in tandem with Rick St. Croix, and Harrison reflected on their differences: "Ricky has always been a wonderful technical goaltender. He was very, very studious, even back in our junior days, always striving to improve and working on his game. Whereas I just stopped the puck. 'Shoot it, I'll stop it,' that's about how much thought I put into it, I think."

During that 1975–76 rookie season, which he split between the North Stars and the Providence Reds of the American Hockey League, Harrison did a lot of watching. And standing up for himself. "Then when I turned pro, everybody and their uncle was trying to turn me into a stand-up goalie. Hell, the reason I'm here is because of the way I played," he said, referencing his hero, Glenn Hall. "I can't play a stand-up style. It felt so awkward for me. I played everything off my edges and reactionary. I was pretty quick for a big guy and that helped me eventually."

Harrison only saw a couple of NHL games the following season, but he did lead the AHL in wins and minutes with the New Haven Nighthawks. In 1977–78, he finally got to the big squad for good and went 6-16-2 in his 27 appearances. It was enough to convince the Maple Leafs that he would be a worthy backup to Mike Palmateer in Toronto, and Harrison was dealt for a fourth-round pick in the 1981 entry draft in June 1978.

Over two seasons in Toronto, Harrison saw a decent amount of action. "My stats aren't exactly wonderful, but I'm proud of them just the same. Just getting into as many games as I did, playing behind Palmy—I had 55 games over two years with the Leafs—and Mike was obviously our starting goaltender, so that's not too shabby for a backup goalie in that environment," he said.

Palmateer had wonky knees and didn't always practise with the team, and coach Roger Neilson worked Harrison hard. He said, "I can remember doing line rushes, and there's only one goalie, so they'd do the line rushes down one end and then I'd have to skate like a mad fool to the other end to do the line rushes the other way. Just getting out there every day and facing Lanny MacDonald's freaking shots in practice for an hour and a half—I should have been paid more just for that!"

But those Leafs weren't world beaters, and neither were the Penguins (1981–82) or the Sabres (1982), his other destinations. His best year actually came in 1980–81 with the Central Hockey League's Dallas Black Hawks, where he was a Second-Team All-Star and shared the Terry Sawchuk Trophy for the best team GAA. Harrison said, "I played on some good teams and maybe some not-so-good teams, but lots of quality people, a lot of good, solid people. All of my goaltending partners over the years were great guys."

"Harry-O" spent the 1982–83 season with the AHL's Rochester Americans and called it quits. With two young children at home, he needed to find work. Enter the police force.

Paul Harrison eyes the puck, heading toward Yvon Lambert of the Canadiens.
(Courtesy Paul Harrison)

"There was no money back then. We played for the love of the game, and it was fun. It was fun to play in the National Hockey League, the travel, the teammates, after-practice stuff. It was just a hoot. It was a great way to make a living and just tour around the world," said Harrison.

He has a lot of pride in his 109 NHL games: "I honestly felt that I was the hardest-working goalie around. Every time I got on the ice, I did the best I possibly could. So I have no regrets. If it didn't work out, it didn't work out, but it wasn't for lack of trying."

Ed Staniowski in a different uniform while stationed in Afghanistan in 2008. (Courtesy Ed Staniowski)

ED STANIOWSKI Ed Staniowski

is one of the few who can say his military career had to be put on hold because he'd been drafted.

During his junior days, when he stopped pucks for the Regina Pats, Staniowski already had aspirations of joining up, wishing to pursue a family tradition. "My father had served in the Second World War, and I had a brother who served in the Canadian Forces, so it was a natural fit for me," said Staniowski, explaining that his father was in the Polish army during the Nazi invasion. His mother also served, as a nurse.

If he didn't get picked by an NHL team, Staniowski intended to enroll in the Royal Military College in Kingston, Ontario, and get a commission in the Canadian Armed Forces.

Born on July 7, 1955, in Moose Jaw, Saskatchewan, Staniowski won the 1970 provincial midget title with his hometown club and went on to star with the Western Hockey League's Regina Pats. An All-Star, he played on the Pats' last Memorial Cup winner in 1974 and was named the inaugural Central Hockey League Player of the Year, the only goaltender to capture the prize. He'd also earn a silver medal at the 1975 World Junior Ice Hockey Championship and was named best goaltender of the tournament.

The third goalie picked in the 1975 entry draft, Staniowski was the St. Louis Blues' first selection, taken 27th overall. The rival World Hockey Association's Cleveland Crusaders also took a run at him, but they made it clear he'd be serving mostly in a support role to number-one Gerry Cheevers. Staniowski's concerns over that league's stability, his desire to play, plus a lucrative offer from St. Louis made him an NHLer.

"For me, it turned out to be a great opportunity and I loved St. Louis. I still have a lot of friends out there and I get back there a couple times a year," he said.

There, he'd come under the tutelage of Mr. Goalie himself, the great Glenn Hall, whom he proudly says remains a friend today:

"One of the great aspects of his approach to coaching goalies, from my perspective, was that he noted your style and complemented it," Staniowski said, explaining Hall would tell his charges how to build on their styles instead of changing them. He also mentored in a way that built confidence.

Staniowski made Winnipeg his new home after Mike Liut became the clear-cut starter in St. Louis and the Blues sent him and future NHL Coach of the Year Paul MacLean to the Jets. Winnipeg had had a miserable previous season with only nine wins, but Staniowski joined a much-improved squad, as rookie sensation Dale Hawerchuk and first-year man Thomas Steen lifted the club, alongside Lucien DeBlois and former Montreal Canadiens All-Star defenceman Serge Savard, into the playoffs. The Jets' 48-point year-over-year improvement established a new NHL record, and Staniowski won 20 games with his new team.

"It was exciting. We had Dougie Smail, Dale Hawerchuk, Scotty Arniel, Paul MacLean, Fergie brought in Serge Savard, which gave us a lot of maturity. We were young and we believed in ourselves, and we went out there and played the game with reckless abandon," Staniowski said.

Also hard to forget was another former Hab, John Ferguson, the Jets GM who'd brought him over from St. Louis. Staniowski explained,

You always knew where you stood with Fergie. He didn't hold any punches. I remember one night in Winnipeg, he was always up in the box at centre ice, and I let in a questionable goal, and all I saw were a bunch of papers come floating down from up in the box.

I never even had to look up. I knew that he was not pleased with me for letting that goal in. When he came into the dressing room, if the door opened and it looked like it was coming off the hinges, you knew he was going to have something to say. But a heart of a lion, a heart of gold. He'd go to bat for his players. He expected a lot out of you, but he was the first guy in your corner when you needed him.

As Doug Soetaert—with whom Staniowski had shared the goal-tending duties at the World Juniors and with whom he now shared them with the Jets—increasingly saw most of the action, Staniowski would be on the move again, this time to Hartford, where his old Blues boss Emile Francis ran the club.

After he retired, his last season coming in 1984–85, he finally got to achieve his original goal of becoming a military man.

Less than a year after playing his last NHL game at the world-famous Madison Square Garden, Staniowski was a basic recruit training in Petawawa, Ontario. He'd just turned 30, and the 25-year-old sergeant giving him drill shouted, "You've got to be one of the most uncoordinated things I've ever seen in my life!" Staniowski was tempted to reply, "Oh, so you saw me in the NHL," but demurred.

He joined the Canadian Forces Primary Reserves as an officer cadet in the Royal Regina Rifles and found his new career a perfect fit.

"I loved every minute of it—jumping out of airplanes, training with soldiers, very physical. Everything I've been able to do in the military, I really, really enjoyed," said Staniowski. His military peers reminded him of his hockey ones in their focus, dedication, and fitness: "I know guys like Mark Napier and [Bob] Probert and Tiger [Williams] and others who would make great soldiers, and I know some soldiers, if they had the ability, they'd make great hockey players. There's definitely an overlap there."

But Staniowski also had trying times in the military, and assignments in Africa, Afghanistan, the Middle East, and the Balkans have left indelible marks on his psyche.

There's some places that I've been to that were very, very sobering. I was in Sierra Leone, where there was a terrible civil war, with a lot of suffering. And the Balkans, when the Serbs and Croats were going at each other. Afghanistan came with its own challenges. Canada's paid a pretty significant price with our allies in Afghanistan. I would say I've seen the best young Canadians have to offer and, unfortunately, I've seen the worst that the world can throw at [Canada] and each other.

His hockey experience—working within a team structure and dealing with pressure situations and making quick decisions—proved immensely valuable to his military career.

Staniowski explained, "When you're on operations in places like Afghanistan, Balkans, and Africa, things happen very quickly and you have to be trained and prepared. You and those around you have to react very, very quickly. You're never by yourself, you're always part of a much larger organization or unit, and it's very satisfying to have reliance on others and have them look to you for decisions and such as an officer and leader."

Now a lieutenant colonel, Staniowski is one of the directors at the Command and Staff College in Kingston, where regular and reserve officers in the Canadian Army are trained for higher command.

"We basically teach them the art and science of war. Everything from peacekeeping to war fighting," Staniowski said, adding he's used lessons and approaches Glenn Hall provided all those years back: "Perhaps his greatest contribution to me was his insight into dealing with the pressures of the game. Being nervous was part of the game, but it was what you did about it that mattered. The big thing was focus on what you have control over before the game, and once the game starts, it will take care of itself. . . . Before operations, you do all you can to prepare, focus on what you have control of and once you're in the fight, your training will take over."

His old GM, Francis, wasn't taken aback in the least by Staniowski's long service and rise through the ranks: "It doesn't surprise me, because he was very disciplined, very well organized, and a hard worker."

Regina hockey hasn't forgotten his accomplishment either, as the Pats retired his and teammate Clark Gillies' numbers in 2000; in 2005, Staniowski was inducted into the Saskatchewan Sports Hall of Fame and Museum. He'll never forget that night, especially a "Hot Stove Lounge" session with Hall and Johnny Bower.

"Sitting between two of the greatest goalies to have ever played in the NHL and moderating their bantering and memories was incredible. The stories never ended, the laughs were long and the humility of both of these NHL Hall of Famers was genuine. I considered it an honour to be in their presence and it remains one of the highlights of my life."

CHAPTER 5

FROM THE NET TO THE BROADCAST BOOTH

BOBBY "THE CHIEF" Taylor cracks wise when asked why so many goaltenders end up as analysts, covering hockey games on radio and television: "Probably because we're so full of bullshit."

But when the colour guy for Tampa Bay Lightning is pressed, he explained, "I think a lot of it is because we see both sides of the game," said Taylor, who played from 1971 to 1976. He added, "Obviously, we really pay attention to the defensive side of the game, because that's what our success hinges on. But also too, we get the offensive side, because of the guys that are coming at you all the time. When you look at it, we're the only position player that's on the ice for 60 minutes of the game."

It seems everywhere you turn, there's an ex-goalie spouting off about this or that; it's not an exclusive club by any means, as ex-coaches and ex-players are equally loquacious.

It was John Davidson who started the ball rolling when he was hired by *Hockey Night in Canada*, initially sitting in as the third man with Bill Hewitt and Brian McFarlane for a Toronto broadcast from Maple Leaf Gardens. He would go on to a stellar career in the United States, and in 2009 he was presented the Foster Hewitt Memorial Award by the Hockey Hall of Fame.

"I always had a feeling that goaltenders would make the best analysts, because they saw the whole rink when they played," wrote *HNIC* producer Ralph Mellanby in his memoir. He added, "John was the first that we hired, and he paved the way for a flood of others: Glenn Healy, Darren Pang, John Garrett, Kelly Hrudey, Kay Whitmore, Chico Resch, Bobby Taylor, Daryl Reaugh . . . the list goes on and on. And all of those guys owe John a vote of thanks."

For a time, Ken Dryden was a high-profile, articulate announcer in the U.S., especially with his coverage of the Olympic Games. He told writer Roy McGregor in 1996 that it was a natural progression: "The broadcast booth in baseball is filled with pitchers and catchers. In football, it's the quarterback. These are the people who see the whole game."

One of the highest profile of them today is Kelly Hrudey of *Hockey Night in Canada*, who seemingly learned the inner workings of Hollywood while playing for the Kings. He served as a commentator for four playoff seasons before getting a full-time gig for the 1998–99 season.

Hrudey believes that any goaltender has to be able to understand options, the multiple ways a play could unwind, which translates to the broadcast studio. "It's all just watching and analyzing and trying to figure out what might happen. That's basically why most good analysts are former goaltenders, because it's all just watching and figuring out the options that a guy might have, and reading a play. I think that's pretty simple. For the guys that played in the net, if you're going to have any longevity, you have to read a play," said Hrudey.

For Brian Hayward, who covers the Anaheim Ducks and played in the 1980s, time on the bench as a backup was invaluable to his development of his skills as a broadcaster. "Goaltenders don't play every game, so can sit on the bench, hear what their coaches are saying all the time, hear the interaction between the coach and the players. I know that in my career, I was able to listen and hear what Pat Burns was saying, for example, behind the bench—and for the entire game, everything that he said. Not only what happens inside the locker room. I think those are all contributing factors," said Hayward.

As good as goalies can be at analyzing, retired Devils broadcaster Chico Resch said that the best of them aren't necessarily in the booth.

"I think people that have analytical minds find the goaltending position really fascinating. You take Kenny Dryden, who wrote a really introspective book, *The Game*. He summed up the way the goalie mind works. But he could say it a little bit better than the rest of us, so he wrote a book and the rest of us just an article," said Resch.

JOHN DAVIDSON Personable only begins to describe John Davidson. In another life, he would have been a politician—he is that good at making connections, listening, and kissing babies. Instead, he found his way into hockey—a 6-foot-3 giant when goalies were not sought out for their height—and parlayed his love of the game into a decent career (a 123-124-39 record) on a few mediocre teams, with one magical spring in 1979 and a run to the Stanley Cup Final, a Hall of Fame–worthy broadcasting career, and, now, a move into management.

"It is absolutely impossible to be nicer than Ranger goalie John Davidson. Some people can tie for first place, but nobody beats him out," wrote Stan Fischler in 1983, just before J.D. retired and moved into the booth.

Davidson, born in Ottawa on February 27, 1953, grew up in Calgary, a Montreal fan in a sea of Maple Leafs loyalists in the pre-expansion days. An injury to a teammate resulted in him trying goaltending. "I fell in love with the position," Davidson said.

After two seasons with the Lethbridge Sugar Kings in the Alberta junior league, he moved up to major junior, with the Calgary Centennials. His breakout year was 1971–72, when he was a workhorse with a league-leading 3,970 minutes in 66 games and had

A rookie John Davidson suits up with the St. Louis Blues in the 1973–74 season. (IHA/Icon SMI)

a Western Canada Hockey League–best eight shutouts and 2.37 GAA. When the rival Edmonton Oil Kings needed a goalie for the Memorial Cup, the Centennials loaned them their stud. An All-Star in both his WCJHL seasons, Davidson was on everyone's radar for the 1973 NHL entry draft.

With the WHA having shaken things up, many teams needed goaltending. Boston seemed a likely destination, with Jacques Plante bolting to the rival league and Ed Johnston off to Toronto. The Canadiens, with the cerebral Ken Dryden in its net, didn't need

Davidson, but they didn't want to see him go to a rival either. The St. Louis Blues, picking eighth, made a deal with the Habs to hop over the Bruins into the fifth spot and claim Davidson. At the time Blues GM Chuck Catto said, "I think his size gives him the confidence which he displays on the ice. He stands up in the goal and he's tough to beat. In fact, when he's on his knees, he's almost as big as most goalies standing up."

By debuting early in the 1973–74 campaign, Davidson became the first goaltender to spend a full season in the NHL directly from the juniors without any minor league experience. J.D. played 39 games and learned a lot from the Blues' other goalie, Wayne Stephenson. In 1974–75, Davidson finally got to the minors, in seven games with the Central Hockey League's Denver Spurs, and he saw his first playoff action. In short, he looked like the Blues' goalie for the future.

If his trade to the New York Rangers in June 1975 was a shock, it was nothing compared to what was to come in the Big Apple. "It was hard at first, because I came in there in my third year pro. It was hard because it was a different culture. Growing up in Calgary, then living in St. Louis for two years, very Midwestern, very quiet," he said.

An added challenge was replacing Eddie Giacomin, claimed by the Red Wings on waivers in October. "That was a tough thing to do. Especially after the first week, he came back in with Detroit after he had left and beat us 6-3 in the Garden. He stopped about 55 shots. I was awful," said Davidson. Madison Square Garden rang out with chants of "Eddie, Eddie," and it would not be too far down the road when those same passionate New York fans would lift him to his highest point.

During his regular season time with the Rangers, Davidson split the netminding duties with Dunc Wilson, Wayne Thomas, Doug Soetaert, Steve Baker, and Gilles Gratton. But in January 1979, coach Fred Shero anointed him the starter, and the team gelled. In 1979, Davidson said, "When I was given the number one job by the team, no pressure was put on me. I was told I would start the next six or seven games. If I didn't do very well, I would still be playing. If I blew a goal, I was still able to relax." But then a blood vessel exploded in his left hip, pressuring his sciatic nerve. The blood drained over the next six weeks, and he was ready for the playoffs.

The Rangers were underdogs against the Philadelphia Flyers in the quarterfinals and against the league-leading Islanders in the semis. With Davidson on fire, the team made it to the Stanley Cup Final and faced the Montreal Canadiens, who were on a three-year Cup streak. Though the Rangers lost in five games, Davidson—who hurt his knee in the series—still considers it a special time.

"That year we went to the finals in '79, that was one of the remarkable periods of my life. We were kind of underdogs, and we captured the whole city—we captured Manhattan, we captured New York. That was unexpected, just a pleasure, something that I'll never forget, ever," he said, jumping ahead to his time calling games. "Being there in '94 [as a broadcaster] when the Rangers won it after 54 years of not winning, just to see what it meant to people. I mean, we're talking millions and millions and millions and millions of people that were just captured by our run in '79 and in '94."

But '79–80 was not like the previous stellar year at all. Davidson struggled, and after just six games, he demoted himself to the minors, playing with the American Hockey League's New Haven Nighthawks. "I just want to get the feeling of the game again. You can't turn it off after the playoffs and sit around for three or four months and then expect to turn it on again," Davidson told the *New York Times*. And Davidson was never one to sit around and rest in the off-season. He and his wife, Diana, owned the White House Hotel in Windermere Lake, BC, at the time, and Davidson was always one to lend a hand to a charitable cause. Later, he started the Columbia Valley Rockies hockey team and ran a hockey school in the Columbia Valley.

After 41 games, and another nine in the playoffs in 1979–80, Davidson only got into 14 more NHL games before hanging up the skates in 1983. His body was a mess, with four knee operations and two back operations in three years. "I still want to play hockey. I'm only 29, although my body is 45. I still have the Rangers' blood in me," he told Fischler in early 1983.

Producer John Shannon hired Davidson for *Hockey Night in Canada*. In his memoir, *HNIC*'s Ralph Mellanby wrote, "From my perspective, Davidson was a good hire politically because he was from the west and had just retired from the game. I also found him to be a gregarious character, full of life, with a great sense of humour. I didn't think he'd be the greatest hockey analyst in TV history, but that is exactly what he became."

Davidson threw himself into the new job. In 1986, *HNIC* executive producer Don Wallace told *The Hockey News*'s Bob McKenzie that "John Davidson knows more about what goes on day-to-day in hockey than anyone else in the game. And I mean anyone. I also know that some management people in the National Hockey League will call him to get his opinions on players before a trade or a move. He's the best in the business. His work ethic is second to none. . . . His preparation is incredible. He's constantly obtaining information, making notes."

After two seasons, J.D. went to the MSG Network, calling Rangers games in the rink where he had once been lauded. He spent time on various networks (NBC, including the Olympics, Global, TBS, FOX, ABC, OLN/Versus, ESPN, SportsChannel), and then the honours started coming, including Emmy Awards and a CableACE Award, as well as the Lester Patrick Award for his contributions to ice hockey in the United States. The culmination of his achievements was the Foster Hewitt Memorial Award from the Hockey Hall of Fame in 2009.

Open to new challenges, Davidson was courted by the St. Louis Blues to become the team's president of hockey operations. He signed on in June 2006 and became the face of a dismal franchise; he deserves a lot of credit for the club's turnaround over the following years.

Being back in St. Louis after so long took some adjusting. He admitted, "When I came here as the president of the team, one of the first things I did was go to a baseball game, when the Cards got beat 11-2 by the Marlins, and nobody booed. I'm going, 'What the heck is this? They'd want to blow your house up in New York!'"

When ownership changed in St. Louis, Davidson's contract was seen as a financial burden, and all parties agreed a change was necessary. When he left the Blues in October 2012, the team's captain praised his contributions: "His savvy, his connections, his ability to connect with people is remarkable. The position that we're in now compared to when he got here the year before me and since I've been here, it's been phenomenal. It's definitely been aided by his work, his efforts. . . . It's sad to see him not be part of the Blues and the St. Louis community," David Backes told the Canadian Press.

He wasn't out of a job for long, as the Columbus Blue Jackets hired him within days as the team's president of hockey operations.

BRIAN HAYWARD The headaches that Brian Hayward went through in junior hockey don't exist any longer. He was one of the highest-ranked teenage goaltenders in Ontario and heavily recruited by Ontario Hockey League teams. Hayward turned them all down, knowing that he had the grades and aptitude to go to an Ivy League school and get an education along with hockey.

A Toronto native, he felt pressure from the Marlboros to play for them, and the London Knights drafted him, even though he said he'd be going to university. At one point, the Markham Waxers cut him, took his equipment away, and said, "We're not trading you."

"They were allowed to do that, because they were still trying to pressure me to play in the OHL," said Hayward. Now all Junior A players are guaranteed a scholarship for tuition, textbooks, and compulsory fees toward an undergraduate degree for each year played.

After a stint in Junior B, there was a happy ending. The Guelph Platers ponied up a higher-than-usual transfer fee to get Hayward out of the Marlies organization, and the team won the 1978 Centennial Cup.

And Hayward did get to Cornell and holds a degree in business

John Ahlers and Brian Hayward share a laugh on-air. (Courtesy Anaheim Ducks)

management. Despite his best efforts, though, he never got back there for the MBA he wanted.

Hockey, broadcasting, and other career choices got in the way.

Today, Hayward can be seen as the colour analyst on Anaheim Ducks broadcasts, but it hardly defines him. For a while, he worked with a manufacturing company that made sports novelty products like half-scale hockey helmets. There was a gym with his brother in Georgetown, Ontario. Now, it's apps, apps, and more apps.

"Broadcasting affords you some time to do some things on the side. This is now my third business," Hayward said of B3Connect, a mobile development/advertising company that has deals in place with a number of NHL and NBA teams. Naturally, the Ducks, owned by Henry Samueli of Broadcom Corporation, were an early adopter of the app. Hayward explained, "The Ducks seemed like a real natural to introduce this concept and this product to the world, and they've been very supportive. I'm all in on mobile right now, especially as it applies to team sports and the potential to customize a product that really allows the fans in the stadium to change the whole experience, allows them to become participatory on a number of different levels. Ticketing, concessions, all facets are right around the corner on mobile devices. It's a fun space to be in."

The 5-foot-10, 175-pound Hayward, born June 25, 1960, got his start in net playing with his older brother and his friends in Toronto's Rexdale neighbourhood. "It was instant positive feedback and a chance for a little guy to play with the big kids," he said.

Following four years with the Big Red at Cornell, Hayward signed as a free agent with Winnipeg on May 5, 1982. In retrospect, Hayward believes the time at Cornell helped him more than major junior would have: "I think back to when I was draft-eligible, physically I don't think I was ready to be a pro. My focus really was on education. You practice so much in college, especially at an Ivy League school. You don't play nearly as many games, so you really practice, and the hours in practice are long. You really have an opportunity to improve your fundamentals as a goaltender with all the practice time." Hayward gives a lot of credit to Cornell's assistant coach, Lou Raycroft, for developing himself and the other keeper, Darren Eliot, who also played in the NHL.

The wide-open hockey that "Hazy" experienced in Winnipeg and the high-flying Smythe Division of the 1980s meant a lot of action.

"Unfortunately, we were in the same division as Edmonton and Calgary, and they also had great teams. We couldn't get out of our division in the playoffs. I really think we were one of the top five teams in the league, but unfortunately, you had the Oilers and the

FRANK BRIMSEK, as "Mr. Zero" rhymes with "hero" for this young fan.

GUMP WORSLEY gets treated by trainer FRANK PACE
for severed tendons in his hand in February 1960. (© IHA/ICON SMI)

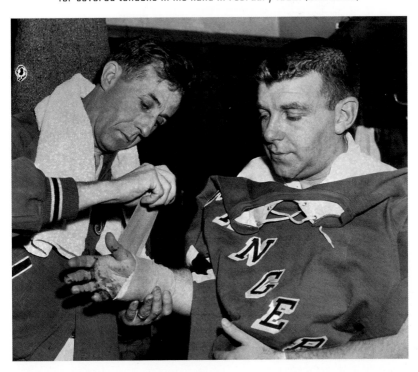

GORDIE HOWE lines up to the right of his Houston Aeros goaltender RON GRAHAME. (COURTESY CHARLOTTE GRAHAME)

CHARLIE HODGE tended net for the expansion Oakland Seals
in the 1967–68 season. (© IHA/ICON SMI)

Both JARI KURRI of the Oilers and MURRAY BANNERMAN of
the Hawks look to see where the puck went. (© IHA/ICON SMI)

In New York
with the Rangers,
the scrutiny on
GILLES GRATTON
was intense.

(© IHA/ICON SMI)

Cleveland Barons goalie
GILLES MELOCHE scrambles to get to
his feet as JIM NEILSON comes in to
help against the Bruins during
the 1976–77 season.

(© IHA/ICON SMI)

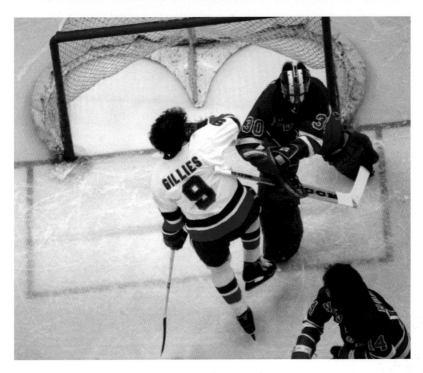

JOHN DAVIDSON of the New York Rangers steers the Islanders CLARK GILLIES away from the net. (© MECCA/HOCKEY HALL OF FAME)

MARTIN BRODEUR concentrates on the puck, allowing Devils captain SCOTT NIEDERMAYER to do his job. (© GEORGE TAHINOS)

Team Canada's CAREY PRICE consoles JONATHAN QUICK of Team USA at the 2014 Olympics in Sochi, Russia, after Canada won 1–0 to advance to the gold medal game. (© QMI AGENCY/ZUMAPRESS/ICON SMI)

Flames there too. I played some great games against the Oilers and gave up six, seven goals," he said.

To most, the trade to Montreal in August 1986 came out of the blue, as he'd played 52 games with Winnipeg and taken the team to the playoffs, but there was a connection that many wouldn't know about. Serge Savard, the Habs' general manager, had been Hayward's roommate in the rookie's first year with the Jets.

"He made the deal and it ended up being a great trade for my career to go to Montreal, to essentially work with this prodigy, Patrick Roy, who had won the Conn Smythe the year before, but was still a kid. It was a perfect situation for me. I could come in, push Pat, but at the same time, it was a great team in Montreal, a great defensive team," said Hayward.

The Canadiens had won the Stanley Cup the year before Hayward got there, and they were a stacked team. Hayward said,

Philly beat us in the conference final the one year when Ron Hextall won the Conn Smythe, and he outplayed both Patrick and myself—both of us played in that series. I think it's the reason we didn't get to the final. They ended up losing to Edmonton in seven, and Hextall was brilliant. But that was a great team we had in Montreal. At the time when we lost to Calgary [in 1989], I thought, "How could we possibly lose to them? We're so much better than they are." I've watched a bunch of games from that series and Calgary had a top team. I think Haakan Loob was playing on their third line at the time. They had Nieuwendyk and Gilmour. That was just a great, great team. Plus you had Lanny McDonald sitting in the stands. That was just a great team in Calgary, and I don't know if I feel any longer that that was the one that got away from us. We had our chance in Montreal.

Hayward played 37, 39, 36, and 29 games behind Roy in his four Montreal seasons. He said, "I'm quite proud of that. People will argue that he might be the greatest goaltender, or one of the greatest goaltenders of all-time. During my time in Montreal, I was able to compete with him."

In November 1990, he was peddled to Minnesota, the year the Cinderella North Stars made the Stanley Cup Final against Mario Lemieux's mighty Penguins. "We had no business playing against Pittsburgh in the final. They were so much better than we were. It's tough, it's a tough league to win in," said Hayward.

The new San Jose Sharks franchise claimed Hayward the following year in the NHL Dispersal Draft. Hayward is still trying to figure it all out: "It was a complicated deal, and I didn't know this, but when Minnesota traded for me, I actually became property of the San Jose Sharks. I didn't know that. So I was in Minnesota temporarily, and then because of this deal with the Gund brothers and the NHL not wanting them to move the franchise from Minnesota, instead awarding an expansion franchise, the Sharks were able to get five or six players off the Stars roster."

But the Sharks were getting damaged goods, explains Hayward.

I think I have a genetic issue with my back. My father had terrible back issues his whole life. I had some issues when I was in Montreal, so I think it was just starting to deteriorate. When I went to Minnesota, there were a couple of flare-ups, but nothing of significance. But right from the first training camp in San Jose is when I full-on herniated a disc for the first time. The discs were wearing down, they were bulged, but they weren't herniated. My first camp in San Jose is when it really broke down on me, and I never really recovered from it. I went through long periods where I couldn't get off the floor, months at a time.

At the time, surgical procedures on backs were not what they are today, and Hayward found that the top surgeons wouldn't touch him. (It wasn't until 2003 that he was fixed up for good.)

With the stereotypical macho mindset, Hayward rushed back to action. "I always thought I could win games, no matter what. I was playing in a full-on corset in San Jose; it literally was tied up to my armpits in a corset and couldn't rotate. Looking back, it was just dumb," he said. He felt he owed it to Jack Ferreira, the GM of the Sharks, who had convinced him to come to San Jose.

When the Sharks turfed Dennis Hull, their TV colour commentator mid-season, the injured Hayward was asked to fill in; after all, he was already on the payroll.

With an eye to the future, Hayward applied and was accepted to do his MBA at Cornell. But then the Mighty Ducks called. "Disney was awarded a new franchise in Anaheim and they convinced me to come out and talk to them. When I got here, it was my ex–general manager from the Sharks, Jack Ferreira, and I turned the job down; I didn't think I wanted it. Then Jack said, 'Then how about we make you the goalie coach at the same time? We'll throw some extra dollars into the pot,'" he said.

Hayward deferred his MBA for two years, thinking it would be a short-term gig with the Ducks. He's still there on TV, but he quickly learned the dual job of broadcaster and goalie coach doesn't work.

"After two years of being the goalie coach here, there was an obvious conflict with my broadcasting career; it was tough to talk to the other coaches on the other team and have them give you anything when you're a member of the opposite coaching staff," he said.

He has heard the criticisms that he is a homer for the Ducks. He responded, "I would say that regional announcers, especially in American markets, tend to be more pro home team than other ones. I don't think there's any question that all of us are slightly biased. But I would say that most of those comments come from Kings fans who hate me."

Hayward also noted that an announcer calls the game differently based on whether it's a regional or national broadcast. And he would know, having worked for *Hockey Night in Canada*, NBC, and ESPN.

His current broadcasting partner with the Ducks, John Ahlers, said that Hayward's reach is beyond just the booth. Ahlers, who often teases Brian about being ousted from the Goaltenders' Union for being outspoken, said,

> He's actually done a very good job and been a big part of marketing every level of the game since he's been here—he's been here 20 years now as broadcaster with the Ducks. He's not afraid to point out ways that he thinks would increase scoring in the game today, because he does believe that we need more goal scoring to be a popular game and to make the game more exciting. And he points out when he thinks goalies are cheating from an equipment standpoint; he points out the things that he thinks aren't right, because in his day it wasn't that way—and he constantly does it on the air.

The Ducks' Stanley Cup win in 2007 was a magic moment for Hayward, who got close but never won the Holy Grail himself. He said, "It was special to me as a broadcaster to see the team in Anaheim win, and to see what some people have called one of the truly great teams ever assembled in the league. I'm more aware of the struggles they had to overcome to win that Cup than most people realize."

KELLY HRUDEY Kelly Hrudey wavers when asked about the highlight of his 15-year NHL career. Most assume it is the 1993 trip to the Stanley Cup Final, where his Los Angeles Kings lost to the Montreal Canadiens.

"There were a lot of highlights, and that would clearly be one of them. But it was also my worst hockey memory," said Hrudey, referring to the two overtime losses at home that sunk the dream. He continued, "There's no question that if you go all the way to the finals, and you're up one game to nothing, and almost two nothing, and then lose in five, well, I know I'll never get over that disappointment. There's just no way you can. That's why I always hesitate when people say that about my most exciting time."

That is a big reason why, during the Kings' 2012 Stanley Cup,

Hrudey was an unabashed homer, wearing his heart on his sleeve despite his supposedly impartial job as a commentator on *Hockey Night in Canada.*

You can't be impartial, he said, "Not under those circumstances. That's your complete life, other than your family and your kids. You live that every single day, playing and competing with your teammates. It was a big part of my life."

A native of Elmwood, in Edmonton's west end, and born January 13, 1961, Hrudey was given a copy of Jacques Plante's famous textbook on goaltending as a 12-year-old and was hooked; up to that point squash had been his sport. He was not an overnight sensation and didn't make a rep team until he was 16 and the team was desperate for a keeper. A workhorse in three seasons with the Western Hockey League's Medicine Hat Tigers, the Islanders chose Hrudey 38th overall in the 1980 draft.

Hrudey (pronounced Ru-dee) is a classic example of a can't-be-denied-prospect needing a chance at the big leagues. At the start of the 1983–84 season, New York Islanders general manager Bill Torrey had little choice but to bring the 22-year-old goalie up from the Indianapolis Checkers of the Central Hockey League, where he had shared the Terry Sawchuk Trophy for best team average with Rob Holland and taken the Tommy Ivan Trophy as MVP in 1982–83. The Checkers players nicknamed him "Mattress" for his love of sleeping; a later nickname was "Manners."

So Islanders coach Al Arbour, always a believer in goaltenders sharing the responsibility during the season, found himself with three keepers: Billy Smith, Roland Melanson (who had shared the William Jennings Trophy the previous season), and the kid.

In a January 1984 article the rookie said, "I'm sure Rollie and Smitty aren't happy because it's a situation they're not used to. I'd probably feel the same way if I was in their shoes. But complaining won't change things. I'm just happy to be here and I want to stay here for a long time."

Looking back now, Hrudey can't believe how lucky he was. "You could bounce things off them and they were great that way. When Rollie was traded, it was Billy and me for a while. Not only were we a tandem on the ice, but we became great friends off the ice as well. I worked and I wanted the job, but Billy was such a competitor that he made me work really, really hard to get it. He was not giving away the starter's job," he said.

Hrudey would play 241 games for the Islanders, with a record of 106-90-26, a 3.47 goals-against average and six shutouts. A memorable moment was the four-overtime period Game 7 against the Washington Capitals on April 18, 1987, in which Hrudey made 73 saves en route to a 3-2 Isles win in the game that ended at two in the morning.

On February 22, 1989, the Kings made a bold trade for Hrudey, surrendering defenceman Wayne McBean and goalie Mark Fitzpatrick along with future considerations. "We believe, and I think the fans believe, that the Kings have their best shot ever at competing for the Stanley Cup this season and Kelly Hrudey is a very important piece in completing that puzzle. Whenever people talk about who the top four or five goaltenders in the NHL are, Hrudey's name always comes up," said Kings general manager Rogie Vachon after the deal.

Los Angeles suited the popular, photogenic Hrudey, who wore a trademark headband under his helmet to keep his hair at bay and sweat under control. Hard to believe in the early days, he was a shy introvert.

In a 1993 interview, Kings coach Barry Melrose described Hrudey's drive: "He channels his criticism into motivation. People that don't handle those kinds of things properly feel sorry for themselves and go into a shell. Kelly stands up and battles."

In his last years in Los Angeles, Hrudey found himself in the Billy Smith role, mentoring young goaltenders like Jamie Storr and Byron Dafoe. His last, mostly forgotten, stint came in San Jose, where he shared the net with veterans Chris Terreri, Ed Belfour, and Mike Vernon, getting in 48 and 28 games during 1996–97 and 1997–98, respectively.

"That was pretty easy. That was just having a friendship and becoming good friends off the ice," he said. As well, Hrudey took Patrick Marleau under his wing, letting him live at his home. Hrudey said, "That was his first year and my last year in the NHL. Boy, what a great experience that was. I always think about that as some of my most pleasurable times in the NHL, just being around him. He kind of rejuvenated me a little bit. At the end, I just knew it was time to go. Practice was a lot harder than it ever was. I had to really focus because I was playing with young guys, and it came naturally to them and not as naturally to me anymore, so it was a good time to leave the game."

But Hrudey didn't completely leave the game, of course. He instead became a high-profile announcer on CBC broadcasts. His in-studio work in Toronto, full-time since 1998, morphed into becoming a colour commentator for Western broadcasts—handier given his home is in Calgary, where he lives with his wife, Donna, and their three girls, Jessica, Megan, and Kaitlin. Those 677 regular-season games and 85 playoff games in the NHL give his analysis a lot of weight. For a time, his "Behind the Mask" segments in the second intermission were a great balance to the bombastic Don Cherry in the first.

It turns out he had been planning for the role all along. Back in Medicine Hat, Bob Ridley was the team's bus driver and handled play-by-play duties, and Hrudey would bend his ear about the broadcasting business.

His thoughts on the pressure of being a goaltender actually echo his talents as a broadcaster as well. Hrudey concluded, "Pressure and consistency, I think those are the two things. You can always have a good game, but you have to follow up a good game with another good game, and another one, and another one, and another one. That's how you last in the game. Any guy can come up from the minors and play great for a game or five games, but it's extremely difficult to last for more than a couple of years."

CHAPTER 6

THE '80s AND '90s

IF YOU WERE a goalie in the 1980s, chances are your goals-against average was not the greatest. It was the days of wide-open offences and defenceman who would abandon their stations to try to goose their stats.

Grant Fuhr is in the Hockey Hall of Fame and had a marvelous career by the standards of any era—especially for his inarguable starring role in four Stanley Cups with the Edmonton Oilers. But according to sportswriter Frank Orr, who is also enshrined and saw Fuhr in action many times, he was as good as he had to be on a given day. "The Oilers played that game, they'd get ahead by six, and the other team would get five, and then Grant would say, 'I'd better not let in any more.' Then you couldn't beat him when you had to," said Orr.

So without resorting to one of baseball's notorious asterisks, we should note that this timeframe is heavily influenced by expansion. After the surviving WHA teams—Winnipeg, Quebec City, Edmonton, and Hartford—came into the league in 1979, there was a sense of stability for many years. It was a solid 21-team league that may not have cracked the consciousness of the coveted American market, but at least it was on the right track. The deification of Wayne Gretzky was justified; for a time, he was simply the most dominant athlete in the world—in any sport. So his trade to the Los Angeles Kings in August 1989 set into motion a series of events that altered hockey, but it was not the only change.

Between 1991 and 1994, the San Jose Sharks came into the league, followed by the Ottawa Senators, Tampa Bay Lightning, Mighty Ducks of Anaheim, and Florida Panthers. Additional talent became available with the changes in Europe, the dissolution of the Soviet Union, and the lure of playing in the most financially lucrative hockey league in the world. Sergei Priakin of the Calgary Flames was the first Soviet permitted to join an NHL club, officially opening the barrier that had already been stealthily evaded by Alexander Mogilny and Sergei Fedorov. From there, franchises moved (Minnesota to Dallas; Quebec to Colorado; Winnipeg to Phoenix; Hartford to Carolina), and firsts came along, like Jaromir Jagr as the first European to win the scoring title, as well as lasts, like Craig MacTavish, the last remaining helmetless player in the NHL, who retired. An additional referee was added to the game, as well as teams in Nashville, Atlanta, Columbus, and Minnesota.

For goaltenders, equipment went through major advancements, getting lighter, more flexible, more durable, and bigger. The masks went from just covering the face to hybrid-style baseball catcher masks to the highly adjustable, colorfully painted masks of today.

More teams meant more movement, more trades, and the money went up substantially, making goalies even more highly desirable commodities.

And, unlike a lot of their predecessors, there were many more jobs in hockey waiting for goalies after their playing careers, whether in management, scouting, coaching the goalies, or even in broadcasting, which had also expanded to meet the needs of a 30-team NHL.

RICK ST. CROIX

RICK ST. CROIX Rick St. Croix has gone full circle, from the shooting gallery inside the Toronto Maple Leafs nets during the dreary '80s to teaching the club's young goaltenders some of the finer points of the position 30 years later.

Replacing outgoing goalie coach François Allaire for 2012–13, St. Croix seemed to be entering an unenviable position on a team that hadn't made the playoffs in nearly a decade and owned the second-worst goals-against-per-game record in 2011–12. In fact, the Leafs ranked among the worst for years in goals given up, and with Allaire out, St. Croix was expected to shore up the situation.

"I won a Calder Cup with Rick many years ago," GM Brian Burke said at the time of St. Croix's hiring, referring to the two having won an AHL championship with the 1977–78 Maine Mariners. Burke added, "He was calm, intelligent—a student of the game. I think he'll be a great addition to our coaching staff."

"We are extremely pleased to add Rick St. Croix to our coaching staff. We trust his knowledge and experience with today's model of goaltender and the Leafs are fortunate to get a person of Rick's calibre," said Leafs coach Randy Carlyle.

By the start of the lockout shortened 2012–13 season, the Leafs were starting with a fresh slate, as Dave Nonis took over as GM and Carlyle, who had become coach late the previous year, would be behind the bench from start to finish. St. Croix was well acquainted with Carlyle, having served as a goalie coach for the Winnipeg Jets while Carlyle was still a defenceman there, and later for the minor league Manitoba Moose while Carlyle was the club's coach and general manager.

Despite their praise for the outgoing Allaire, Toronto's goaltenders thrived under St. Croix, and Toronto's goals-against average fell half a goal per game.

"He has a lot to teach and I have a lot to learn, and together we're trying to figure out what tweaks we can make or what things we can do to get better," starter James Reimer told the *National Post* early in the season.

Backup Ben Scrivens said, "Ricky's all about playing your game. He's not trying to break you down and build you back up. . . . He's trying to help you play to your strengths."

Reimer shone in the playoffs in a seven-game battle against the Boston Bruins that went right down to the wire, overtime in a Game 7 that the Bruins would win. The Leafs had been down three games to one and wouldn't have evened the series without Reimer's outstanding play.

A native of Kenora, Ontario, St. Croix was born January 3, 1955, and spent his junior days with the Oshawa Generals. Drafted by the Philadelphia Flyers in the third round of the 1975 draft, he started his pro career with the International Hockey League's Flint Generals in 1975–76 before graduating to the Maine Mariners of the American Hockey League. St Croix played seven games with the Flyers in 1977–78 and two in '78–79.

He became a full-time NHLer thereafter, backing up Pete Peeters and working in 27 and 29 games in two seasons. He recorded a 2.49 GAA in those 27 games and assumed a starting role in the playoffs, appearing in nine games and recording a 2.99 GAA.

It was in Philly that St. Croix had his first taste of goaltending coaching, coming from none other than Jacques Plante. "That was one of my special memories of my career, being around Jacques Plante," said St. Croix, who remembered Plante as fairly rigid in his methods.

When Pete Peeters was traded to Boston in June 1982, St. Croix fully expected to take over as Philly's number one. But Pelle Lindbergh surprised Flyers management with his outstanding abilities and usurped St. Croix's role. Unhappy as a backup, St. Croix requested a trade.

St. Croix admitted, "I found that disappointing. I wanted to play more. I liked my time in Philly and I probably look back with some disappointment that it unfolded the way it did, but it's only because I wanted to play more. That in itself is not bad. I'd been eight years with the organization, and I think I'd been a faithful, loyal soldier. Who knows? You make your decisions and move along."

St. Croix explained that he told his agent, Max Kaminsky, about his frustrations, and his agent "took it upon himself to say we're gonna do this. And I didn't stop him. So I guess by not stopping him I said okay."

If St. Croix was looking for more action, he'd get just that and then some with the Maple Leafs. Traded for Bunny Larocque, who also sought a fresh start, St. Croix joined a young team that gave up a lot of chances each and every night and almost needed their net bricked off for a chance at winning.

In his first start in Minnesota, he faced a whopping 41 shots and was awarded the game's first star in a losing cause as the Leafs fell 2-1. He also played well in his next game, against the Red Wings in Joe Louis Arena, but his 31 saves weren't enough as Detroit beat Toronto 4-3. Coach Mike Nykoluk at the time said St. Croix was excellent in both games. But the losses eventually got to St. Croix, who suited up in only 48 games for the Leafs and saw far more action in the minors, finally finishing his playing days with the IHL's Fort Wayne Komets.

"It was just the fact that we weren't winning, and I had been winning in Philly. I just thought work hard and work harder and that would be the answer," said St. Croix, who wore himself down mentally and physically, putting increasing pressure on himself and practicing more to improve his performance. "I think for a while there I was playing the best goal I'd ever played and was still losing. I didn't understand that [I should] sit back and just recognize you can't win every game without the team scoring some goals for you."

Those were tough times for St. Croix, but it was an important learning experience, one he put to good use when he became a goaltending coach, starting with the Winnipeg Jets. His ex-Leafs coach, Dan Maloney, had become bench boss in Winnipeg and was in the market for someone to help out his goalies. St. Croix, living in Kenora and working as a real estate agent, met with Maloney and joined the Jets for two seasons. In Winnipeg, he worked with Daniel Berthiaume and Eldon "Pokey" Reddick, basically a couple of kids in their early 20s, not unlike the young goaltending duo he'd met in Toronto who'd been thrust into a high-pressure situation, Allan Bester and Ken Wregget.

"Daniel could have had a better career than he had if he had been allowed to just mature more, both on and off the ice. I think they just rushed him," St. Croix said, emphasizing the importance of slowly nurturing young players in developmental leagues until they're ready.

After the Jets cleaned house with the firing of GM John Ferguson and coach Maloney, St. Croix was out as well. He opened a goalie school and then received another chance to work with the pros, this time for the IHL's Manitoba Moose. He also, however, worked with the Dallas Stars' IHL affiliate in Utah, and he decided to work for Dallas when Carlyle objected to the arrangement.

The Dallas opportunity arose thanks to another ex-teammate, this time his one-time partner in the Toronto goal, Tim Bernhardt, then a Stars scout.

St. Croix said, "I'd say he was responsible for putting my name in a hat. I liked Timmy a lot. I think he did a great job in Dallas all those years. So [coach Ken] Hitchcock called one day and asked me if I'd be interested."

St. Croix was a part of Dallas's 1999 Stanley Cup championship, but he doesn't take credit for making the Stars' Eddie Belfour a better goalie: "I learned more from him than I taught him. I didn't do a lot for him—I did most of my work with the other guys in the system. He was on top of his game, he was the best in the world. You'd just sit and watch and go, 'Wow!' I learned a lot watching how he prepared, how he tracked pucks. He was sure of himself. He had a good team in front of him and he was good at the other end."

St. Croix would eventually return to the Moose, now in the AHL, and his efforts with Cory Schneider and Eddie Lack put the job of Roberto Luongo, of the parent club Vancouver Canucks, in jeopardy.

"After a while, it doesn't become coincidence that all the goalies he's had in the last three or four years were either All-Rookie or All-Stars in the AHL. He's got a great ability to not just teach a system, but is able to adapt and work with what he has been given," said Jets assistant GM Craig Heisinger at the time of St. Croix's hiring in Toronto. Heisinger, who knew St. Croix while still an equipment manager with the original NHL Jets, was GM of the Moose during St. Croix's second go-round with the club.

When the Moose became the St. John's IceCaps, and the affiliate for the new Jets, St. Croix worked a week to 10 days a month there while also scouting. As his position evolved into something more full-time, the Leafs came calling.

Hockey seems to run in the St. Croix blood. His youngest son, Michael, is a scoring star with the Edmonton Oil Kings of the Western Hockey League and a New York Rangers draft pick. Older brother Chris, a scoring defenceman for the Kamloops Blazers, was a Calgary Flames draft selection and played in the North American minor-pro circuit and Europe. His youngest daughter, Richelle, played defence for Minnesota State University.

MURRAY BANNERMAN Replacing a living legend
can be an unenviable task, even more so if the fan favourite is still around to remind fans of days gone by.

Speaking about having to follow Tony Esposito, Murray Bannerman said, "It was extremely difficult, especially when he was still there. From a standpoint of the fans, if you were having a bad game, they'd be chanting for Tony. But you learn to deal with that. I think that was more a respect thing for him than a negative for me. But it's not easy. He set a very high standard, and sometimes it's tough to live up to those standards."

Bannerman certainly had his share of success with the Chicago

Black Hawks, playing in two All-Star Games and reaching the Campbell Conference Final three times, but he never completely got out of Esposito's shadow.

Born April 27, 1957, in Fort Frances, Ontario, Bannerman was drafted by the Winnipeg Jets in the 10th round, 88th overall, in the 1977 WHA amateur draft. Apparently low on the team's list of priorities, he signed with the Vancouver Canucks, who drafted him in the fourth round, 58th overall in the same year's NHL draft.

"You never know, but things have their own way of working out," Bannerman said about the possibility of having joined the Jets in their WHA heyday, had they gotten in touch with him.

Bannerman only played a single game for the Canucks in 1977–78, spending most of that season in the International Hockey League with the Fort Wayne Komets. Glen Hanlon had a lock on the Vancouver netminding position, and Bannerman became expendable, moving to Chicago in 1978 as part of the previous year's Pit Martin trade between both teams. "Vancouver needed a centreman with some experience. Tony wasn't done by any stretch of the imagination, but he was getting older and Chicago needed somebody for the future," Bannerman said.

Bannerman felt good about heading to a solid Original Six franchise with an opportunity to crack an NHL lineup, but playing behind Esposito was a mixed blessing.

Bannerman said, "It was good and bad. It was good because the experience and the opportunity to learn the position from somebody like that was a wonderful thing. When I say it was bad, it was bad because I didn't play much the first couple years. As a goaltender, it's a difficult proposition. For any player it's difficult, but especially as a goaltender; it's difficult to be sharp if you're not getting some kind of game action."

He played a couple of seasons as a backup, and during that second season, 1981–82, he got a chance in the playoffs and responded well, helping lead Chicago to the semifinals, playing against the Vancouver Canucks, who took the series in five.

After splitting the 1982–83 season with Esposito, Bannerman became the starter, leaving the Hawks former workhorse in a secondary role. Some contend Esposito's failing eyesight forced him to the sidelines. Bannerman said,

> I think he probably had some issues with [nearsightedness]. He had his lenses and was forever having them changed or this and that. On most goaltenders, you would try to get the puck right in the slot and work it into the best possible scoring position. Oftentimes [with Tony] other teams would say, "Shoot the puck from the blue line" or whatever. But I think a lot of that was overblown. It probably started when Montreal scored on him [from centre ice in the '71 final]. Yeah, he probably struggled a little more than some guys on long shots, but in tight and from the areas where teams shot from all the time, he was phenomenal. I don't know if that was all that much a big of a deal or that much of a detriment. It couldn't have been—look at the career he had and look how successful he was.

According to Bannerman, no inherent resentment existed between Esposito and his replacement. "We had a good relationship. We were friends and we're still friends. I see him every now and again," Bannerman said, adding Esposito dispensed tips, but only if asked. "If you wanted advice or you asked for advice, he would freely give it. He wasn't the type of guy who was going to say, 'You should do this, you should do that.'"

Bannerman shone in the nets, getting selected to two consecutive All-Star Games, in 1983 and '84. The Hawks excelled as well, and in 1982–83, under coach Orval Tessier, they won the Norris Division title with a 47-23-10 record, their best regular season in a decade. But Tessier feuded with Esposito, which eventually led to Esposito's forced retirement as the club wouldn't trade him and didn't offer to bring him back the following year.

"I think both Tony and Orval had pretty strong personalities and I think at times they clashed. I don't know if they necessarily saw eye-to-eye on things. . . . They definitely had their differences of opinions at times and had a bit of a rocky relationship every now and again," said Bannerman.

The Hawks reached the semifinals again in 1983, this time against the Edmonton Oilers, who swept the series. The Oilers took the first two games by a wide margin, scoring eight goals in each, spurring Tessier to lash out against his charges in the media, telling reporters he was "going to call the Mayo Clinic and see about getting 18 heart transplants for our players."

The Mayo Clinic comment proved to be Tessier's undoing, as the club floundered in 1983–84. He was then fired during the '84–85 season. Bannerman explained,

> If he says that in the dressing room, he's upset and he's mad at us and he makes a comment like that in the dressing room, it stays there, which is where that type of stuff should stay. When he made the comment to the press and it comes out in the papers, it's kind of like, if we win, we—including him—are really good. And if we lose, well, those guys don't want to do as I tell them to do.
>
> I think the damage from what Orval did there was going to the press and [making out] it wasn't his fault, it was our fault. Because of what he did, he lost some respect of players. . . . You don't have to like the guy you're playing for as a coach, but I think you do have to have respect for him, and I think that ultimately led to his downfall going forward.

With GM Bob Pulford taking over from Tessier as coach, Chicago again advanced to the semifinals to take on the Oilers, this time losing in six to the eventual champions.

"I believe that that stretch when we were playing them in the semifinals that they were better than us. . . . But I really think we were probably the second best team in the league. People might argue that, but I really believe that at that point in time," said Bannerman.

Bannerman's last season with Chicago was '86–87, when Bob

Sauvé began getting more of the starts. "It was tough . . . because you wanted to play. I wanted to be the guy in there playing, not the guy sitting there and watching," said Bannerman.

Goalies saturated the Blackhawks' 1987–88 training camp. Sauvé had moved to New Jersey, but Bannerman still had to contend against Bob Mason, Darren Pang, Jimmy Waite, and a young Eddie Belfour, among others. Mason and Pang took over in nets, and Bannerman got demoted to the American Hockey League. The writing on the wall couldn't have been clearer.

"You'd have to be pretty stupid because they went out and signed Mason and they signed him to a pretty big contract for three or four years—and a significant amount of money for that era—so you gotta figure they're not going to go out and spend that kind of money on a guy if they're not planning on him being their number one goalie," said Bannerman.

Bannerman wanted a move to another NHL team, and while Pulford promised he'd do what it took to accommodate him, Bannerman felt he didn't follow through in good faith.

"Making every effort to trade a guy is to make it easy for the team that's trying to get you to trade for you," Bannerman said, explaining some clubs may have shown interest but weren't willing to pay the price Chicago demanded. He added, "You look in today's game, when they get rid of somebody they don't necessarily want, they're trading him for a fifth-, sixth-, seventh-round draft pick. Most teams are going to say that's fine. But if they're looking for a player off their current roster, depending on where he fits on that roster, it's not an easy thing to do."

It would be Bannerman's last year. His son was starting first grade, and, given few good opportunities, he hung up his pads.

He said, "I probably could have gone over to Europe for a couple years, but with a wife and kids involved . . . I had a decent career, and at some point in time you gotta move on with your life, so might as well do it here as opposed to bouncing around here and there and the other place for a few years and come back. Shortly thereafter, the salary structure in the NHL kind of went crazy, so in hindsight, maybe I should have bounced around for a few years!"

These days, Bannerman's in sales but keeps his hand in hockey as a Blackhawks alumni. But he hasn't strapped on the pads for an old-timers game in years, and he isn't about to, considering the lack of protection his old gear provided.

"From the time the season started until it ended, you'd have bruises somewhere. It wasn't serious injuries, but it's painful. It hurt. And obviously with today's game, it's different. You never would have seen a guy back in my era go down and actually let the puck hit him if he could get his catching mitt or blocker on it," Bannerman said, adding today's equipment has changed the way goaltenders can play, "simply because the puck can hit you in the upper body and not hurt. Back in the '60s, '70s, and the '80s, the guys stood up a lot more as a necessity because you really didn't want to get whacked off the shoulder or the chest."

He found practices threatened his well-being even more than actual games:

When you're playing in a game, there's one puck; you focus on one puck and watch one puck. In practice, there's all these guys and pucks out there. And quite frankly, I got hurt in practice more. You'd stop one shot and somebody'd shoot [another] puck from the corner or side.

Plus, you don't get situations in a game very much where a guy skates halfway down the ice and then winds up and shoots it as hard as he can. Usually game situations happen a lot quicker, so guys don't have that much time. There's a lot of differences between practices and the game.

So if Bannerman ever does get asked to participate again, he's insisting on getting some modern goalie gear: "I actually told Cliff [Koroll, president of Blackhawks alumni], 'The only way I'm going to play is if somebody gives me a complete set of equipment, the new stuff the guys wear in today's game. If that happens, I'll be more than happy to play because I know I'm not going to get killed. Otherwise, I think I'm out.'"

CLINT MALARCHUK Imagine suffering from compulsive thoughts, playing one of the most high-pressure positions in sport, *and* having nearly been killed in the line of duty.

Clint Malarchuk doesn't need to. He's lived it.

Born May 1, 1961, in Grande Prairie, Alberta, Malarchuk graduated from the Western Hockey League's Portland Winter Hawks to play over 300 NHL games with the Quebec Nordiques, Washington Capitals, and Buffalo Sabres.

Obsessive-compulsive disorder may have assisted his rise to the NHL, but it also nearly caused his undoing. OCD, an anxiety disorder characterized by repeated thoughts, images, and/or rituals, pushed Malarchuk to train like an Olympian during an era when it wasn't unusual to see ashtrays in dressing room stalls. He sought any edge he could get, from reading books about positive thinking to pursuing extracurricular instruction.

"When I broke in, there was still a lot of that old-school mentality where after practice the guys would go for lunch, which would be beer and a sandwich. There wasn't the training that was involved yet. I was also one of the guys who was working out and doing stretching. I remember Moose Dupont, I was stretching on the floor in the locker room, and he said, 'Hey kid, what are you doing? You lose a contact lens?'" said Malarchuk.

In the summers, while many other pros relaxed and got fat, Malarchuk trained up to six hours a day, which he now admits was "probably ridiculous."

"I think it helped in some ways, but probably hurt me in a lot of ways too—you wear down the body. I'd get up and go to the gym at 6:00 a.m. and do my weight training, and then I'd go run, and I was running 20 miles a day, almost every day. I joined a boxing club for conditioning, I did circuit training. I was pretty extreme. But I was also in phenomenal shape," said Malarchuk.

Early on as a Nordique, Malarchuk came across a book called *Sports Psyching*, and he immediately adopted its six-week program of mental exercises and skills to improve concentration, an asset he considered vital for goaltending and that taught him how to handle pressure.

He explained, "That book really, really helped me. Because I was playing pretty darn good in the American League, but when I'd go up to the NHL, I'd do okay, but the pressure was so much more magnified. You're in the big arenas and in front of TV cameras. I give that book a lot of credit."

Malarchuk never contented himself with the status quo, even looking for ways to improve his abilities as an established NHLer and get ahead of the curve. While a Washington Capital, he learned Soviet legend Vladislav Tretiak would be holding a hockey school in Montreal. When the Caps refused to expense the trip, he paid his own way. Malarchuk said,

> It was funny, because I was on the ice with 14-, 15-year-olds, and here I was in the NHL. But I wanted to go to that hockey school so bad, and I did. I was the guy that tried to do anything and everything to be the best I could. And having OCD probably helped me with some of those things.
>
> If I wasn't so obsessed with trying to find an edge to get better and better in any way I could, I wouldn't have gone to that hockey school, I wouldn't have learned from Vladislav Tretiak, I wouldn't have done research to find one of the best sports psychology books.

Even if his habits could be over the top, he maintained, "It made me feel good. It's like you've got these rituals, and for me it was training and doing everything I could to be the best I could be. But it was also a lot of stress—if the schedule changed and I couldn't get my certain routine in, it would really bother me."

Although unaware of his malady, OCD would turn his life into a roller coaster after a freak accident during one fateful night in March 1989 at the Buffalo Memorial Auditorium. He was tending the nets for the Sabres, the team he'd been traded to by the Capitals only weeks before, but wouldn't finish the game. St. Louis Blues forward Steve Tuttle collided into him and his skate sliced into Malarchuk's throat, severing his jugular vein. Circumstance and skill saved his life, as Malarchuk happened to be on the side of the ice near the dressing and training rooms, and he received the quick response of trainer Jim Pizzutelli, a former medic in the Vietnam War.

Despite receiving 300 stitches to close his wound, Malarchuk was back on the ice, skating during practice mere days later. Not long after that, he returned to game action. While physically able, he was far from mentally sound, obsessing and haunted by thoughts related to his near-death experience.

Malarchuk said, "There was a point in Buffalo I couldn't sleep. I went 10 days without sleeping. It just got out of control with my life. I had a hard time leaving the house. Things just got really bad. And when I say I didn't sleep, I did not sleep. I was just wired. Within two years after the accident, I definitely spiraled. So the accident definitely brought it [OCD] to a whole new level."

He mostly played a backup role for his next three seasons with Buffalo before the Sabres traded for Dominik Hasek, leading to Malarchuk getting sent down to San Diego in the IHL. Malarchuk did not take the move well. He admitted, "When I got sent to the minors with San Diego, I was ready to pack 'er in; I was an emotional wreck."

Luckily for him, his former Sabres coach, Rick Dudley, awaited him in the "I." Dudley comforted his goalie, who was in tears, and promised to find a doctor who could help him. Fortune struck again, for the leading doctor in this field practised in San Diego. Recognizing a chemical imbalance and depression in Malarchuk, his doctor prescribed him medication that lifted him out of his depths.

"I couldn't believe how I'd suffered for probably two years, really, really bad suffering, and this guy just said, 'No problem, we know what to do,'" said Malarchuk, who weeks later felt like a new man. "So this is what it's like to be normal," he remembered thinking.

Malarchuk went to Las Vegas the next year, promoted as the Thunder's "Cowboy Goalie." He even had his own fan club and, after finishing his playing career there, got behind the Vegas bench as an assistant before taking over the head coaching duties.

"It was fun. I was there for the inaugural season. We did a lot of charity work and really got a pretty good fan base going—those first couple years, we were getting anywhere from 9,000 to 12,000 people a game," Malarchuk said.

He spent a couple more years as a head coach for the Idaho Steelheads in the West Coast Hockey League before starting his career as a goalie coach, first with Roberto Luongo in Florida, with another assist going to Dudley, who was then the Panthers' general manager. After three years there, the Cats dismissed him, much to Luongo's chagrin.

"Clint was my very good friend. He knew me, he knew how to handle me, and it was disappointing for me to see him go because we had such a good relationship. [He] could always keep me on an even keel, not get too high or too low. We worked together as a team," Luongo told the *Palm Beach Post* after Malarchuk's firing, during a period when he was struggling in net.

Malarchuk recalled Luongo buying him a watch, a gesture that at first touched him but then turned to shock when he learned it was a Breitling, a luxury brand of Swiss watch.

He said, "Roberto Luongo, what a great kid he was. Even now in some interviews he'll give me credit for helping him."

Malarchuk's career would take him to the Blue Jackets, where he'd work with Pascal Leclaire and Fredrik Norrena. Malarchuk said, "Leclaire had his best season in the NHL under me and we formed a really tight bond. We still keep in touch."

But it was while in Columbus that Malarchuk's life nearly went off the rails. He shot himself after an argument with his wife in 2008, an incident he still maintains was an accident.

"I had really regressed bad, almost to where I was before," said Malarchuk, who believed that while living in Nevada, he'd been over-prescribed by a new doctor. He continued, "When I was doing really good, I was on 80 milligrams of Zoloft, and all of a sudden I'm on 300 milligrams of [one thing] and 250 of another thing."

He pointed out that it's no wonder pharmaceutical companies include disclaimers on their TV commercials about antidepressants possibly causing suicidal tendencies. While in hospital recovering from his self-inflicted gunshot wound to the head, Malarchuk met with a psychiatrist, who opened his eyes to the effects of trauma and how it can affect someone predisposed to OCD like himself.

Dudley, seemingly Malarchuk's guardian angel, came down to help his old goalie through his latest crisis. Malarchuk said,

> Rick would do just about anything for anybody. People look at Rick, and he's been a GM, head coach, and player in the NHL. . . . For whatever reason we don't think those people understand or would take the time like Rick does. He's a wonderful person who happens to be a very successful hockey man and former player. Rick can relate to people. He got it with me, he understood my pain. I know there's people out there, we all have down days, but when you say, "I suffer from depression," well, okay, pull your socks up and get going. And it doesn't quite work that way—it's a chemical imbalance. It's like diabetes, or any other thing, where the body doesn't produce enough of certain things. They call it mental illness, but is it really?

Malarchuk made a comeback as an NHL goalie coach, joining Atlanta in 2010, hired by, you guessed it, Rick Dudley, who was serving as Thrashers GM. When Atlanta moved to Winnipeg, the new owners made a clean sweep, but Malarchuk wasn't out of work for long, as the Calgary Flames picked him up in 2011.

He's gone full circle, returning to his home province and reconnecting with Jacques Cloutier, a fellow netminder in Buffalo and now an assistant coach in Calgary.

Malarchuk said, "Him and I laugh because he's had some partners that were kind of high maintenance guys. But him and I are a lot alike. . . . We got along great together there [in Buffalo]. We talked about it, [I said,] 'Jacques, you must have been glad when you got me as your partner.' He laughed and said, 'Oh my God, I've had a few beauties to play with.'"

PULLING THE GOALIE: INTO MIKE KEENAN'S MIND

As a coach, Mike Keenan had a well-deserved reputation for being rough on goaltenders, yanking them from the net seemingly on a whim. He swears there was method to his madness: "I pulled goalies for a lot of different reasons, and most often it wasn't because of their play. I used it as a tactic for timeouts. I used it as a tactic to talk to the team, to take a timeout. I used it as a tactic to throw the opposition off. I used it as a tactic to alert our own team if they were flat. I used it sometimes, for example, if we were going to lose a game and I sensed it, and we had another game the next night, I'd pull the number one goalie out so he'd be more prepared and physically ready for the next game."

A loophole in the rules, since closed up, was another reason Keenan pulled goalies. He explained, "Sometimes, and I haven't told too many people this, I would pull the goalie if I didn't like the official's call. So it would give me time to make my point. At that time, there wasn't the hurry-up, get the other goalie in there on the fly almost, it was, take your time, take your gloves off, take your helmet off. Of course, the other guy's got to take his time putting his gear on. Then I would put the other guy right back in. I'd say, 'You're only going to be here for one shift, so take your time and get a rest.' Then away you go again. The team was quite in tune to what I was doing."

Jacques Cloutier was one of those goalies "in tune" with Keenan. "You always had to be prepared with him. Every game day with Mike, I was preparing myself, 'I might be playing tonight.' Because with him, you never knew," Cloutier said.

ALLAN BESTER The worst thing that might have happened to Allan Bester was fulfilling the hopes of just about any young goaltender: instant success.

The Toronto Maple Leafs called up the 19-year-old junior in 1983–84 as an emergency replacement for starter Mike Palmateer, and he quickly got the attention of fans and owner Harold Ballard, whose patience had long worn thin, by performing well and stemming the bleeding of constant losing. Bester returned to junior after Palmateer recovered, but his stay was brief as Ballard overruled his general manager, Gerry McNamara, in bringing the kid back to the bigs.

"When the Leafs were losing and I was playing junior . . . they [the fans] were chanting my name. They'd introduce Mike Palmateer and they'd boo and start chanting 'Bester! Bester!' during the games. So Mr. Ballard turned around and said, 'We're not going anywhere, we're not going to make the playoffs, they want Bester, bring him back.' He made the call," said Bester.

Bester shouldered the majority of the weight from that point on, but it was no picnic for a greenhorn teenager, as he faced a barrage of pucks, including 65 against the Hartford Whalers and 52 in Boston in a win at the Garden. "I saw a lot of shots—I averaged 38 shots against per game. It was a real baptism of fire," said Bester.

Putting it in perspective, Bester said that in a way, it was easy. The pressure to perform wasn't great as he hadn't been the club's number one draft pick, and no one on the team expected him to carry that lineup to a championship.

Bester explained, "This team was going nowhere. They were trying to put pieces together for the next year. I was going in there knowing I was going to get lots of shots, and if I lost 8-1, no one was going to blame me. If we won 3-2, I was the hero. . . . I walked in every game thinking I'm just going to play the best I can. I've got nothing to lose."

But after looking like an NHL-calibre goalie, he did have something to lose: his reputation, his place on the team, and ultimately his confidence.

And that's just what happened, as Bester would be jerked between the Leafs and the American Hockey League Saints farm club for a couple years, before he spent a few more years as backup to Ken Wregget, another young goalie tagged as the next possible Leafs saviour. And when Bester finally inherited the starter mantle, he struggled through one of the most frustrating times of his professional life, until he was chased out of town by jeering fans and reporters.

Allan Bester was born March 26, 1964, in Hamilton, Ontario, the youngest of eight children. All his brothers were 10 to 20 years older than him, which left him stuck in the net whenever they played hockey. He became a fan of the position, cheering for such luminaries as Rogie Vachon, Eddie Giacomin, Tony Esposito, and Ken Dryden, the lawyer/netminder of his favourite team, the Montreal Canadiens.

Bester admired Dryden not only as a talented goalie but also as an intellectual, and he wanted to follow in his path by pursuing a college career. Never seeing himself as NHL material, Bester believed he might earn a degree on the back of his goaltending. But it wasn't to be, as no university gave him an offer. Bester believed his diminutive size—just over 5-foot-6 and 135 pounds at the time—held him back.

But the Brantford Alexanders took a flier on him, selecting him as a late draft choice. His first year was a learning one, as he saw action in only 19 games, but he blossomed in his second, playing 56 games and getting named to the Ontario Hockey League's First All-Star Team.

That breakout season made him the second-highest-rated goaltending prospect in the 1983 draft by the NHL Central Scouting

Mike Bullard of the Flyers gets sandwiched between Leafs Darren Veitch and Allan Bester during the 1988–89 season. (IHA/Icon SMI)

Bureau, behind only Tom Barrasso. And that's the way it followed on draft day, as Buffalo took Barrasso in the first round and Toronto selected Bester in the third.

The year after his promising rookie showing, Bester figured he had a lock on Leafs goaltending duties. Club brass seemed on the same page, opting to start the season with two 20-year-olds, Bester and Wregget. But when the team failed to get off to a good start, the goalies were the ones blamed. In Bester's case, the Leafs explained they were demoting him to save his confidence, a dubious claim considering Bester had just won the Molson Cup for best Leaf of the month only days before.

Bester struggled in the AHL, his confidence seemingly shattered as he played behind a poor team coached by a neophyte in Claire Alexander. But the next year, 1985–86, Alexander was replaced by John Brophy, and Bester revived his game.

"Broph was great. He just said, 'Allan, I don't care how you do it, stop the puck. I'm not going to tell you how to play goal [because] I don't know how to play goal. Stop the puck and everything will be good.' I played for Broph and loved it," said Bester.

Brophy took over the Toronto reins in '86–87 and brought Bester with him. Bester shared goaltending duties with long-time rival Wregget, whom he'd once faced in a Memorial Cup and whom he battled for starting time with Team Canada's junior squad. He admitted he and Wregget weren't an ideal tandem: "It was an open fight. And Kenny and I had very different personalities. At that time, I was very high strung and probably hard to take on a one-on-one basis. . . . I don't know if my personality and his meshed very well. We didn't dislike each other, but we weren't close."

One of Bester's fondest memories under the Brophy regime came in '87–88, in the final game of the season against Detroit, which Toronto needed to win to make the playoffs. Wregget started the contest and within the first 10 minutes, the Leafs were down 3-0. Bester came in relief, and despite having been out for a couple months with a knee injury, he proceeded to put on a clinic, shutting out the Red Wings as the Leafs rallied to win 5-3. Bester said it was "definitely one of the highlights of my career in the NHL. I honestly stood on my head."

Surprisingly, another highlight for Bester was his relationship with outspoken owner Harold Ballard, who often found himself vilified by frustrated fans and the press. Ballard seemed to go out of his way to build a reputation in the media as a terrible ogre, but Bester liked him.

"I had nothing but respect for Mr. Ballard," Bester said, referring to him as Santa Claus for generous gestures like giving plane tickets away to the players every Christmas. "I went to Hawaii twice because of Mr. Ballard."

Maybe most touching to Bester was the fact that Ballard and his constant companion King Clancy showed up at the funeral of Bester's brother, Paul, in Hamilton. Bester said, "That touched me. Not expected whatsoever. They just showed up at the funeral."

Professionally, things seemed to be looking brighter for Bester: Wregget got traded to Philadelphia, and the team was improving. In 1989–90, the Leafs reached their high-water mark for the '80s by going .500, and Bester recorded his personal best in wins with 20. The Leafs that year played exciting hockey for fans, but much less so for the goaltenders, as defensive play seemed a dirty word.

"We had a great offensive team, I was seeing a lot of shots, and I was letting in a lot of goals, but we were winning because we had a very good offensive team," Bester said, remembering shaking hands with the forwards before games as he didn't expect to see them again until the final siren.

That year, like others for Bester, could best summed up by a quip from Don Cherry, who once said Bester saw "more rubber than a dead skunk on the Trans-Canada highway."

"For years I'd been stopping pucks in my sleep and punching my wife in the face," Bester joked about his fitful sleeps, brought on by nights when he'd see 40 or more shots per game.

But despite the team and Bester putting together what were

good numbers for the Leafs, Bester clashed with new coach Doug Carpenter. He mocked Carpenter, whom he felt fancied himself a "goaltending guru" and bristled against his employing a three goalie system of himself, Mark Laforest, and Jeff Reese. "There's a man who decided to play mind games with goaltending. That was a *bad* time for me," Bester admitted.

Carpenter took his issues with Bester to the media, including pointing out his biggest perceived weakness—his five-hole. But by going public to hang Bester, he not only undermined his starter, he essentially openly invited all NHL shooters to test his claims. When the trading deadline came and went and the Leafs didn't acquire a new goaltender, Carpenter offered a *mea culpa* of sorts, telling Bester the media had overblown what he'd said. As far as Bester was concerned, Carpenter figured he was stuck with him so he'd say anything to repair what was a permanently broken relationship. "He was *the* worst coach for a goaltender probably ever," said Bester.

Besides feuding with his coach, Bester was also fighting a battle in finding a pair of skates that didn't aggravate bone spurs in his ankles and heels. It became a point of contention for the Leafs— Bester insisted the problem was serious, the training staff disagreed about its severity, and teammates just wanted it fixed.

"The rest of us were just getting sick and tired of having to watch him walk around in the dressing room in his skates and [saying] nothing was right," said Mark Osborne.

What finally did Bester in as a Leaf was letting in a Sergio Momesso shot from the blue line in overtime of Toronto's third playoff game against St. Louis, the Leafs' first-round opponent.

Osborne said, "Carpie [coach Carpenter] was frustrated with that and I can't [blame him]. We all were. I think part and parcel with bone spurs, quirkiness, letting soft goals in, it was just all a part of the package that year."

While still hearing about that Game 3 all these years later, what's gone largely unsaid is Bester's fine outings in Games 1 and 2, as well as the fact that future Leaf Curtis Joseph, playing for the Blues that night, indicated that what looked like a blown save really wasn't Bester's fault. "Serge has a great shot and he used their defenceman as a screen. It's a tough shot to stop," Joseph said after the game.

"I had Lou Franceschetti standing about halfway between me and Momesso, and Momesso lets the shot go that I don't see at all, and next thing I know it's in the net between my legs. I ran into Curtis Joseph who was on the other end, and he goes, 'I can't believe you're getting crucified for that goal, that thing dropped about three feet—I could see it from the far end,'" Bester said.

His teammate, defenceman Brad Marsh, felt Bester deserved credit for enduring those topsy-turvy Maple Leafs years of continual turnover in players, coaches, and general managers.

"It just seemed it was such a circus atmosphere within the organization. It really took a lot to keep focused on hockey and not the distractions. A goalie has to have that much more focus to keep his head on straight. With Al, his focus was very strong," said Marsh.

The next year at training camp, Peter Ing got Bester's job and Bester was sent down. Toronto proceeded to go 1-9-1 in its first 11 games, and Carpenter was fired. In March, the Leafs traded Bester to Detroit. The deal was likely at the behest of owner Mike Illitch, who'd watched Bester shut down the Red Wings in past outings and didn't want him doing likewise in the playoffs for Minnesota or Chicago. Other than playing a handful of games with the Wings, Bester was cast out of the NHL and sent to the minors.

With a fresh start in Adirondack in 1991–92, Bester excelled under the best coach he ever had: Barry Melrose. Whether Bester had a bad night in goal or not, Melrose supported him, and Bester's confidence returned. The club advanced all the way to the final, winning the Calder Cup, and Bester took home the Jack Butterfield Trophy as playoff MVP.

"He was just a rock. Absolutely focused that nothing was gonna get by him. He made very timely saves," said teammate Mike Sillinger.

While with the Orlando Solar Bears of the International Hockey

League, Bester received the opportunity to briefly see NHL action once again. Although initially reluctant, a sweetened deal from the Dallas Stars convinced Bester to give the NHL another shot. He filled in admirably on a Stars team desperate for quality goaltending after their regulars, Andy Moog and Darcy Wakaluk, went down to injury. His 10-game stint ended with a respectable 4-5-1 record and a 3.00 GAA, which came as no surprise to his Orlando general manager. "I know how good he can be, because I've watched him carry our team," coach Don Waddell said at the time.

After getting back to Orlando, he and the Bears marched all the way to the IHL Turner Cup Final.

In retirement, Bester managed to transfer his experience into a hotel career, but every now and again, he'll still strap on the pads and flash that quick glove hand once again.

BILL RANFORD For all his great accomplishments, Bill Ranford never quite achieved the celebrity and recognition of the greats of his time.

Despite winning a Stanley Cup as a starter on a Wayne Gretzky–less Edmonton Oiler squad and leading his country to international triumphs, he would always be mentioned after the likes of Grant Fuhr and Patrick Roy, and he was all but forgotten when Martin Brodeur and Dominik Hasek hit their stride.

Born in Brandon, Manitoba, on December 14, 1966, Ranford spent his early childhood without a permanent home as he followed his military father from base to base, from Germany to several Canadian locales. It was Bill Sr.'s influence that put Ranford on skates, but not hockey skates—at least, not right away. "My dad was a big Bobby Orr fan and Bobby figure skated first. And so it was important to skate properly first," said Ranford.

In his first year of organized hockey, Ranford played defence but took up goaltending after watching a friend of the family play in the nets with the Armed Forces. He'd root for Ken Dryden and Mike

Palmateer, two goalies who couldn't be much more different from each other, with one a 6-foot-4 quiet intellectual who used his size to flick away shots like bugs and the other a cocky 5-foot-9 acrobat.

By the time he hit his teens, Ranford was taking a run at following them to the NHL. A third-round pick of the Boston Bruins in the 1985 entry draft, Ranford would play three seasons of major junior with the New Westminster Bruins before getting the call from Boston GM Harry Sinden. Ranford said,

> I think I was 19 at the time and I got called into Harry Sinden's office. The team wasn't in the playoffs yet and he said, "We just wanted you here after your junior season to get used to the NHL shots and see what you could do, so keep working hard on your game and you never know what could happen." As soon as I walked out of Harry's office, he called my dad and told him I was playing the next afternoon so get to a satellite TV to watch the game. They didn't tell me till I got to the rink the day of the game in the morning. I basically showed up and I saw a jersey hanging in the stall with my name on it, and the coach called me in to let me know I was starting that night.

The Bruins took on the Buffalo Sabres at Boston Garden, and they and Ranford came out victors with a 2-1 win. Ranford not only played in four of the Bruins' last five regular season games, he also started the second and third games of the playoffs against the Montreal Canadiens.

"There's no doubt I was nervous playing in the Montreal Forum for my first NHL [playoff] game. But as far as realizing that I could play at that level, I was a bit more comfortable than I was my first game in the Boston Garden against Buffalo. It was pretty intimidating," said Ranford.

After playing 41 games and another two in the playoffs in 1986–87, Ranford was sent down to the American Hockey League

Bill Ranford hugs his post during the 1995–96 season. (IHA/Icon SMI)

the following year. Terry O'Reilly took over as coach from Butch Goring and determined Ranford needed to pay his dues.

"I didn't even get a chance in training camp, they sent me right to the minors. To go from the starter the previous year to not even getting a chance was a little bit of a rude awakening," said Ranford.

Looking back, though, Ranford believes it probably was the best thing that could have happened to him. Instead of truly learning the game like he needed to, he was going game to game functioning on adrenaline. With the Maine Mariners, he could learn how to really play at the pro level.

But when the Bruins acquired Reggie Lemelin, it appeared Ranford's opportunity to prove himself would need to come elsewhere. At the deadline, the Bruins moved him to the Edmonton Oilers. The news was met with mixed feelings.

"Like any young player, you want to get back to the NHL as quickly as possible. I have to admit I was excited about going back to the NHL," said Ranford, adding it was exciting to be heading back closer to home, as his parents lived in Red Deer, Alberta. He concluded, "But the aspect of Grant Fuhr being the number one there and the number of games he played, I was a little skeptical about how much playing time I would actually get."

Fittingly, the Oilers and Bruins would meet in the final, with Lemelin and ex-Oiler Andy Moog, who was involved in the Ranford transaction, splitting the series Edmonton swept. But Ranford would be watching from the bench, where he spent the entire 1988 playoffs as Fuhr played every game.

"I think once we got to the playoffs, it's a learning experience and seeing how it wears you out as the playoffs go further and further on, you watch and learn and learn from the best. I think it probably helped me out hugely two years later in '90, learning what it's about because it's definitely not easy," said Ranford.

The following season, Fuhr again played most of the games, but injuries and a suspension would open the door to Ranford again.

In 1989–90, Fuhr underwent an emergency appendectomy in training camp that would keep him sidelined for several weeks, leaving Ranford to start the season in his place. When Fuhr returned, he injured his shoulder and was sidelined again. With Fuhr re-injuring his shoulder before the playoffs, Ranford became Edmonton's de facto starter, backed up by Eldon "Pokey" Reddick.

Ranford stumbled out of the gates, and the Winnipeg Jets, traditionally the warm-up act for the Oilers, blitzed Ranford for seven goals to take Game 1.

"I didn't play very well. I definitely took my licks in the post-game media scrum. . . . After I sat in front of the media for probably 15 or 20 minutes, [GM] Glen Sather stepped in and said, 'You've taken enough chunks out of this guy and he's had enough,'" Ranford said.

The next day, the coaching staff put together a video highlight package of big saves Ranford made during the season and made it plain to the players that Ranford was their guy.

"They beat us pretty good in the first game. Bill Ranford was just horrible," Oilers coach John Muckler said in Dick Irvin's *Behind the Bench*, adding, "Our back-up goalie was Pokey Reddick and I remember Peter Pocklington coming in after the game and asking why I hadn't pulled Ranford at the end of the second period. I told him I didn't think we could win the Stanley Cup with Pokey, and I was going to stick with Billy and go all the way with him."

The Oilers rallied from a three-games-to-one deficit to take the series, riding that momentum all the way to the final. There, the Oilers again faced the Bruins, this time a much-hyped match between Ranford and Moog.

"The funny part is that trade was mainly Moog for Geoff Courtnall and I was kind of the throw-in. Two years later, the trade was myself for Andy Moog. I was always got a good chuckle out of that because how quickly things change," said Ranford.

The Oilers won the first game 3-2 in triple overtime and Ranford stood on his head.

"The only other performance I can compare with it was when Grant Fuhr shut out the Islanders 1-0 when we won our first Stanley Cup," Muckler said in *Behind the Bench.*

Oilers teammate Martin Gelinas said, "He was such a competitor when he got on the ice. That run, when we won the Cup in '89–90, he was incredible. He just had that presence, just one of those goalies where you know he's going to make the save all the time. In the dressing room, he was pretty loose."

The Oilers took the series in five, and Ranford played a major role in defeating his former club, which made the Cup victory extra sweet. He also won the Conn Smythe as the most valuable player of the playoffs.

A one-year suspension handed to Fuhr by NHL president John Ziegler over substance abuse parachuted Ranford into the starting role again the next season. However, his star came crashing down when that suspension was commuted to a mere 59 games, and Muckler went with a hunch to start Fuhr in the playoffs.

"It was tough to swallow," Ranford said, but added it's also hard to question starting Fuhr, who'd won four Stanley Cups to his one. He continued, "Was I disappointed? No doubt. But it's about being a teammate, respecting your teammates. And I think I gained a lot of respect from the guys in the room because I was just a good soldier, and made sure that I was ready to play if I needed to play."

Fuhr took Edmonton all the way to the Campbell Conference Final before that year's Cinderella story, the Minnesota North Stars, knocked them off. Gone but not forgotten, Ranford again took over the number-one mantle when Sather traded Fuhr to Toronto.

Ranford said, "They're moving away from one of the greatest goalies of all time. It was a huge vote of confidence."

But the team Ranford officially inherited bore little resemblance to the one with whom he'd won a Cup. Glenn Anderson was included in the Fuhr trade, Mark Messier and Adam Graves would both head to the Rangers, and Muckler accepted a coaching position with Buffalo. It was the start of numerous lean years in

Edmonton, during which Ranford would enjoy far more success on the international stage than with the Oilers.

Prior to training camp in 1991, Ranford led Team Canada to a Canada Cup victory, and in 1994, after the Oilers missed the playoffs, he helped Canada win its first gold at the World Hockey Championship in over 30 years. In both tournaments, Ranford was named MVP.

"Being the first Canadian team since the Trail Smoke Eaters to win the World Championship was probably a little more special than the Canada Cup. But it's very hard to distinguish between the two," Ranford said.

Rod Brind'Amour told ESPN, "I played with him in the World Championships and he was a guy that would always make you look at him because he was making a spectacular kind of save. He's a very acrobatic goaltender, so it's difficult for you to figure where to [shoot] on him."

Back in Edmonton, the Oilers had shed the team of high-priced veterans as they rebuilt with young prospects. Ranford had hoped to see them develop and be part of a winning Oilers team again, but with Curtis Joseph waiting in the wings, Ranford became expendable.

After trading Ranford to the Bruins in January 1996, Sather said, "It became evident it was going to be increasingly difficult to do this deal as time went on. Part of the difficulty was the evidence other teams were watching Billy's save percentage decrease over time. That was a factor in this whole thing."

Ranford's value continued to decline at the World Cup of Hockey in the summer of 1996, as his poor play relegated him to spectator status. "That wasn't a great experience for me. I didn't play a single game, but I think maybe I had my best year that season in Boston, so I don't think I'd lost anything," he told the *National Post*.

A nagging shoulder injury led to his departure from Boston, and his list of injuries lengthened in Washington, leading to Olaf Kölzig taking over top spot. He led the Capitals to the final while Ranford sat out. Ranford said, "I was getting it back last year in Washington at training camp and then I got hit in the nuts in the first game of the year in Toronto and everyone knows what happened from there."

His $2.8-million contract proved too rich for Washington, and Ranford continued wandering through the league, first to Tampa Bay and then to Detroit, which was looking for veteran insurance for Chris Osgood.

"I had a terrible year [in Tampa] and I'd be lying to you if I were to tell you I didn't have doubts, but that was a terrible situation for everyone. It's no fun just to come to the rink and hope to stay close and not even think about winning. Nobody plays well under those circumstances," Ranford said to the *Post*.

The most influential player on his new club, Steve Yzerman, was far from won over, describing Ranford's style as "goaltending of the '80s," adding, "He hasn't had a place to play for a while. In Washington, in Tampa, it wasn't right, and he doesn't have a place here really. I don't know what the future holds for him."

It turned out Ranford would finish the string out back in Edmonton, backing up Tommy Salo. In retirement, he played the hockey scenes in the movie *Miracle* in the role of U.S. Olympian Jim Craig. After filming wrapped up, Ranford started his second hockey career, that of goaltending consultant, first with the Seattle Thunderbirds of the Western Hockey League. His goalie coaching career would blossom after he joined the Vancouver Giants, and in 2006–07, Ranford returned to the NHL, joining the Los Angeles Kings as goalie coach. L.A. was struggling, with starter Dan Cloutier going down to injury early in the season, which encouraged the Kings to grab Sean Burke to shore up the position late in the year.

Burke said, "I really have a lot of respect for him as a goalie coach. He's one of those ex-players that really puts a lot of time and effort into learning new things about the game. The game's always changing and you've got to change with it. And Billy does an excellent job."

After the lockout, L.A. revamped its goaltending in a major way, making Jonathan Quick its starter. Quick would rewrite the Kings' record books and win two Stanley Cups in three years.

"It was huge. [After] five years working with Quickie, it was a special moment," Ranford said of his protégé winning a Cup and Conn Smythe Trophy in 2012. "You get that bond going and that trust that you have between the goalie and goalie coach, and I was just like a proud papa when it was over."

SEAN BURKE "They did it! They did it! The Devils make the playoffs for the first time in their history!"

New Jersey broadcaster Gary Thorne had come unhinged after John MacLean's monumental overtime winner against the Chicago Blackhawks in New Jersey's last game of the 1987–88 season, which vaulted the Devils past the New York Rangers for the eighth and final playoff berth in the Patrick Division.

Coming to join the celebration was rookie goaltender Sean Burke, who'd just played in his 13th professional game. He led the Devils to 10 wins in their last 11 games and would take them to within one win of the Stanley Cup Final.

"We heard the way he had stoned the Russians and how well he played for the Canadian Olympic team. Just the fact he was with us gave us confidence," said Devils 46-goal scorer Pat Verbeek.

While holding the fort all the way to Game 7 of the Wales Conference Final against the Boston Bruins, Burke found himself compared to Ken Dryden. The comparisons were obvious: both towered over their peers at 6-foot-4 and were unheralded first-year men who took the league by storm. Heading into the Boston series, Rangers general manager Phil Esposito opined Burke's accomplishments actually overshadowed Dryden's during the Canadiens' miracle 1971 championship year. "Look at what Dryden had in front of him," Esposito said at the time.

"Of course I found that very flattering. As a young guy, Ken Dryden was one of the guys that I watched and one of my favourite goaltenders growing up," said Burke.

While both Burke and Dryden were nearly identical in proportion, Burke was unable to win the Cup that year, or any other. Both enjoyed success on the international stage, but Burke went through some lean years playing behind squads that nowhere near resembled the dynastic Canadiens of the '70s.

Born January 29, 1967, in Windsor, Ontario, Burke toiled as an amateur for Canada's National Team after a couple Junior A seasons with the Toronto Marlboros. It was Max McNab, then New Jersey's general manager, who favoured Burke's apprenticeship in the Olympic program over the minor leagues.

Burke said, "It was really his idea, and looking back, it was pretty wise of him to look at that option because at the end of the day, I did develop a lot quicker playing with the national team. I had such great experiences against what were probably the best players in the world outside of the NHL, playing against the Russians, Czechs, and Swedes. A lot of their best players hadn't come over to the NHL."

Burke shared the goaltending duties with Andy Moog, who walked out on the Edmonton Oilers, at the 1988 Winter Olympics in Calgary. Working alongside an established pro and Stanley Cup winner like Moog turned out to be a huge plus for Burke's development. When the Devils tapped Burke to take over the nets in 1988, he wasn't overwhelmed by the pressure and played like an old hand despite his lack of professional experience.

"I looked at it as an exciting opportunity to come in the NHL to get a chance to play. And when we started winning and moving along through the playoffs, it was a wonderful experience to come into the NHL," said Burke.

After that amazing run, Burke played the majority of Devils games for the next couple seasons, but neither he nor the team returned to their previous form. He'd be relegated to backup duty behind Chris Terreri in 1990–91, his last season with the Devils.

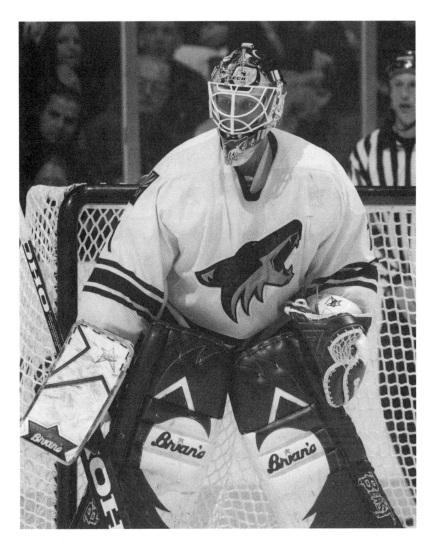

Sean Burke played five seasons with the Phoenix Coyotes and later returned as the team's goaltending coach. (Courtesy Phoenix Coyotes)

"I did struggle at times for the next couple years to try and get my game back to where it was. I don't even know if it was that my game was so good [during the playoff run], but it was just the enthusiasm and energy that went along with that that helped get us to that point. But when the reality of the regular season settled in again the next year, and you've got to play 80 games to make the playoffs again, I battled a little bit with trying to be consistent," said Burke.

Burke wondered if perhaps he hadn't been able to appreciate his early success because he assumed it would return every year. Becoming an instant NHL sensation might not have been unequivocally beneficial and might actually have hurt him in some ways too, he believes.

When Terreri usurped him as number one, Burke looked for a change in scenery. New GM Lou Lamoriello offered Burke a good contract, but Burke had decided he needed to get back to enjoying the game. It was another Olympic year, and Burke rejoined Canada's national team, with whom he ended up winning the silver medal in Albertville, France.

A trade to Hartford brought him back to the NHL, and his game returned to its previous excellent form. But while he enjoyed great personal success, being named the Whalers' most valuable player for four out of his five seasons in Hartford, the team itself struggled.

"An MVP on a losing team, a team that doesn't make the playoffs, is really not that satisfying," Burke said. As much as he enjoyed the city, the fans, and atmosphere, "At the end of it all, we never made the playoffs. I guess I established myself in some ways as a top goaltender, but I wasn't able to get the team into the playoffs and we weren't able to win anything, so in hindsight, how much success did I really have?"

Burke's chance at team success again came by representing Canada internationally. At the 1997 World Championship, he was the starter on a gold medal–winning squad made up of players who didn't make the NHL playoffs or whose teams were bounced out early.

He quickly came crashing back down to Earth the following season, 1997–98, which was one of turmoil. The Whalers moved to Carolina, and Burke's trade to Vancouver was followed by another one, to Philadelphia.

"Vancouver was a really tough situation at the time. I was having some personal issues and I didn't go into Vancouver in the right frame of mind to be a good player," said Burke, who was dealing with a domestic assault charge stemming back to an incident in Carolina. He added, "With the experiences I had in the game, I didn't go in there and add anything to that dressing room. I didn't play well, but I also wasn't much of a factor, the leader or anything like that. At the end of it all, it was a short stay. Did I get a fair shake? I probably got a fair shake, I just didn't deliver."

His situation didn't improve much after he went to the Flyers, where he joined incumbent Ron Hextall. For Burke, there is no more difficult place to play goal than Philadelphia, where the over-hanging sentiment among the fans and media is that the club's goaltending has been sorely lacking ever since Bernie Parent and the Broad Street Bullies last won the Stanley Cup in the mid-1970s.

He felt the criticism before ever pulling on a Flyers sweater. After arriving in Philly and hopping into a cab, he heard the doubters question his ability and the Flyers' decision to acquire him on a sports talk radio program.

Burke said, "The first thing I heard was the guy that they're talking to, he says, 'I don't know what we traded for this bum for, he's no good.' And I was sitting in the back of the cab thinking I haven't even gotten to the rink yet. I had played in the league for 10 years; it's not like they were trading for some guy that had never done anything. It's something I couldn't get used to, I couldn't get used to the negativity in Philadelphia. And that's really what it is."

Hextall was only too glad for someone to share the pain. "He didn't want to play at that point! He was happy that I was coming in to take the burden of negativity; he was more than happy to have that passed on to somebody else. He had had enough of it himself," said Burke.

The Philly experience, however, would be short-lived, and after another short stint, this time with Florida, Burke joined the Phoenix Coyotes, with whom he'd again be counted among the best. In 2001–02 he was named a finalist for the Vezina and Lester B.

Pearson trophies, and he also finished fourth in Hart Trophy voting for NHL MVP. He credited Coyotes goalie coach Benoit Allaire for his recent rise in the ranks. He said,

> I think it had a lot to do with Benny; it was a lot to do with maturing.... Like a lot of people, I'm stubborn, I think that I know how to do things the right way most of the time, especially when it comes to playing goal. I was able to put that ego aside and realize there were a lot of things I needed to work on. Benoit had a way of presenting it to me that allowed me to realize these are some of the things I need to do to become a top goalie in this league, and if I'm not going to do them, [I'll] continue to be inconsistent.
>
> Benny came along at the right time for me where I was willing to learn and he was able to teach me the right stuff.

Burke starred for another gold medal Canadian team at the World Championship in 2003, and those international successes have become his Stanley Cups.

"The most exciting thing about the winning is the guys that you did it with and the memories that you have. I don't want to make it sound like I'm pining away and disappointed every day because I didn't win a Stanley Cup. Yeah, that would have been wonderful, but at least I did have some winning experiences in international hockey that I'm very proud of," said Burke.

Midway through the 2003–04 season, he made an unwanted return to Philadelphia, where Jeff Hackett had been forced to retire. While Burke found the Flyers to be a first-rate, classy organization that tried to build a winner every season, the undo pressure on the goaltenders from fans and media made playing there miserable.

"I can say that in all the years I played, the two times I was in Philadelphia were the most unenjoyable experiences that I've had in the National Hockey League," he said.

After the 2004–05 lockout, Burke signed with Tampa Bay to replace Stanley Cup–winning goalie Nikolai Khabibulin, who'd signed a four-year deal with the Chicago Blackhawks. Burke had previously replaced Khabibulin when the latter was a holdout in Phoenix, but this time, the fit proved poor.

"The team had won the Stanley Cup and now they had a whole year of a lockout and they came back and they lost Khabibulin, and I was one of the few guys that was coming in new. It just never felt comfortable, it never felt like I was part of the team. I felt like I was just a guy filling a hole and it's hard to play that way. When you're a 17-year veteran, you want to feel the organization is behind you and they believe in you and expect you to perform, and I just never felt that way in Tampa," said Burke.

In his second year, Burke was sent down to Springfield of the American Hockey League, where he rarely played. Burke's career got a reprieve from the Los Angeles Kings, where Bill Ranford was serving his first year as the team's goaltending coach.

Ranford said, "I was actually a big part of bringing him in. I'd been on a scouting trip and ran into him and we had some injuries and needed some goaltending help, so I called our GM."

Burke brought stability to a struggling franchise that had gone most of the season with untried netminders after starter Dan Cloutier went down to injury. His presence paid immediate dividends.

At the time, L.A. coach Marc Crawford said, "Since Sean Burke arrived, we've been a lot better. He's come in and taken that burden and it's given us a better feel for our team. Sean's played well for us and he makes us more confident on the ice, which makes a difference."

The Kings' leading goal scorer, Alexander Frolov, echoed Crawford's praise: "He makes so many great saves for us. It's much easier to play when you're not afraid of what's going on in your zone."

Burke's retirement from hockey was brief, as he would return to the Coyotes' fold, but this time in a suit and tie. After starting out in prospect development, GM Don Maloney pegged him to coach Ilya Bryzgalov and Jason LaBarbera. In his first year working with the duo, 2009–10, the Coyotes allowed the fewest goals in the Western Conference. Bryzgalov thrived under Burke, finishing runner-up for the Vezina and fifth in Hart Trophy voting and setting new franchise goaltending records.

"My experience with Bryz was really good. . . . I found myself watching him some nights thinking this is a guy with a lot of potential to be a better player than he is right now. And I could identify with that," Burke said about his initial reflections.

LaBarbera is a fan: "Burke gets it, he understands what the guy's going through. He goes to bat for you. If you work hard and you do perform, he'll go to bat for you."

Burke's later work with Mike Smith was impressive too. Smith had previously backed up Marty Turco in Dallas and split duties in Tampa, so he'd never really established himself as a starter in the NHL. That would change under Burke, as Smith won 38 games his first season and backstopped the Coyotes to the Western Conference Final, the furthest the franchise had ever advanced in its history.

Burke said, "With Smitty, he's an incredibly gifted athlete—size and skill. He's kind of a rare combination of a guy that's a goaltender; he's built like he could play defence; he's competitive in every aspect, practice, games; he's just got a really, really good combination of raw ability. So he wasn't a lot of work technically, it was more to get him to believe he can be one of the best in this league. And he started to see that and his confidence started to grow."

Possibly following in Burke's footsteps is his son, Brendan. Father originally tried to dissuade son from stopping pucks, steering him toward having some fun as a goal-scoring forward. But even after two years of lighting the lamp, Brendan's ambitions to block shots rather than fire them remained unchanged and his father gave in. Brendan's since grown to resemble his father's playing days' physical dimensions, and, appropriately enough, he was picked by the Phoenix Coyotes in the 2013 entry draft.

"I think the advantage he's going to have is he really understands the games. He can read the play, he knows what he's seen, and he's been around it his whole life, so that's going to work to his advantage down the road," said Burke, the proud father.

BOB ESSENSA Goalies are often victims of their coaches'
whims, and not even turning around their team's fortunes and taking them to the playoffs are enough to automatically give them a post-season starting assignment.

Picked for the All-Rookie Team in 1989–90, Bob Essensa helped the Winnipeg Jets rebound from their horrendous previous year, playing a major role in their securing a playoff berth. But in the first round, coach Bob Murdoch inexplicably platooned Essensa and backup Stéphane Beauregard. The Jets would take a commanding three-games-to-one lead over the Edmonton Oilers, with Essensa winning all three of his starts. But the Oilers took the next three— with Beauregard in net for two of those, including the pivotal seventh game—and would eventually go on to win the Stanley Cup.

At the end of the 1991–92 season, Essensa was nominated one of the most proficient among his peers, but his stellar play wasn't enough to earn even a single playoff start against the Vancouver Canucks.

Another coach, John Paddock, went with another hunch, starting backup Rick Tabaracci ahead of Essensa. The move looked brilliant after the Jets once again went up three games to one, but like Edmonton, Vancouver battled back and took the series in seven. Tabaracci started every game.

Born January 14, 1965, the Etobicoke, Ontario, native eschewed the local Maple Leafs in favour of the Philadelphia Flyers and their brilliant goalie, Bernie Parent. While still a Junior B goalie with Henry Carr, the Jets drafted him in 1983 in the fourth round, 69th overall. Although drafted by Major Junior's Cornwall Royals, Essensa pursued the college route, heading to Michigan State, where he starred, won championships, and set school records. But turning professional would be an eye-opener for Essensa, who dominated in his four years with the Spartans.

"My first year pro, I was down in Moncton with about 16 rookies, because it was Winnipeg's first year of having their own farm club. We were very young and green, and it showed in our results. I think we won four out of 40 road games. Just abysmal," Essensa said.

In his second year, Essensa got shipped out to Fort Wayne. But when Jets incumbents Daniel Berthiaume and Eldon Reddick struggled to regain their previous years' form, coach Rick Bowness—who had been behind the bench in Moncton during Essensa's first year—called him up and threw him into the breach.

There'd be no waiting for a soft opponent, as Bowness started Essensa against the Detroit Red Wings at Joe Louis Arena. Although Essensa had played there as a collegiate, that familiarity didn't initially translate into a good omen. "My first shot on goal, they scored," Essensa said, remembering Dave Barr's goal in the opening 25 seconds of the first period.

It looked like it would be a long night when his third shot was a penalty shot from none other than Red Wings captain and future Hall of Fame sniper Steve Yzerman. He cruised in to score high glove side.

"So three shots into it and only a few minutes into my first game, I've already given up a couple, so I'm trying to figure out if I get two days' pay or only one before they ship me back to Fort Wayne," said Essensa.

The Jets, however, somehow turned it around to even the score and allowed Essensa to earn a tie in his first NHL game.

He'd stick around for the rest of the season, and by training camp the following season, 1989–90, he figured he had the inside track on an NHL job. He didn't. New coach Bob Murdoch chose Berthiaume and Tom Draper to open the season, and Essensa found himself back in Moncton. The Jets, however, staggered out of the gate. Essensa was recalled, and he didn't waste much time making his mark.

He impressed with his domination of the reigning Stanley Cup–champion Calgary Flames and earned his coach's and captain's

Bob Essensa is a study in concentration. (IHA/Icon SMI)

admiration after stopping 49 shots in a 2-1 Jets victory at the Saddledome in late 1989.

"Call the cops," Murdoch reportedly told waiting journalists.

Dale Hawerchuk told the *Calgary Herald*, "Those guys [goalies] are usually a little goofy, but you know what? He's a normal person. He just quietly goes about his business. You can see him really coming into his own lately."

Hawerchuk's enthusiasm for his goalie continued after Essensa helped steal the first game of the Jets' best-of-seven playoff series against the Oilers. "Goaltending in the playoffs is like World Series pitching, and we had an ace going today," Hawerchuk told the *Edmonton Journal*.

In his first ever NHL playoff game, Essensa stopped five breakaways, allowing Winnipeg to come out on top 7-5. Murdoch, however, was intent on carrying on his practice of rotating his netminders.

Essensa said, "We religiously flip-flopped myself and Stephie Beauregard. I don't know if a team's tried to do it since. It was certainly unusual. Bob was confident that would give us an edge and not overtax one of us. We were both young and green, so from that perspective, I understood it. To do that, flip-flop back and forth, from a team perspective, I'm not sure that's the greatest thing. But I think it was more just trying to throw the Oilers a curve ball."

But Edmonton hit Murdoch's juicy pitch right out of the ballpark when they eliminated the Jets from the playoffs.

"[Essensa] fell victim to the worst coaching call in Jet NHL history when Bob Murdoch, Alpo Suhonen, and Clare Drake chose Beauregard over Essensa for game seven in Edmonton," said Curt Keilback, who called the action in the broadcast booth for the original NHL Jets.

For the Jets, 1990–91 proved disastrous, and they missed the playoffs, but they returned the following year, Essensa's Vezina-finalist season.

"Essensa covers a lot of net and plays the angles extremely well," Maple Leaf and former Jet Dave Ellett marvelled after Essensa and the Jets won a 3-1 decision at Maple Leaf Gardens. He continued, "Because he plays in Winnipeg, he doesn't get as much attention as he should, but I think the NHL is starting to respect him now."

Not quite *everyone*. Despite repelling 36 of 37 Leaf shots and earning First Star honours, new Winnipeg coach John Paddock didn't seem to see what the big deal was. "I don't think he was particularly sharp. I thought he was going down too soon early in the game," Paddock said after the game.

That harsh critique didn't surprise Keilback in the least. He said, "I remember John Paddock would never give him credit publicly. When Essensa played a particularly good game and Paddock was approached about it, he had a stock answer: 'He's paid to stop the puck.' I always felt that Paddock was under orders from ownership to downplay Essensa's performance, to keep his contract price down."

Despite Essensa sharing the league's shutout lead that season with five, Paddock shocked the hockey world by starting Tabaracci in the Jets first-round playoff series against the Canucks, claiming Tabaracci outplayed Essensa in games versus Vancouver. Essensa saw a grand total of 33 minutes in the nets as Winnipeg again squandered a series stranglehold and made an early playoff exit.

For the next two seasons, Essensa would carry the load for the Jets in the regular season, seeing action in 123 games, and frustrating opponents with his unorthodox style.

Keilback said, "What I remember most about 'Goalie Bob' was his style. He was as apt to stop a puck with his butt as he was with his stick. He was often like a beached whale, but somehow made the save. He was fun to watch. He was a popular guy with his teammates. He was also accessible at any time, unlike some goalies who keep their distance on game day."

The fans too revered him.

"For whatever reason, Winnipeg really took me into their own and I'll be forever grateful. I was lucky enough to come back when they invited me back when they closed the old Winnipeg Arena. It was certainly from my perspective some of my most enjoyable hockey years," said Essensa.

But the Jets resisted paying him the sort of salary he deserved, and the club and Essensa got embroiled in a bitter contract arbitration in 1992–93. Before the '93–94 trade deadline, he was dealt to the Red Wings. "My contract was up and was most likely one of the main reasons I was traded," Essensa speculated.

The original NHL Jets never came close to becoming a playoff force, having won only two series between 1979 and 1996. So when Essensa was traded to Detroit, he took the move as a positive step in his career: "At the time, I thought going to an Original Six team was maybe the right thing to do. Obviously it didn't work out as I expected."

Motown could be a tough place to tend goal in those years. Tim Cheveldae, who went to Winnipeg as part of the deal, had been so mercilessly booed at the Joe Louis Arena that the coaches would only start him on the road. Detroit was the class of the league during the regular season, but they hadn't come close to the finals, and the goalies shouldered most of the blame for the team's playoff shortcomings. Essensa didn't endear himself to coach Scotty Bowman, going 4-7-2 down the stretch. In the Wings' first-round matchup against the San Jose Sharks, Bowman gave Essensa the start, but when the Sharks won the opener 5-4, Essensa took the brunt of the blame and was sat in favour of Chris Osgood. Detroit still lost the series in seven.

When Mike Vernon joined the Wings in the summer, Essensa became the odd man out. He felt management already had their rotation decided before training camp and didn't give him a chance.

"I actually had myself a pretty good training camp.... I remember Stevie Y skating up to me after one of the exhibition games and saying, 'You're going to screw everything up and actually make this team.' But it was clear to me my days were numbered if not already done in Detroit," Essensa said.

He spent the next two seasons in the IHL, two leagues below the NHL, and feared he might be buried there for good: "My first thought was maybe I'm done. Maybe it's time for me to move on to other things."

But a good attitude and a solid year in Fort Wayne gave him a reprieve; Edmonton came calling, trading for Essensa's rights and making him an Oiler for the next three years.

When GM Glen Sather brought Bill Ranford back into the fold in the summer of 1999, Essensa signed with the relocated Jets franchise, the Phoenix Coyotes. It was an enjoyable year for Essensa, as he played 30 games while sharing the duties with Sean Burke. It was also his first experience with a full-time goaltending coach—Benoit Allaire.

"I echoed Sean Burke's comments at the time that I wish I'd met this guy 10 years prior, because he did wonders for Burkie and his game and for me and mine. Even that one year I spent with Benny was terrific and invaluable," said Essensa.

Essensa's last hurrah, though, would come in Vancouver. Signed on to back up Felix Potvin, Essensa's stature would grow in his fans', teammates', and coach's eyes, as Potvin faltered while he shone.

"Starting out as the number two and really coming in and taking over number one, he did more than what was expected," Canuck defenceman Murray Baron told the *Vancouver Sun*. "He has done everything asked of him."

"When we signed Bob, we expected him to give us quality starts and he has given us more than what we asked for," said his coach, Marc Crawford, who would credit Essensa with getting the Canucks into the playoffs.

Essensa claimed, "Vancouver was another one of those cities that was very good to me. And maybe because I was the underdog. When I went there, I was clearly the backup but got to play almost 40 games. I was more surprised that they didn't have me back after that year than any of my other surprises."

Canucks GM Brian Burke and goalie coach Andy Moog weren't convinced Essensa could handle the workload of a starter. Vancouver opted not to re-sign him in the summer, and Essensa caught on with Buffalo, where he languished behind number-one Martin Biron. Essensa had started only three games by Christmas break and never won the confidence of coach Lindy Ruff. The end had come.

While his playing career was done, his days in the NHL weren't over yet, thanks in part to his old Winnipeg coach, Rick Bowness. "It's not like these guys don't know you, but they'll forget about you in a couple years' time," Essensa remembered Bowness telling him.

In Boston, Essensa's former Coyotes teammate Mike Sullivan was taking over as coach, and with Gerry Cheevers retiring from his goaltender consulting duties, Sullivan coveted a familiar face to fill the open spot. Enter Essensa, who in 2005–06 started working with the Boston and Providence Bruins goalies. He drew on his playing experience, including the toughest times, when he was buried in the minors. He explained,

> I got pushed right out of the league entirely, sent to San Diego right after the lockout, and the following year, spent the entire year in Fort Wayne. To be honest, I think it made me into a better goalie coach because now I understand what it takes to be a good number one, a good backup, and to be good down in the minors. There's all sorts of challenges, and I draw a lot from those experiences when I deal with the guys in our Bruins organization, whether they're down in the East Coast league, Providence, or in Boston.

The Bruins struggled the first couple of years but turned into a powerhouse, with Essensa along for the ride. They'd win a Stanley Cup in 2011 with student Tim Thomas taking the Conn Smythe, and they returned to the final again in 2013, falling in six with Thomas's former backup Tuukka Rask standing on his head in a losing cause.

DOMINIK HASEK During his Hall of Fame broadcasting career, Sabres announcer Rick Jeanneret has seen them all, but Dominik Hasek, he says, was the best: "Hasek was the greatest goaltender I ever saw—in the years he was in Buffalo. He'd say, 'You guys go out and get one, and we'll win.' That was his approach to the game."

Confident to the point of arrogance, Hasek brought a unique style, and a touch of European flair, to the game, and he bridged the gap between the scrambler goalies of the past and the butterfliers of today.

Clint Malarchuk said, "He kind of changed the game in a lot of ways. He went against every goaltending rule that I was brought up with—stand up, play the angles. He would stay on the goal line—later on he learned to play outside, thanks to Mitch Korn—but he was just total reflex, flop around, stop the puck, it doesn't matter how you look. He defied everything that goalies were supposed to do, coming up in that era. But the thing is, he had success."

If anything, the praise underplays "the Dominator's" accomplishments: Czechoslovakian Goaltender of the Year (1986, 1987, 1988, 1989, 1990); Czechoslovakian Player of the Year (1987, 1989, 1990); Czechoslovakian First All-Star Team (1988, 1989, 1990); IHL First All-Star Team (1991); NHL All-Rookie Team (1992); NHL First All-Star Team (1994, 1995, 1997, 1998, 1999, 2001); William M. Jennings Award (1994, 2001); Vezina Trophy (1994, 1995, 1997, 1998, 1999, 2001); Lester B. Pearson Award (1997, 1998); Hart Trophy as NHL MVP (1997, 1998); NHL All-Star Game appearances (1996, 1997, 1998, 1999, 2001, 2002); Hockey Hall of Fame (2014).

Then there's the 1998 Olympic gold medal in Nagano, Japan, the first to feature the stars of the NHL. All told, Hasek only let six goals—total—into the Czech Republic net he was guarding, and only two of those goals were in the medal round; he had two shutouts and a .961 save percentage. In the semis, there was a dramatic shootout victory over Team Canada, as he stoned Theoren Fleury, Ray Bourque, Joe Nieuwendyk, Eric Lindros, and Brendan Shanahan—who have a combined 2,625 goals in their NHL careers.

"When the game ended, I just threw my stick. I was so happy. When I saw the flag go up, I saw my whole career flash before my eyes from the first time my parents took me to a game until now," Hasek said after the game.

Before the Olympics in Turin in 2006—his fourth and final Games—Hasek recalled the post-victory scene for CBC.ca: "The celebration in Prague in 1998 was the biggest ever in my hockey career. Vaclav Havel [the Czech president] called me an hour after we won the gold medal. He told me people were in the streets chanting, 'Hasek to the Castle!' I told him his job wasn't in jeopardy because I had no plans to run for president."

In 2002, while a Detroit Red Wing, Hasek became the first European starting goaltender to win the Stanley Cup; on the way to the title, he set a post-season record for shutouts with six (since broken by Martin Brodeur). It was a full decade after he first played in a Cup Final, when he filled in for Ed Belfour when the Chicago Blackhawks lost to the Pittsburgh Penguins.

And neither of those is even his most famous Stanley Cup appearance. That was in 1999, when he took the seventh-seeded Sabres past the Ottawa Senators, Boston Bruins, and Toronto Maple Leafs and into the final against the Dallas Stars, the league's top team. His counterpart in the Stars' net was Belfour. The sixth and deciding game went to triple-overtime, with Hasek and Belfour counting 50 and 53 saves, respectively, before Brett Hull's notorious foot-in-the-crease goal ended the game and gave the Stars the Cup.

Make no mistake, the Sabres were Hasek's team at that point, said Jeanneret. At one morning skate, the players were taking shots on the goalies. In the dressing room after, some players started boasting about how their team had won. "Dom said, 'Bullshit! You did not win!' He took them all right back out on the ice again. The guys are almost getting out of the shower, made them all put their stuff back on, and go back out on the ice and complete the game that his team won. It will give you some idea of the respect that the players had for him that they would do that. I mean, who's going to get out of the shower and have to put wet stuff back on and go back out on the ice? But with Dom saying 'Yes,' then yes, it happens," said Jeanneret.

Born January 29, 1965, in Pardubice, Czechoslovakia—now the Czech Republic—Hasek was tall for his age, and when he was just six years old he was the goalie for nine-year-olds. Learning the game as he went, without the benefit of a goalie coach, at age 16 he became the youngest player ever in the Czechoslovak Extraliga when he suited up for HC Pardubice. The HC won two league titles, in 1987 and 1989. For 1990, he was drafted into the Czech army and played

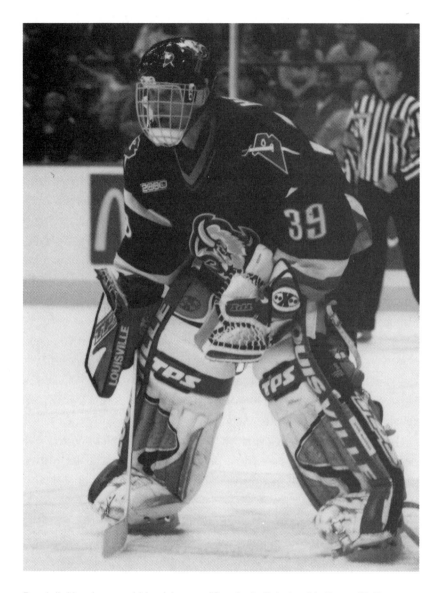

Dominik Hasek earned his nickname "Dominator" during his time with the Buffalo Sabres. (George Tahinos)

for Dukla Jihlava and the national team. International attention first came his way in April 1984, when the Czechoslovakian team with Hasek in the net beat the Russians 7-2 in the Sweden Cup tournament, handing the Soviets, with the famed KLM line of Vladimir

Krutov, Igor Larionov, and Sergei Makarov, its first loss in international play in two and a half years. On North American shores, he was the starter for the Czechs at the 1984 Canada Cup. By the 1987 Canada Cup, the 5-foot-11, 168-pound Hasek was getting raves from the likes of Tony Esposito: "As far as Europeans go, he's by far the most talented. He moves really well, seems to be well coached, and he has a very good glove," Tony O told the *Globe and Mail*.

The Blackhawks were ahead of the curve, taking Hasek 207th overall in the 1983 NHL entry draft, a risky move given that players from behind the Iron Curtain usually didn't get a chance to play abroad. It wasn't until 1990–91 that he made his way over, an All-Star with the International Hockey League's Indianapolis Ice. He also got into five games with the Hawks that season.

At the time, Ed Belfour was the goalie of the future in Chicago, however, and Hasek got into just 20 games and three playoff tilts as the Hawks marched to the final. Mike Keenan was the coach of the Hawks, and he said, "I had Dominik Hasek who was just learning to speak English and had this crazy style."

In the book *Without Fear: Hockey's 50 Greatest Goaltenders*, the desperate switch to Hasek from Belfour, after the latter let in two goals in the opening six minutes in Game 4, is recalled:

> We were all looking at each other, wondering, "Who is this guy?" recalls Scotty Bowman, then coach of the Penguins. As the commotion continued, Penguins sniper Jaromir Jagr glided slowly toward the bench, his complexion ghostly, his eyes glazed over, his face frozen in fear. Staring directly at his fellow Penguins, he spoke with terror dripping from his words. "We have to win this game," he said in a pleading tone.

Jagr, a Czech native, knew all about Hasek. While the Pens put four goals past him in the Cup-winning game, it did foreshadow Hasek's effect on the league.

The Hawks, electing to go with Belfour and Jimmy Waite, traded

Hasek to Buffalo for goalie Stéphane Beauregard and future considerations (a draft pick, Éric Dazé). In Buffalo, Hasek was initially stuck behind Grant Fuhr and Tom Draper, but when Fuhr got injured, Hasek got his chance.

Goalie coach Mitch Korn recalled Hasek's early days with the Sabres: "We traded for Dom my second season in Buffalo, and I remember [GM] John Muckler . . . came to me that training camp and said, 'You see this guy, Hasek? He's a little different. Leave him alone. Help him if he wants help. You can talk to him. Work with the other guys. He's just different, leave him alone.'"

Korn, who also managed the arena in Miami, Ohio, was in and out of Buffalo. He caught up with the team near the end of training camp at an exhibition game in Hamilton, Ontario, against the Leafs. He met up with a frantic Muckler: "Instead of saying, 'Hi, Mitch, how are you? What's going on?' John Muckler looked at me as I walked in and said, 'Have you talked to him yet?' I said, 'Talk to who?' He said, 'Hasek, have you talked to him yet?' I said, 'You told me to leave him alone.' 'Don't leave him alone anymore!' 'Okay, John.' That's really when Dom and my relationship really began at that point."

Korn helped Hasek be more patient and created drills to drive Hasek's competitiveness and flexibility. Somehow they worked on making the spectacularly spontaneous saves commonplace. "I've seen him do things that make me shake my head," Pat LaFontaine once said.

In 1999, Hasek told the *National Post*, "He didn't try to change me. Sometimes I have too much flexibility. I try to reach too much. He explained to me that I was a great skater and I could move on my skates."

But the innate confidence, faith in self, cannot be taught—Hasek had it already in spades.

"No one will say he was the greatest athlete, but he brought a mental strength to the game with his positioning, his unorthodox style, all geared toward stopping the puck and winning," said Marty

Turco, decidedly a fan. He continued, "His competitive nature showed through the way he yelled at his teammates, to the way he yelled at the refs, to the way he buckled down after a poor start in the game or not a great start to the season, and then end up being the best goaltender in the league."

Hasek was driven to improve and stave off Father Time. He would stay after practice, after *games*, to take shots, to hone his skills, to address what might have gone wrong. His pliability was legendary and cringe-worthy—while in his gear, Hasek could spread his legs wide and put his chest on the dressing room floor.

"A guy doing the splits, and every male in the crowd immediately grabs for his you-know-what because they can't believe it and it hurts just to watch. Dom used to do it whenever, and it didn't bother him in the least. Entirely unorthodox the way he played the game; it's not so unorthodox anymore," said Jeanneret.

When the Sabres needed to trim payroll, Hasek was shipped to Detroit on July 1, 2001, in exchange for Vyacheslav Kozlov, a first-round selection in the 2002 NHL entry draft and future considerations. With a stacked team in front of him, Hasek set a career high with 41 wins on the way to the Stanley Cup.

Hasek retired in 2002–03 but then came back for 14 games with the Wings, knocking the incumbent, Curtis Joseph and his three-year $24-million deal, out of the net. Joseph ended up back in goal during the playoffs, though, after Hasek got sidelined by groin and ankle woes. The lockout of 2004–05 gave him a year to recover, and he came back for a season with Ottawa, signing as a free agent.

"There is nothing like hockey—being in the net and the feeling of winning after a game," he said in 2005, before suiting up with the Senators. But that year in Canada's capital, things just didn't go right, at least not to the standards he had set for himself.

The Sens didn't invite him back, but the Wings did, though he eventually made way for Chris Osgood; the backup role did get him a second Stanley Cup in 2008 though, as the Wings beat the

Penguins. He retired in June 2008, took a year off, then played two more seasons—one back with HC Pardubice and then Spartak Moscow of the Kontinental Hockey League. The end finally (probably?) came for good on October 9, 2012.

After Hasek's last retirement, Wings GM Ken Holland told Steve Simmons of the *Toronto Sun*, "He made saves no one else made. He would get inside the head of your opponents. And he would break your will. I've been lucky to have been around some all-time great players here. Dom was one of those. He could take his game to another level and when he took it to that level, no one else could take their game to a similar level. And he was in his 40s doing that here. Imagine how great he was before that."

An appropriate, lyrical coda for a stellar career comes from Ed Willes, in a 1998 *New York Times* profile: "Like a great jazz musician, the Czech goalie has mastered the basics of his trade—positioning, anticipation. But it is what he does in his moments of improvisation that set him apart."

PELLE LINDBERGH The Philadelphia Flyers tandem

of Pelle Lindbergh and Bob Froese were about as different as two goalies can get. Lindbergh was a hot, young star from Sweden, a high-living bon vivant with quick reflexes whose talent came easily. Froese was raised a Mennonite Brethren in St. Catharines, Ontario, and his work ethic and consistency was what kept him in the NHL. Together, they had gotten the Flyers to the Stanley Cup Final in 1984–85, losing to the Edmonton Oilers in five games. Lindbergh earned praise for his play.

Post-hockey, Froese earned a bachelor of science in religion from Liberty University and followed that up with a master of arts in religion at Liberty's Baptist Theological Seminary, and finally a PhD in biblical counselling from Trinity Theological Seminary. He is now the pastor at Faith Fellowship Church in Clarence, New York.

Froese's spiritual growth allows him to look back on the sudden death of the 26-year-old Lindbergh in a car crash in November 1985 perhaps differently than many of his peers.

"A week before Pelle died, he and I went out. Just he and I. We just spent a good portion of the night together, just talking. We basically, if you could say this, buried the hatchet. We were so competitive, not that we ever fought or anything like that, but there was tension, two guys wanting one spot. He was more talented, and I was probably more the, I don't know, the hard worker," Froese said.

They bonded over idiosyncrasies and superstitions. Froese could use any stick and didn't have a particular set routine. Lindbergh had to use a certain stick, favoured a worn-out cloth glove inside his blocker, and refused to take off his equipment—any of it—between periods.

The coach of those Flyers was a young Mike Keenan, in the first of his many NHL jobs. His own career having stalled, he coached the Ontario Hockey League's Peterborough Petes for one season, until being tapped to helm the American Hockey League's Rochester Americans. It was there that Keenan got to see Lindbergh play for the Maine Mariners, where he was the AHL MVP for 1980–81.

When he was hired by the Flyers, Keenan found confidence in the 5-foot-9, 166-pound Swede, who had replaced Rick St. Croix as Philadelphia's starting netminder in November 1982. The Flyers dealt St. Croix and the ascending Pete Peeters, committing to Lindbergh. "Iron Mike" butted heads with Froese as the goalie sought more playing time. The team's goalie coach, Flyers two-time Stanley Cup hero Bernie Parent, had already helped Lindbergh through a shaky second season and was a mentor to the youngster.

It's not like Froese didn't have the stats to be the starter. As a rookie, he set the NHL record for most consecutive games without a loss from the beginning of a career—13 games, 12-0-1—in 1982–83. (The record was broken by Patrick Lalime, who notched 16 consecutive wins in 1996–97.)

In the 1984–85 season, Froese actually had a better GAA than

Lindbergh, 2.41 to 3.02, though in 17 games to Lindbergh's 65; Lindbergh lead the league with 40 wins and three shutouts.

So going into training camp for the 1985–86 season, Froese didn't expect to win Keenan's affection, and he resigned himself to backup status for a stacked team that was once again a legitimate Stanley Cup contender.

And then Lindbergh died.

Early in the morning of Sunday, November 10, Lindbergh left a team celebration at the Coliseum, a restaurant-athletic complex where the Flyers practised, following the Flyers' win over the Bruins, a 10th straight victory for the squad. Froese had been the goalie that night. With no game scheduled until Thursday night, the team let loose.

Lindbergh actually went home after the game with his fiancée, Kerstin Pietzch, but returned later that night. The goalie departed the party with two other passengers, Edward T. Parvin, 28, and Kathyleen McNeal, 22, in his two-seater red Porsche 930 Turbo. Just outside an elementary school in Somerdale, New Jersey, the car slammed into a three-and-a-half-foot-high concrete wall.

Lindbergh was taken to John F. Kennedy Memorial Hospital in nearby Stratford. He had severe brain and spinal cord injuries, a fractured skull, and broken legs. The estimate was that his brain had gone without oxygen for 15 minutes and there was no hope of recovery. The passengers were not as severely injured. The goalie was hooked up to a life-support system as news of the accident travelled through the Flyers.

Team captain Dave Poulin called his coach, who had only just heard about the accident from Murray Craven. Keenan and Poulin lived in the same neighbourhood and went to the hospital together. Teammates trickled in throughout the early morning as they heard the news. Froese was in church Sunday morning when he learned of the accident. He had not been at the bar with his teammates.

With general manager Bobby Clarke and the owner, Ed Snider, out of town, it fell to Keenan to call Lindbergh's parents. "I was the only part of the management that was around," said Keenan.

Lindbergh's mother, Anna Lisa, and his fiancée arrived at the hospital, followed by his father, Sigge, who came in from Sweden. By Tuesday, his parents had given permission for the plug to be pulled and his organs harvested for donation. Lindbergh's blood alcohol content was measured at .24 per cent, according to Dr. Edward Viner, the team physician; in New Jersey, a motorist with a level of .10 is considered legally drunk. To a man, the Flyers defended their teammate, avowing that he was not a drinker, and instead attributed the accident to Lindbergh's need for speed and his customized car.

The Flyers regrouped and gathered as one. At the time, general manager Bobby Clarke said, "We thought it would be right to explain to the players what happened in one official meeting. Some had gone to the hospital right away. Others found out over the radio. There were a lot of tears."

The funeral was at Old Swedes Church in Philadelphia, conducted in English and Swedish. Poulin delivered the eulogy.

He managed to do what most of us won't be able to fit into a much longer lifetime. He travelled all over the world, and wherever he went, he made friends. Pelle left his mark. We'll remember him for his wide grin. And his zest for conquering the world. If Pelle wanted something, he got it. If he wanted to go somewhere, he went. We'd all joke about his ways, but I think we were all envious. By challenging life, he managed to see a great deal more than most of us will.

Poulin closed off with the Swedish words for "I love you," *Jag älska du.*

Before the family and Flyers defenceman Thomas Eriksson returned to Sweden for another memorial service, the Flyers had a game against the Edmonton Oilers at the Spectrum.

An emotional roller coaster of an evening started with memorial cards handed out to the fans, with a head shot of Lindbergh in black and white on one side, and "In Loving Memory of PELLE

LINDBERGH Our Goalie, Our Friend 31" on the opposite, with two small Flyers logos in the bottom corners. The 17,211 tickets were not torn up either, just marked with a black line, as, coincidentally, Lindbergh's picture was on the ducats.

With Lindbergh's number stitched onto their jerseys, and the Oilers wearing black armbands, the Flyers pulled it together for a 5-3 win.

The surprise starter was Darren Jensen, who had been the regular in the team's AHL squad in Hershey. He was flown in by private plane from Montreal, at the last minute, after Froese had gotten hit in the groin in practice and broken his protective cup and blood had been found in his urine.

Jensen, who had known Lindbergh a little, having suited up as his backup a bit the year before, said, "Bobby Clarke and Mike Keenan were at the airport. I wanted to go on the ice in the morning, just to practice with the guys, get a feel of the NHL calibre before I went into the hornet's nest. They said no, there was too much press, 'You have to go back to the hotel.' It was really, really difficult."

Jensen, in only his second-ever NHL game, led the Flyers onto the blue and orange carpet leading to centre ice under dimmed lighting. The pre-game ceremony took more than half an hour.

Parent told the crowd, "As I stand before you, our hearts are one. Every single one of us has lost someone we respect, someone who made us happy, and someone who made us proud."

Pausing occasionally to dry his tears, Parent said Pelle's death was the single hardest thing he had ever had to deal with, like the death of a son. He said, "I have flashbacks of a young goalie from Sweden relying on me to teach him how hockey in America is played. The paper said I was his hero. I wish I could tell you how much I admired him. I wish I could have told him this . . . how much I admired him and how much I cared."

Lindbergh, born on May 24, 1959, in Stockholm, grew up playing in the Hammerby hockey organization, and he actually made a trip as a bantam player to Aurora, Ontario. He always maintained that

Parent was his hero, and he wore a white face mask as a tribute throughout his career. Lindbergh was also always adamant that he would play for Fred Shero and the Philadelphia Flyers.

After playing for the bronze medal–winning Swedish team in the 1980 Winter Olympics in Lake Placid, Lindbergh was so confident in his abilities that he chafed at being sent down to Maine at the start of the 1981–82 season. At the time he said, "I'm going, but I don't think I can get any better there. I want to be in the NHL. I'm good enough to play in the First Division in Sweden and I think I should be in the top league here."

It was Parent who brought Lindbergh along.

Keenan said, "Bernie Parent was Pelle Lindbergh's hero, and I brought Bernie in as the goalie coach. He didn't go on the ice a lot with them—he did from time to time—but he was somebody that Pelle could talk to about the position and Pelle tried to emulate the style of Bernie, which he did well and played well. They had a great relationship."

At the NHL All-Star Game on Long Island in January 1983, Lindbergh was lit up for seven goals, four of which were to Wayne Gretzky. One went in over his head. After the game Pelle said, "The All-Star Game was embarrassing. You don't expect to be super in a game like that, facing all those shooters, but you don't think you're going to give up seven goals, either. I mean, I wasn't ruined, it wasn't the end of the world, but it wasn't easy, anyway."

In 1985, Lindbergh was an All-Star for the game in Calgary, stopping Gretzky four times as the Wales Conference defeated the Campbell Conference 6-4. "I kept telling myself that no matter how many goals they scored on me, it was still an honour to be here," he said post-game. (Lindbergh was also posthumously voted the starting goalie for the Wales Conference in the All-Star Game in Hartford in January 1986.)

The 1983–84 campaign was a rough one on Lindbergh. Philadelphia beat writer Jay Greenberg summed it up in February 1984: "They have the guy, in Pelle Lindbergh, who can be great. And

Pelle Lindbergh was superb in the 1984–85 season, when he won the Vezina Trophy. (IHA/Icon SMI)

Bob Froese, who, on the whole, is just happy to be here. But their roles have been reversed. Lindbergh, except in flashes, hasn't been wonderful since a Russian skate bent back his wrist last January. And Froese has, for now, taken over the number one job."

But Lindbergh would put it all together in his Vezina-winning season and trip to the Stanley Cup Final. The reward was a six-year contract, estimated to be worth $1.5 million; after the accident, the Flyers announced the team would still honour the deal.

Lindbergh's stall in the Flyers dressing room, with its gear still hanging, stayed untouched for the remainder of the 1985–86 season. The same was not true for the Flyers roster, which soldiered on as best it could.

Keenan said, "We did the best we could, our coaching staff, Teddy Sator, A.J. McGuire, Billy Barber, Bernie Parent, we just tried to hold the team together as well as we could. I had no professional training in grieving, counseling for grieving, and nobody else did. We just tried to be as humane as possible and still have the team ready to play and meet the expectations of the Philadelphia fan base and the organization." In fact, some of the stories from the time blow a hole in the "Iron Mike" mystique; he personally served the meals on the plane to his team on the first post-Pelle flight to Hartford.

But Keenan and Froese did not see eye to eye, and Jensen wasn't Lindbergh.

"I worked hard. He was just, I couldn't do anything right," Froese said of his coach. He added, "Then all of a sudden Pelle dies in a horrific car crash, just something we would never foresee coming, and it's hard to, it's like someone saying, 'Now I'm on your side,' and it's hard to trust that person. I think within that, Jens and I just really took solace in the fact that we realized we were fighting basically an uphill battle, but that we were doing the best we could."

The decision to trade for Glenn "Chico" Resch from the Islanders would pay dividends, as Resch mentored the next-great Flyers goalie, Ron Hextall.

Resch said it was an "emotional" time:

I was caught in the middle. You have Darren Jensen, who is trying make his career, and Bob Froese, who thinks that he does deserve the position—and did—and was actually a really good goalie. It's just that Pelle was special and he was playing all the time and Bob didn't get that opportunity.

When I went in there, I also felt the tugs of these people's lives, those two players' lives. They're saying, "Hey, we're trying to make it here. Your career is winding down." It was hard for me to know exactly what my role was.

Goalies are pretty loyal to other goalies. I don't know that I went in there hungry to take the position from those guys, as you sometimes have to be. I still felt it should be fair, that if I play really well and if I earn it, but if Bob plays better than I do, then he earns it, or Darren.

In the end, Froese played 51 games, lead the league in wins, with 31, and shutouts, with five. Jensen played 29 games, going 15-8-1, with two shutouts; his 3.68 GAA was probably the biggest strike against him. Resch only saw action in five Flyers games. In the playoffs, Froese played all five games in the first-round loss to the Rangers.

The O-Pee-Chee hockey card from the 1985–86 set reads 1959–1985. In April 1986, the Hockey Hall of Fame received a pair of goalie pads, hand crafted by a friend of Lindbergh's in Stockholm and worn by the goalie as a rookie in the NHL during the 1982–83 season, and his plain white mask.

That mask made an impression on future Canadian Olympian and NHL keeper Corey Hirsch. "I loved Pelle. He was awesome. He had the coolest mask. I loved it. I loved how athletic he was," said Hirsch.

Bobby "the Chief" Taylor was a Flyers broadcaster that season. A former NHL goalie, he reflected on the whole "what if?" of the tragedy: "Pelle was just starting to get good. He was really, really fast. He wasn't very big, but he was so quick and he could recover so quickly. He looked like he finally understood the game, understanding how to play at the NHL level until that tragic accident. I think his story is more on the potential that was missed as opposed to the body of work that he'd had coming up to that time."

Taylor was around the team afterward and paused to think about what the death of Pelle Lindbergh did to the Philadelphia Flyers:

> I think athletes are pretty resilient people first of all, because you deal with adversity so often. . . . There are always those mountains that you climb and those cliffs that you fall off in a sense. I think that you can compartmentalize a lot of things in your mind if you're going to be successful. I think it was a lot harder for players when Pelle went down on a personal level, because he was such a popular guy . . . I think sometimes that can really affect you and your play.

DEBUNKING THE FLYERS GOALIE CURSE

There is no curse for goalies in Philadelphia. It is a fallacy brought up again and again by overwrought, frustrated fans who have not seen their team win the Stanley Cup since 1975. The facts bear this out.

Since 1967, when the Flyers entered the NHL, the team has used 49 goalies as of the end of the 2013–14 season. Two of those goalies, Bernie Parent and Ron Hextall, played more than a decade with the team.

Compare those numbers to the four existing teams from the same expansion year: Minnesota/Dallas has also used 49 goalies; the state rival Penguins have used 58, with Dennis Heron and Tom Barrasso lasting 10 and 12 seasons, respectively; the Los Angeles Kings have put 62 people in net; and in St. Louis, perhaps they should be singing the goaltending Blues, with 64 goalies over the years, not one lasting more than six seasons, and a grand total of zero Stanley Cups. And in Toronto, where the famed chalice lives at the Hockey Hall of Fame, but not with the Leafs since that very 1967 expansion, there have been 57 goalies used since the league doubled in size.

Now, is Philadelphia tough on goalies?

Absolutely, said Sean Burke, who did two tours of duty there: "The goalie in Philadelphia really needs support, I don't care who it is. I can name [John] Vanbiesbrouk, [Hextall], Garth Snow, myself, there's four or five guys that have come through there and yet everybody there goes, 'Oh they haven't had a goalie since Bernie Parent.' Well, they've had lots of good goalies come through there. But there has to be a support system for the goalie in Philadelphia. It either has to come from management or the goalie coach or wherever, because it's a hard place to play."

Equally tough is the local media, from the newspapers to talk radio and, more recently, bloggers and the new media, with its penchant for reaction first over analysis and thought.

CHAPTER 7

FATHERS
AND SONS

STUCK BEHIND TERRY Sawchuk and Glenn Hall in the depth chart, Dennis Riggin played a grand total of 18 NHL games during two stints with the Detroit Red Wings during the 1959–60 and 1962–63 seasons. Back home, he had two sons who were hockey mad. One, Larry, "might have been too intelligent to be a goaltender," joked Dennis, and while the other, Pat, ended up backstopping in the WHA and NHL from 1979 to 1988. Riggin Sr. said, "We always thought he was going to be an announcer."

It turns out Pat, the young goalie-to-be, passionately followed the Hamilton Red Wings of the Ontario Hockey Association and would get out a feather duster to call the play-by-play in his own manner.

In the end, the son followed his father into the goaltending fraternity and then to the extra-exclusive club of father-sons who both played goal at the top level.

"His 18 games in the league seem to be better than my 400," joked Pat Riggin, adding, "I keep teasing him though, 'You're a legend with 18 games and I played 400 and they don't even mention me.' But that's just dad."

Dennis Riggin played 18 games in the NHL for Detroit. (Courtesy Dennis Riggin)

To date, there have been four other father-son NHL combos: Sam and Pete LoPresti, Bob and Brent Johnson, Ron and John Grahame, and Bob and Philippe Sauvé. They aren't likely the last, either. To name but a few, the sons of Martin Brodeur, Sean Burke, and Bob Essensa are all wearing the big boy pads at various levels. And let's not forget that Denis and Martin Brodeur both earned

Olympic medals for Team Canada for their heroic efforts in net. As well, there are a number of NHLers whose fathers were capable goalies in junior or the minors, like Jamie Storr and Braden Holtby.

There is understandable tension in filling out your father's skates and pads.

Philippe Sauvé said, "It used to frustrate me when I was very young. It comes to a point where it's not about what your father did, nobody's going to give you anything. That's part of maturing and growing into your own person. After a while, when I was a teenager, it didn't bother me anymore."

What about pressure from Dad?

"Maybe a little bit, but I always felt it was a little bit of a shortcut to getting some good information. After, when you get to the pros, you maybe resort back to things he told you. Then you gain a whole lot of other stuff from goalie coaches too, which made it a little bit confusing," said Pat Riggin.

To John Grahame, who dedicated himself to being a netminder at around age 11, having both a mother and a father who understood the challenges he was facing was an excellent outlet.

"It's tough for people who never lived the position or been in it a hundred per cent to understand the little nuances of what goes on," said John Grahame, who played in the NHL from 1999 to 2008 and then hung around the AHL and in Russia for another couple of years. He added, "Just to have that kind of sounding board, someone who's been through it, they can relate to every situation. It could be something that happened at a game or a practice, or you're tweaking something and they see a change in the positioning; the mental side of things. It was invaluable for me—on both sides, with my mom and dad."

There is a unique connection between John Grahame and his mother, Charlotte—they are the only mother-son tandem listed on the Stanley Cup. John won his Cup with the Tampa Bay Lightning in 2004, when he was the backup to Nikolai Khabibulin. Charlotte

Ron and John Grahame pose with the Stanley Cup, which John won with the Lightning. (Courtesy Charlotte Grahame)

was an executive with the Colorado Avalanche from the day the team moved from Quebec City. Poor Ron never got close to a Stanley Cup, but he did hoist the WHA's Avco Cup in 1975 and was the playoff MVP. Following tradition, Ron has never touched the Stanley Cup, despite the multiple visits the famed chalice has made to his home. "I don't know that I'll ever be in a position where I would be contributing to the success of winning it, but I'm not going to jinx it by touching it," he said.

Now that his own career has ended, John Grahame—who took on Brent Johnson on February 4, 2006, marking the first time two second-generation goaltenders faced each other in an NHL game—says he appreciates what he and his father accomplished more: "It was kind of a cool fact. It was something that me and him could share in quiet moments, 'Hey, we did this.' It was just a father-son thing, no pressure whatsoever. I think that's one of those things, us growing up, things were so natural, there was just never any pressure in any situation. It was just a natural progression. I was thankful to have someone who'd been there, done that, to lean on."

Brent Johnson can remember being really down after a game in junior and calling his dad in tears. Dad's response: "This is how it goes. This is the life of a goaltender."

The tough love paid off, and Brent played 306 NHL games to his father's 66 in the NHL and WHA; Bob married Sid Abel's daughter, Linda, making Brent a third-generation NHLer. There are strange parallels to the careers of Bob and Brent, though: both started with St. Louis, and both finished in the NHL with Pittsburgh. Both also won their first games on the road against Vancouver.

"Isn't that what we want with all our children, to do better than us?" said Bob Johnson.

CHAPTER 8

RECENT GOALIES

GOALTENDING TODAY IS as much about science as it is about stopping the puck. The unprecedented advancements in, well, just about everything are pretty incredible.

The skates are better, the pads are lighter, the masks offer better protection, and the players are in better shape, with their personal trainers and chefs and year-round exercise regimens.

But the mental aspect of playing goal hasn't changed a lot over the decades, and the stress of the job has been altered but not lessened, now that every team has a goalie coach (or two) working with netminders throughout the system.

David Marcoux, the goalie coach with the Calgary Flames from 2003 to 2009, is an example of the fundamental switch that happened in the early 1990s—the educator hadn't come from the NHL ranks.

"I was a teacher, maybe the psychologist a little bit. But I was not intimidating," said Marcoux, whose star pupil, Miikka Kiprusoff, took the Flames to the 2004 Stanley Cup Final. Marcoux added, "The trust that we could create was 'Hey, I am here to help.' We all say that as goalie coaches, the former goalies and the non–former

NHL goalies, but I think there's a way of going through your daily routine where he did not sense that I was a threat or judging."

The work necessary in the video room has increased exponentially over the years, with every game, every goal, every shot from every angle now available for review. Not every goalie wants to watch it all on their iPads, but there are those who do.

And the old dogs do need to learn new tricks. Martin Brodeur is a case in point. According to his goalie coach in New Jersey, Jacques Caron, they watch together: "Certainly, the videos are very important for Martin to address his deficiencies. We have a 'meeting' before each practice and watch videos from the last game. As they say a picture is worth a thousand words," Caron explained in an interview on Brodeur's website.

The other big difference that gets noticed is size—the height of the players and the size of the equipment.

Dave Prior, goalie scout for the Washington Capitals, said, "Some teams, they won't draft goaltenders unless they're 6-foot-2 or something. We're not of that mindset. I think the pool is too small and many big guys are handicapped with quickness and agility issues to get to the higher levels of hockey. Yet smaller guys who have those qualities sometimes don't have the mass to play in the NHL game."

At 6-foot-2 and 200 pounds, Brent Johnson is pretty typical of goalies of today. Recently retired from the NHL, he has seen changes just in his lifetime.

"The new style right now is big friggin' goalies that are on their knees. For you to score five-hole or catch a hole, you get a goalie that says, 'Well, I was there, but it was a hell of a shot. I applaud you.' Now you've got guys that are 6-foot-7, you've got your [Anders] Lindbacks, just huge, huge goalies, who are playing that style," Johnson said.

The size and the style tests the human body. Johnson added, "You're seeing more hip injuries than ever in goaltending, because there's so much pressure being put on them. You're not only doing it in games, you're doing it for 200-some-odd days of the year at practice."

Size is just one part of the equation, said Bobby "the Chief" Taylor, a 1970s goaltender. "It still comes down to, you've got to stop the puck, whether you're 5-foot-10 or you're 6-foot-10, you've got to stop the puck. That's the key," he stressed.

Are we far away from a sumo wrestler in net?

"How many times, especially when you're in a non-traditional hockey market, have I heard that? They all ask that. 'Just put a great, big fat guy in there,'" laughed Taylor.

GOALIES AS GOONS

The Goaltenders' Union has always had its share of surly members, but to be fair, if you had people firing 100-mile-per-hour frozen rubber at you and preventing you from doing your job by bumping you, blocking your vision, and even falling on you, you might be in a bad mood too.

Paddy Moran was one of the original big league bad boys, slashing and chopping at enemy skaters who ventured too close to his crease.

Terry Sawchuk, infamous for his terrible practice habits, didn't brook high shots from teammates, which could elicit a flying goalie stick in response.

Billy Smith was no different in that respect, sending fellow Isles fleeing when they saw his heavy goal stick whirling at them like a helicopter blade. He didn't distinguish between teammate and opponent when they stood in his way either, slashing away at any ankles when he felt crowded.

Isles teammate Billy Harris said, "Billy was just a natural talent, but wacky. He just liked to hurt people. He was just nuts. He'd come back in and brag about how he almost took a guy's eye out, and the rest of the guys on the team are going, 'That's really cool, Smitty, that was really great.'"

Smith also happily tussled with forwards, even trying his luck against tough guys like Tiger Williams and Dave Semenko.

Bad-tempered Smith was just following in the footsteps of Boston's Gerry Cheevers, who, while more congenial, wasn't afraid to join his fellow Big Bad Bruins when brawls erupted, even taking on the Leafs' Forbes Kennedy *twice* in Kennedy's record penalty-setting game.

A number of goalies in the 1980s emerged as real threats to knock someone's block off, with Ron Hextall, Clint Malarchuk, Ed Belfour, and Sean Burke leading the way. All four were big, with Malarchuk a fitness nut to boot at a time when ashtrays still sat in dressing room stalls. Garth Snow, a 6-foot-4 giant for his time, would follow.

Snow's Canuck teammate Brad May told the *Vancouver Sun*, "There's no question that Garth is not a typical goaltender who is passive. Garth likes the action and provokes it for the most part. When I was with Buffalo and he was with Philadelphia, we had three or four five-on-five brawls, which all started in front of the crease—his."

Patrick Roy didn't shy away from the action either and was right in the middle of the wars between the Detroit Red Wings and his Colorado Avalanche. He took on starters Mike Vernon and Chris Osgood in centre-ice brawls, and he once even tried to get at Dominik Hasek, although he was restrained by officials from making it a hat trick.

Roy may have been more game than effective as a fighter. The same can't be said for Dan Cloutier and "Sugar" Ray Emery, who might be the finest fighters in league netminding history.

Baby-faced Cloutier built his fighting resumé in the junior and minor leagues and wasn't tamed by the NHL. "If Dan was a winger, in junior he probably would have had 300 penalty minutes," Todd Warriner, who played with Cloutier in Tampa Bay and Vancouver and against him in the OHL, told the *National Post*.

As a rookie with the New York Rangers, Cloutier pummelled cross-town rival Tommy Salo before challenging the entire Islanders bench.

One-time Islander Scott Lachance told the *Regina Leader Post*, "It was something. A lot of guys already knew Danny had a short fuse. That pretty much solidified his reputation."

Emery's antics received multiple plays on highlight show reels. He gave Buffalo goalie Martin Biron a thrashing and thereafter took on Sabres enforcer Andrew Peters. After both fights, Emery's wide grin suggested he'd had a ball.

He seemed far more serious years later when, as a Philadelphia Flyer, he skated all the way down the ice to beat on Washington netminder Braden Holtby during a 7-0 drubbing against the Capitals. Holtby had no intention of fighting back, but Emery was undaunted and rained down a flurry of blows.

It was a mugging that drew the ire of NHL commissioner Gary Bettman, commentators, and even other players. Emery, who received 24 penalty minutes but no suspension, weakly justified his actions after the game: "He didn't want a fight but I said basically protect yourself. I didn't really have much of a choice."

MARTIN BRODEUR
During the 1993–94 pre-season, Martin Brodeur, fighting for a job with the New Jersey Devils after a year in the AHL, was asked what he needed to work on. His response? "Trying to stay on my feet. I can cover a lot of net, and my reflexes are good. I have a good glove because I played baseball when I was young, and I learned a lot last year at Utica."

And he stayed on his feet for the next two decades, a throwback to a time when goalies kept to their feet instead of dropping to their knees and butterflying every opportunity. He reacted to the situation, never panicking, never getting flustered.

That is a terrible oversimplification, though. Brodeur has evolved through the years. He learned to butterfly when necessary, his stickhandling improved, and he started really studying video.

But the old-school goalies love him, as they can see a bit of themselves in him.

Clint Malarchuk, who played in the 1980s and 1990s, said, "He can butterfly, he can stand up and play the angles, he can stack the pads. He's done it for 20 years. Billy Smith was the same way—he could butterfly at times, you never knew what Billy was going to do. He might come out and poke-check you. He was unpredictable and guys couldn't get a book on him, really. And it's the same with Brodeur."

One night it could be a toe-up save with the inside lower edge of a pad, another a spectacular stop with his stick, or maybe it was a desperate swing of his blocker to keep the puck out of the net.

"Of all the goalies playing now, Brodeur is the closest to Sawchuk. He gets down low and follows the puck, never gets caught out of position," said Emile Francis in the *New York Times* in 2009, as Brodeur sat tied with Terry Sawchuk atop the all-time shutouts list.

"He's probably the perfect style for any era," said Hall of Fame sportswriter Frank Orr.

You can criticize his technique, said ex-goalie Darren Jensen, but not the results—three Stanley Cups, four Vezina Trophies, five Williams M. Jennings Trophy wins and/or shares, 10 NHL All-Star Games, two Olympic gold medals, and a Calder Trophy as Rookie of the Year. Jensen said,

> You take a guy like Martin Brodeur and he goes against every rule of thumb for the way a goalie's technique should be these days. So my [statement] to everybody, "He's doing it!" He gets up with the wrong leg, he does everything wrong technically. But the guy stops the puck. How do you justify that? They are right with the new technique and everything, however, he's totally playing old-school, and he can do it. He'll do skate saves, he'll do all different things, maybe that's why it's so good because guys don't know what he's going to do. He'll go into a butterfly. Just technically, he's terrible compared to the goaltenders today, like Jonathan Quick.

Martin Pierre Brodeur was born May 6, 1972, in Montreal, Quebec, to Mireille and Denis Brodeur, who had been a goaltender for the Kitchener-Waterloo Dutchmen team that earned a bronze medal at the 1956 Olympics in Cortina d'Ampezzo, Italy, and later was a famed Quebec photographer. As a youngster in the Saint-Leonard Minor Hockey Association, Martin played different positions, finally settling on playing in the net at age seven. When he turned 16, he jumped to the Montreal-Bourassa Midget AAA Team, where the attention from scouts first started and then intensified

Martin Brodeur was the starting goaltender for the Eastern Conference at the 2004 NHL All-Star Game, held in Minneapolis. (George Tahinos)

when he went to Calgary for the National U-17 Hockey Festival in the summer of 1988.

The following season, he played with the Quebec Major Junior Hockey League's Saint-Hyacinthe Laser, making the All-Rookie team in 1989–90. That summer, the Devils selected Brodeur 20th overall at the entry draft. While still a junior, New Jersey summoned him as an emergency call-up for the ailing Chris Terreri and Craig Billington, launching the historic career of Martin Brodeur in earnest on March 26, 1992, when he was in net as the Devils beat the Bruins 4-2. He would play in four regular seasons games and one playoff match, but the next year, he was the regular starter with the American Hockey League's Utica Devils.

Though Utica coach Robbie Ftorek and goalie coach Warren Strelow were initial influences, the arrival of Jacques Caron as the goalie coach in Jersey for the 1993–94 season made a huge difference for Brodeur. Caron, an ex-goalie with 18 years' experience in the big leagues, had run a hockey school in Rouyn-Noranda, Quebec, and served as an assistant coach in Hartford before taking the Devils coaching gig.

According to Caron, Brodeur's early weakness was his mobility, and he worked hard to improve it. "Martin has always been independent and intelligent, so he quickly understood what I showed him. He raised questions, was in control of himself, and offered ideas for improvement. He always loved to practice and especially play. In this case, there was room for improvement," Caron told Brodeur's website, MartinBrodeur30.com.

In an interview with *InGoal Magazine* for the summer 2011 issue, Brodeur spoke about how his game had changed:

> When I was playing junior, my whole thing was the butterfly. I was going down a lot. I had the wide stance, both feet were really wide and my knees were locked in, I was a lot different than I am now, that's for sure. Jacques Caron wanted me to be a more agile, mobile goalie, not just a blocking goalie. It's funny the way you do the shuffle, I don't really do the shuffle with my skate. We T-push everywhere instead of other goalies that drive everywhere, and you don't see goalies T-push anymore. But that's Jacques Caron, that's the way he had to survive when he played the game because he wasn't blessed with great mobility, so he had to stand on his feet and he learned to T-push everywhere to get there on time and make the saves he needed to make. So really, that's something I never did before and when I came into training camp and did the first drill I looked like a peewee. I couldn't do anything because I wasn't used to that, and it's funny now because I've been around a long time with him and every time we have a young goalie coming up, Jacques is trying to teach him this stuff.

And Marty has never stopped trying to get better, said Shawn Chambers, who patrolled the defence for Brodeur from 1995 to 1997 and roomed with him as well. "He's always working on his game. Workaholic is a perfect example," said Chambers, praising Brodeur's work as a third defenceman, able to make tape-to-tape passes. "Shit, Marty made the game so easy for us as defencemen it was crazy."

The other aspect of Brodeur's game that helped him get to the top—and stay there—is his mental makeup.

As a Devils broadcaster, Glenn "Chico" Resch has had a great vantage point to see Brodeur through the years. He compares him mentally to his old Islanders teammate Billy Smith, who was inducted into the Hockey Hall of Fame in 1993: "Smitty and Marty have built something into their system of protection for themselves in that they don't dwell on the fact that it was their fault when a goal was scored. They just had a built-in belief: 'My system's good, my skills are good, goals are going to go by me. Once one goes by me, just go play again. Don't even think about it.' And I'm not saying that either approach is right, but I think the Billy Smith/Marty Brodeur mindset is less taxing, doesn't take as much energy, doesn't mess with your mind as much," said Resch.

The systems enforced in New Jersey through the years, defensive hockey masterminded by the likes of Jacques Lemaire, have helped Brodeur's numbers in a way that is difficult to quantify. The Jennings Trophies for team play are as much a testament to the style of play—like popularizing "the trap"—as the three Cups are. The all-time leader with wins and shutouts couldn't have done it on his own. He has been remarkably injury-free for most of the time too, a hurt arm that sidelined him for four months at the start of his 15th season the most serious issue of his career.

His honours, accolades, records, and feats could fill pages—the rink in Saint-Leonard is even named after him. For a challenge, during the late stages of the 2012–13 season, Brodeur campaigned through his website, Twitter, and the media to be on the cover of EA Sports' *NHL 14* game; more than 23 million fans voted online.

Brodeur told NHL.com, "I think that's the beauty of this for me. Just the amount of fans that voted; over 22 million people voted for the cover. When you finish on top, it feels pretty good. I think it's exciting. I never really realized I wasn't on the cover. There's only one game a year. It's pretty exciting for the fans to be involved and to decide who is going to be on the cover."

As much as his contemporary/rival Patrick Roy is credited with inspiring youth to take up the position, Brodeur has been a major influence as well. Braden Holtby of the Washington Capitals is one of those kids. "I'm more of a reactive goalie, reading where the shot is going, trying to force players to shoot in certain directions. Marty is obviously the best ever. I don't think there will ever be anyone as good at encouraging shooters to aim at a certain spot, but that was the age of goaltending I grew up watching on TV, and that's where I got that from, seeing those guys when I was young and I [was] trying to do it myself," Holtby told *InGoal Magazine* in October 2012.

Brodeur will be a first-ballot inductee into the Hockey Hall of Fame when he does finally retire. After that, who knows? Maybe replacing Lou Lamoriello as general manager of the Devils?

"Marty Brodeur might be one of the best at breaking down all aspects of the game. I think he has the mind of a coach, but I think Marty Brodeur would lean toward management more," said Resch.

After all, there's another Brodeur in the Devils system already: New Jersey selected goalie Anthony Brodeur, with the 208th overall pick, in the seventh round of the 2013 entry draft.

WHEN THE GOAL IS THE OTHER NET

Whereas the chances of a netminder scoring a goal once seemed virtually impossible, it has now become only somewhat rare.

Eleven NHL goalies have scored at least one goal (with more in the minor-pro leagues and elsewhere), and most of those have come in the 1990s and 2000s. But netminders have been trying to pot one for almost as long as the game's been around.

A Pembroke, Ontario, newspaper celebrating Hugh Lehman's 1958 Hall of Fame induction noted it wasn't an unusual sight to see him venture on end-to-end sorties and that he may have even scored on one of them. The newspaper reported, "It was claimed that in Vancouver or Berlin he once scored a goal, but that story, like many that have been told of his exploits on the ice, may be apocryphal."

Fred Brophy went on a similar rink-long dash during the 1905 season in the Canadian Amateur Hockey League, and he did manage to score, beating fellow goalie Paddy Moran. With players from both teams off for penalties, only the goalies were left, and both Brophy and Moran took turns racing the length of the ice for a shot.

Chuck "Bonnie Prince Charlie" Rayner did his best to become the NHL's first netminder to notch a goal. Although try as he might—sometimes he'd even be left out as a skater instead of being pulled for an extra attacker on a delayed penalty—he never did score. He did, however, manage one during World War II, while minding the All-Star Royal Canadian Army nets.

"When I broke in, I remember I was shocked that Rayner would bring the puck almost to your end. He could handle the puck better than some of the players he played with," said Emile Francis in *Without Fear: Hockey's 50 Greatest Goaltenders.*

"When you threw it in the corner, he would just go out and get the puck. He really forced us to change the way we came into the zone. No one else other than Jacques Plante later on was doing that," Gordie Howe added.

Plante, who literally wrote the book on goaltending, assumed Rayner's mantle as the NHL's premier puckhandling goalie about a decade later.

Dick Irvin Jr. first watched Plante when he was a toque-sporting Montreal Royal, and he remembered being struck by Plante's unorthodox wandering and passing. "I thought he was a bit of a nutcase," Irvin said in *Without Fear.*

It was while playing as a teenager for the Quebec Citadels that Plante first tried his hand at puckhandling, a tactic he felt necessary given the lack of ability of the defenders in front of him.

"Somebody had to clear loose pucks, so I began doing the job myself. It worked so well that I kept on roving, all the way up to the NHL—with pro-and-con arguing all the way," Plante explained in *The Jacques Plante Story*.

The NHL finally clamped down on the degree to which a goalie could join the attack after Gary "Suitcase" Smith took an impromptu skate up ice.

Smith dreamed of scoring a goal one day as he took mental notes about rushing up ice while watching Cesare Maniago play third defenceman for the Hull-Ottawa Canadiens, according to *The Last Hurrah*.

Despite being best known for his career spent travelling city to city, Smith changed the way goalies can play one fateful night, December 21, 1966, at the Montreal Forum. Substituting for the Leafs' Bruce Gamble, and knowing his parents were back home watching him on the new colour television set he'd bought them, Smith decided he needed to do something memorable.

That he did, going on a wild dash past centre ice that only ended when J.C. Tremblay knocked him to the ice with a rare body check.

His rush caught the attention of everyone at the Forum—and at league headquarters. What would become known as the "Suitcase Smith Rule" forbade goalies from playing the puck or checking opponents beyond centre ice.

The rule collected dust for years until Patrick Roy of the Colorado Avalanche was penalized two minutes for stickhandling his way past centre in a November 1997 contest versus the New York Rangers. Roy, an excellent puckhandler in his own right, thought he might help out his anemic offence that night by playing quarterback. After deking past Wayne Gretzky and performing a spin-o-rama Denis Savard would be proud of, referee Paul Devorski had to spoil the fun by calling the play.

Rogie Vachon seemingly broke the NHL goalies' goose egg in

a February 1977 game against the New York Islanders, when Bryan Trottier shot the puck into his own net in a delayed penalty situation. Vachon was thought to have been the last King to touch the puck and was awarded the goal, but the historical moment was brief, for the officials would review video of the play and discover Kings centre Vic Venasky had touched the puck last.

Islanders goalie Billy Smith became the first netminder credited with a goal. It occurred in a similar situation in November 1979, with Rob Ramage of the Colorado Rockies committing the goof and giving Smith the goal.

But Ron Hextall was the first to actually shoot the puck into an opponent's empty net, accomplishing the feat against the Boston Bruins in 1987. He'd do it again in a 1989 playoff match versus the Washington Capitals.

Taking his lead, numerous goalies thereafter would take a shot at a net emptied for an extra attacker in the late stages of a game, and goals by goalies became almost commonplace. After Detroit's Chris Osgood scored with a shot on goal in 1995–96, the goals came fast and furious, relatively speaking, with 10 more goals being scored by goalies between 1996–97 and 2013–14.

The trapezoid rule, however, would significantly restrict puck-playing netminders and limit their scoring opportunities. Those teams without the puck-playing talents of a Martin Brodeur, Ed Belfour, or Marty Turco were sick and tired of seeing their dump-ins casually shot back out, and they urged the league, seemingly open to altering the rules of the game at the drop of a hat, to force goalies back to where they felt they belonged.

Introduced in the 2005–06 season, the league's "Brodeur Rule" restricted goalies from handling the puck beyond the trapezoid area behind their nets or in the area in front of their nets.

NHL Rule 1.8, Goalkeeper's Restricted Area, called for a trapezoid-shaped area behind the goal: a 2-inch red line would extend 5 feet outside of each goal crease, from the goal line to a point on the end of the rink 10 feet from the goal crease, and continue vertically up the kickplate. Goalies touching the puck outside of this area would be assessed a two-minute delay of game penalty.

Somehow goalies still managed to score anyway—Chris Mason of Nashville, Carolina's Cam Ward, Brodeur with his record-breaking third, and Mike Smith of Phoenix. Smith, however, was the only one of these to actually shoot the puck himself into the opposite net, doing so against Detroit and with only one second remaining in regulation time in an October 19, 2013, match.

MARTY TURCO It can take ages for a goaltender to go from a nobody on the ground floor to the penthouse as a celebrated All-Star NHL netminder, but going the other way can take almost no time at all.

So it was for Marty Turco, who replaced a legend in Eddie Belfour while in Dallas. Turco performed brilliantly, establishing club records and joining the elite ranks of hockey's best, but he found himself discarded after he and the team slipped. Starting over in Chicago, he quickly lost his starter's job to a young hotshot and disappeared from the league altogether before returning to the NHL briefly, ending his reign somewhat ignominiously as an emergency backup replacement, banned from suiting up for the playoffs.

Born August 13, 1975, in Sault Ste. Marie, Ontario, Turco grew up a fan of hometown hero Tony Esposito, the Chicago Black Hawks Hall of Fame goaltender. Turco always had his eye on goalies, and in sixth grade, he wrote a letter as part of a school project to Philadelphia's Ron Hextall, who wrote back and included a signed player card and photo.

As he moved through the ranks of minor hockey, Turco looked up to the calm, cool Kirk McLean in Vancouver, Toronto's stylish Felix Potvin, and a couple of sensational puck-stoppers in Curtis Joseph and Dominik Hasek.

Turco's own star rose as a goaltender for the Soo Legion, with whom he won a bronze medal at the 1993 Air Canada Cup, a national Midget AAA championship tournament. He'd play a year with the Junior B Cambridge Winter Hawks before receiving a four-year scholarship to the University of Michigan. There he blossomed, starring as a Rookie of the Year, leading the Wolverines to a Final Four appearance in every year he played there, and winning two NCAA titles.

Michigan coach Red Berenson told *Sports Illustrated*, "Marty has a way of making every save he has to when he knows the team needs a little life. He also makes a lot of saves that keep the other team from getting any life."

His record 127 victories certainly gave the Dallas Stars, which drafted him in the fifth round, 124th overall in 1994, a reason to smile.

"When the game is on the line, he shuts the door. That's the quality we're most excited about, and I don't think there's another college goalie close to him," Dallas head scout Craig Button enthused.

Graduating to the pros, Turco tended goal for the International Hockey League's Michigan K-Wings in 1998–99, where he won another Rookie of the Year trophy. After one more season there, Turco joined the big club in 2000–01 and spent two seasons as a backup to Ed Belfour.

"He was arguably the best goaltender in the world at that point," said Turco of Belfour. "He won a Cup, went to the finals back to back, and I got to witness this journey for the Stars up close. I was the third goalie. And then I had a great opportunity to see him every day in practice and playing games."

While Turco looked up to Belfour, the latter seemed to regard the former with suspicion, seeing him as a threat to his position. Reports at the time revealed Belfour physically set himself apart from Turco, sitting in a practice stall separated from Turco's by a cement pillar. He even briefly walked out on the team in 2000–01 when Turco got a start over him and he argued with coach Ken Hitchcock over playing the backup role in the morning practice. Belfour never got close to his backup, let alone mentored him.

"We weren't tight by any means, but the experience was pretty tremendous for myself in the maturation of my game," Turco said, explaining he learned much through observation. "It was more of a job to him than most players, but that's part of the reason why he's a Stanley Cup champion and a Hall of Famer. That's not for everybody; he didn't have much time for many other people, because he put a lot of work and time into his craft."

Belfour had reason to look over his shoulder, as the coaching staff continued to take a closer look at Turco. In 2001–02, Belfour was pulled in the third-to-last game of the season to be replaced by Turco. For the next two games, Belfour watched from the bench as his former backup starred in net. Dallas missed the playoffs that season, and Belfour signed with the Leafs, leaving Turco the new starter.

"I didn't know until Doug Armstrong, the GM at the time, came to my house and told me that Eddie wouldn't be returning and I'd be given the chance to start," said Turco.

It was a pivotal moment for Turco, and as the new number one, he reset his goals. He explained,

> Even though you make it to one level, always the mentality is to take it to the next one and take that challenge. . . . That should be your goal, to play, and play as many games as long as possible in this league. This game is mental—all the guys here have the athleticism and attributes, they are good goaltenders, but the ones that can have the capacity day in and day out to succeed and forge ahead to become better and put those bad days behind them, and work on it, to gain respect from their teammates, those are the guys that have long-term success.

Turco's relationships with his backups would contrast sharply with the one he had with Belfour. He'd have a number of goalies supporting him as backups, including future Coyotes number-one Mike Smith. Turco said,

[Smith] was like my little brother and I wanted him to succeed and push me as much as I wanted him to learn from me and have a prosperous career whenever we parted ways. I'm a social person, no matter what, I'd rather have a strong relationship with my partner . . . the way I looked up to Eddie, I wished we had a closer relationship. . . . I'm as competitive as the next guy, but I play this game to win, and I always thought that two goaltenders were on the team, not just one guy was the man.

Turco replaced Belfour almost seamlessly, as he proved his number-one credentials immediately. In his first season as Dallas's starter, 2002–03, Turco chased Tony Esposito's 30-year GAA high-water mark, beat it, and then achieved the best goals against in 60 years—the NHL's lowest since Dave Kerr in 1939–40—with a stingy 1.72 GAA in 55 games.

Turco also demonstrated his proficiency as a puckhandler and, over time, he would be considered second only to New Jersey's Martin Brodeur. Inspired by expert puckhandlers like Hextall and McLean, Turco worked on becoming equally proficient. But the traditional style they adopted just didn't work for him.

"My speed allowed me to get to a lot of pucks, but I was not able to control them with the efficiency I needed in order to play it and give the coaches the confidence I knew I could play the puck with," Turco said.

In college, he first started tinkering with holding his goalie stick in a different fashion, and in the minors he developed a style that would be copied by other pros. His idea was born out of his frustration at pucks getting sent around the boards onto his backhand. He found the traditional way of holding his glove hand underneath the stick didn't give him much power or control to stop the puck. Turning his catching glove over gave him better leverage, strength, and power, especially on the backhand, and it also worked for forehand saucer passes and rimming the puck off the glass.

"I can't tell you how many times I shot a puck in practice over the years. It would be mind boggling. Some days alone I'd fire over 100 pucks, whether it would be passes, beginning of practice, during or after. The combination ended up being what you saw over the life of my career, which was the confidence my defenceman had to fan out, not to come to me, and the ability of the coaches to utilize it in practice to let everybody get familiar with it," Turco said.

"The guys who played with him say he was like having a third defenceman. In fact, when the backup had a night in, it would change the way Dallas played," said Dallas play-by-play voice Ralph Strangis.

In his first year as starter, the Stars' fortunes reversed completely, as they rebounded from the previous year's poor finish to climb all the way to first place in the Western Conference and second overall in the league. The club, however, fell to the Cinderella Mighty Ducks of Anaheim in the second round.

This became the pattern for Dallas during Turco's tenure, with the club excelling in the regular season but making early exits in the playoffs. In Dallas's series against Vancouver in 2007, the Stars lost in seven, despite Turco recording a record three shutouts.

"That should never happen," said Strangis, blaming the coaches for installing a conservative, defence-first game plan to a team loaded with scoring talent and a goalie who wanted to play creatively as well. "[Dave Tippett's] theory was if they don't score they can't beat us. Well, yeah, but eventually, if you don't score, *you* won't win." According to Strangis, Turco's game thrived on taking a certain amount of risks: "He was imaginative and he wanted the game to be played with pace, and he was going to try to be a weapon." Strangis pointed to Oscar Wilde's quote that "Consistency is the last refuge of the unimaginative."

The club finally demonstrated its promise in 2007–08, getting all the way to the third round of the playoffs, but they couldn't advance past eventual the Cup winners, the Detroit Red Wings. It was the last hurrah for Turco and the Stars, as the following season his GAA bloated to 2.98 and the club missed the playoffs. Dallas missed the playoffs for the second year in a row in 2009–10, a tough one for both the club and Turco.

"We've left our goalies hanging out to dry a lot this season and let some games get away from us. We don't play the same style we used to [protecting leads]," Mike Modano told the *Edmonton Journal*.

Goalie coach Andy Moog continued to believe in Turco as starter, telling the *Journal* Turco still had his focus and attention to detail. "He has got a swagger, a personality. He has got a presence in the net we've relied on for years. It's frustrating for me to watch him and not get the rewards, but I keep encouraging him that it'll pay off in the end," Moog said.

It didn't, and first year general manager Joe Nieuwendyk expressed his doubts: "I think he'd just like to eliminate those goals that you wonder how they get in." Nieuwenduk opted not to re-sign Turco in the summer. "I just felt like it was time we went in a different direction," Nieuwendyk told the *Dallas Morning News*.

A three-time All-Star, Turco left Dallas having established numerous franchise goaltending records, including most games played (509), most wins (262), and most shutouts (40). Only four goalies in history have bettered Turco's six straight 30-plus-win seasons—Martin Brodeur, Patrick Roy, Tony Esposito, and Ken Dryden—leaving him tied with Canadiens' Hall of Famer Jacques Plante.

Strangis called Turco one of his favourite people in 25 years of hockey, adding he was fun to watch, which he felt was a rarity among today's goalies. Strangis said,

> He was artistic, athletic, a showman. He was entertaining. In a game where that position has become, sort of, everybody looks the same, everybody's a butterfly goalie, everybody relies on their size and positioning, it's not always fun to watch—it looks like a big, black hole where pucks disappear into. The way he made saves and especially the way he played the puck, I don't know if I've ever seen a guy that skilled with it, that strong with his passing, and that athletic with his skating to get out that quickly to get out and grab and it and move it.

Turco signed as a free agent with the Chicago Blackhawks, as the club needed to replace Antti Niemi, with whom they'd just won a Cup. But Turco's production there came well short of the buildup, which had come complete with idol Esposito appearing at the press conference announcing his signing. He struggled and went from starter to backup to emerging great Corey Crawford. Turco saw action in only 29 games and received more coverage on television for his pranks—opening the bench door to allow a St. Louis player to nearly fall in, rolling his eyes at TV commentator Pierre McGuire, and betting with a fan on the outcome of a game—than for his play. He believed he got a fair opportunity, but he was vague about what went wrong, preferring to keep any specific complaints to himself.

> If I would have played well, I would have been the guy. A lot of things weren't what I was used to. I needed a little bit of help that I wasn't getting. It wasn't an ideal situation, more than I realized going into it. But those things aren't in your control and I was like whatever, we'll move on. I wish things were a little bit different. But I'll never regret putting on that jersey and playing for that team in that city at any moment. Never. It was cool. It sucks it didn't work out. I'm not really gonna dive into the particulars of it quite yet. I would have liked to have stayed there a while.

Strangis thought Turco's style of play dictated a certain shelf life: "He played deep in his net and he was a very reflexive goalie and when that goes, it's harder to hang on. . . . I think when Marty lost half a step, that was enough. When you look at how Marty ended his career, he really never played again in any meaningful way."

The year after Chicago, Turco was out of the league altogether, playing in Europe for Salzberg. He put his vacation plans on hold when Boston came calling late in their season after their second- and third-string goalies, Tuukka Rask and Anton Khudobin, went down to injury. Turco posted a 2-2-0 record.

"There's no question [with] his qualities as a player, as a person, and as a leader, we're happy to have him on board. It's a great fit," Bruins captain Zdeno Chara told the *Boston Globe* upon Turco's arrival.

After Turco's last game, Milan Lucic expressed to ESPN his appreciation for Turco's contributions: "We've been happy with what he's brought to this hockey team and this organization. He definitely played well for us."

Unfortunately for Turco, he couldn't join the team for the playoffs, as he had signed his contract after the trade deadline. It was a far from an ideal way of retiring. He said, "You draw it up, going out, and you're playing in the playoffs and having some success and playing well."

BRENT JOHNSON One could say that Brent Johnson was a casualty of the 2012–13 NHL lockout. He had been the solid backup to Marc-André Fleury in Pittsburgh for three seasons when the Penguins signed veteran Tomas Vokoun, concerned about Johnson's injury woes. There just weren't many offers for the veteran of 306 NHL games.

"I played the majority in the NHL and I was limited maybe to signing a two-way, which I didn't want to do, and I didn't want to finish in the minors. I was comfortable with my career. I guess you could say my lifestyle, as it is right now, I just didn't want to go through the whole bus thing again, and that was it. I'm comfortable. I'm happy. This time away from hockey has afforded me a lot of time to be with my very young daughter, so it's been especially fantastic in that area. I'm very grateful," Johnson said.

Of course, "time away from hockey" is a funny phrase coming from someone whose father, Bob, was an NHL goaltender and whose grandfather was Hall of Famer Sid Abel. Johnson said,

My grandfather was huge in my early childhood because I got to do what few people get to do—go around the Detroit Red Wings dressing room, the alumni room, at a young age; be with my grandfather while he was sitting and talking to Steve Yzerman. Not many kids get an opportunity to do that and I did. My grandfather always took me around the rink. He lived to see my first game in the NHL, which was huge for me, in '97. He was just such a genuinely nice man and could tell a story about hockey with the best of them. I would be in awe of some of his stories.

His father's tales, not so much. "I have heard my dad re-tell every one of his stories 100 times," he said.

A native of Farmington, Michigan, born on March 12, 1977, Brent Johnson didn't set out to be a goalie like his dad. He played defence and took his turn in net like all the other kids. When he was about nine years old, he decided that's what he wanted to do.

Bob Johnson said, "We got him second-hand equipment; we didn't go out and give him top stuff. He just loved the position the way I did."

Brent shot up to 6-foot-3 quickly and played up in age groups. "Most of the Lower Michigan teams were always asking for him. He was the most requested goaltender during his time, whether it be peewee, bantam, squirt, whatever," said Bob.

From 1994 to 1997, Brent played for the Ontario Hockey League's Owen Sound Platers. In 1996, his coach, John Lovell, told the *Toronto Star*, "He is aggressive and handles the puck extremely well. He is a stand-up and models himself after Philadelphia Flyers' Ron Hextall, and even wears 27."

The Colorado Avalanche selected Johnson 129th overall in the 1995 NHL entry draft, but they dealt him to St. Louis at the draft two years later for a third-round choice. Three seasons with the American Hockey League's Worcester IceCats were interspersed with a sprinkling of games with the Blues.

His first breakthrough came in 2000–01, when he got into 31 games in St. Louis, but his real breakout season was the next one, when he played 58 games and 10 more in the playoffs, falling to the Colorado Avalanche in the Western Conference Final. He set a Blues franchise record with 206:45 consecutive shutout minutes and registered three straight shutouts. In his third playoff campaign, his playing time dropped back down. Johnson explained,

> Throughout St. Louis, I had Joel Bonneville [as coach], and he was great—"You play well, you're staying in." That wasn't my first year, because we had Roman Turek, and he was the prime starter. After he had left and went to Calgary, it was one of those things where they didn't necessarily give me the starting job; it was one of those things where I had to earn it. It maybe looked on paper that I was, but it was never declared, if you will, until maybe going into the playoffs, where I played every game. It was one of those things, you get a game if you have a good game, and you get another one; ride a win or ride a good game. That's all it was the first few years in the league. I had an unfortunate injury my last year in St. Louis and that set me back a whole ton as to where I was in my career.

His goalie coach in St. Louis was Keith Allain, who said, "When I first saw him in the minor leagues, I said, 'This kid's an NHL goalie.' He was big, he was athletic, he could handle the puck, he had a really good demeanor in terms of his approach to the game, liked the pressure of being 'The Guy.' I enjoyed working with Brent."

In early March 2004, Johnson was shipped to Phoenix for Mike Sillinger. He saw action in eight games there and then the NHL shut down operations for the 2004–05 season.

Johnson signed a one-year, two-way deal with Vancouver, but after the 2005 pre-season, he was placed on waivers. He then went to Washington. "The Caps took a chance on me. They kept me up the entire year and I signed a much better ticket the following spring," he said of his time backing up Olaf Kölzig.

"I've always had good numbers, or decent numbers, and sometimes I did actually think that I was the starting goaltender," said Johnson, who played 96 games with the Caps. "It was never declared, but sometimes I had that inkling that I was [the number one] in Washington. A couple of things happen, and you're climbing up and trying to get back in that role. I always had pretty good numbers, and from a winning standpoint, I thought I did pretty well in my career."

Johnson continued in a backup role in Pittsburgh, where he signed as a free agent in July 2009.

Being a backup is tough, especially if you have been a starter. He confessed: "If I would have kept an edge, I think I could have either had better contracts—and I'm speaking totally candidly with you—I think I could have had a better career if I could have kept that edge, but I got shuffled to that backup role. It worked for me for a few seasons, until actually my last year, where I was plagued with injuries that year anyway. I just didn't have that so-called edge."

ROBERTO LUONGO Look no further than Roberto Luongo for proof that the brotherhood of netminders is alive and well. Despite two years of doubt and criticism from management, the press, and fans in Vancouver, Luongo maintained strong ties to his fellow teammates in goal.

In just a matter of a couple years, Luongo went from becoming the first goalie to captain his team since Bill Durnan in 1947–48, winning an Olympic gold medal as a starter, and taking his team to the seventh game of the Stanley Cup Final to being relegated to backup duties and becoming the subject of incessant trade rumours for two years. However, throughout that entire time, Luongo not only maintained his sense of humour but also his relationships with his fellow Canuck puckstoppers.

"Roberto was really open and embraced me as a younger guy when he was playing a lot of games," Cory Schneider told reporter Jim Matheson before his new team, the New Jersey Devils, played his old one. "I learned a lot from him, on the ice and off. He dealt with some tough situations, fair or not, and he put on a smile and did what was best for the team. That's not easy, especially for somebody who has accomplished as much as he has and has as much pride. He supported me and put the team first. I was really impressed with that."

Schneider's agent, Mike Liut (who knows a thing or two about goaltending from his 664 NHL games in net), praised Luongo in Vancouver's *The Province* in May 2012: "He is a veteran secure in his ability and has helped Cory learn what it takes to play goal in the NHL."

A month before, the Canucks had been eliminated in the 2012 Western Conference quarterfinals by the eventual-champion L.A. Kings. But the bigger story was Schneider replacing Luongo in the series. Schneider had already at times usurped Luongo as starter during the 2011–12 regular season. But Luongo, while obviously not thrilled to be warming the bench, continued to support his former backup. "I'm behind Cory and all's good. Right now, we're winning games and that's all that matters. We've got two great goalies here. We both can play. We're both number ones. Obviously, Cory is playing unreal right now and we're winning games. What else could you ask for?" Luongo told *The Province* in December 2011.

The playoff replacement, though, got everyone talking about the chances of Luongo plying his trade elsewhere the following season. Playing on the hype, Luongo, instead of complaining, participated in a hilarious skit with Schneider that mocked the situation. After the Canucks lost to the Sharks in four straight playoff games in 2013 (in which the goalies split the games, Schneider taking over for Games 3 and 4), Luongo told CBC.ca, "We both want to play, that's the bottom line and there's only one net. I think me and Schneids handled it well on a personal level. We didn't let it get in the way of our friendship or relationship. We were supportive of each other, we made it work. I think we did the best we could with what we had."

Luongo expected he'd be on the move that summer, but Vancouver was unable to trade him thanks to a massive, front-loaded contract that could wind up punishing teams taking it on thanks to the new collective bargaining agreement. It was Schneider, and his less onerous contract, who was traded at the 2013 draft.

Although shocked by that turn of events, Luongo returned

without any fuss, only to find another backup breathing down his neck. This time it was Eddie Lack, but Luongo proceeded as per normal: he took the aspiring starter under his wing. The final straw, however, came when Luongo—returning from the Olympics, where he won another gold medal for Canada, this time as a backup—was left on the bench in Vancouver's outdoor Heritage Game in favour of Lack. It was time to go.

"I can say if he had played, maybe the call [to Canucks GM Mike Gillis] wouldn't have happened," Luongo's agent Pat Brisson told TSN radio.

Luongo would return to his old stomping grounds with the Florida Panthers, where he thought he'd team up with his finals nemesis Tim Thomas, formerly of the Bruins.

"Take good care of my boy Eddie Lack for me. He's a great talent and an even better person!" Luongo tweeted before adding, "Me and Tiny Tim are gonna rip it up the rest of the year!!!!!!!"

Before that could happen, however, Florida dealt Thomas to Dallas, eliciting a "NOOOO!!!!!!!!" from Luongo. Once a union man, always a union man.

Born April 4, 1979, in Montreal's Italian east end, Luongo, originally a centreman, didn't start playing net until he was 12 years old. The goalie on the team quit, and legend has it Luongo got a shutout in his first game.

Speaking to *InGoal Magazine* for its summer 2011 issue, Luongo named Grant Fuhr as his idol growing up. But by the time he was 14 or 15, he had decided he wanted to be a more technical goalie, someone more like Patrick Roy: "That's just the way the game is now if you look at, not only the NHL, but everywhere in the world everybody does the butterfly now. The effectiveness of that style, everybody wants to do it and that's what works right now in the NHL and the whole hockey world. That's the style that's most effective for goaltenders."

The Val D'Or Foreurs of the Quebec Major Junior Hockey League took the 6-foot-3, 181-pound Luongo second overall out of

Montreal's Bourassa College in the league's June 1995 draft. The buzz about the tall, lanky goalie, named the 1997 Michael Bossy Trophy winner as the top draft prospect in the Q, quickly picked up. In a Canadian junior showcase game in Toronto in February 1997, opposition coach Don Cherry raved, "Boy, oh, boy, I'll never forget that guy. I thought I was playing against Ken Dryden again" about Luongo's many spectacular, acrobatic saves in a 7-2 win for Team Orr.

"I think the scouts already have seen what I can do, but I wanted to leave a good impression," Luongo said after the game.

A future foe in Boston, Claude Julien, was behind the bench for the Hull Olympiques when Luongo was about to be drafted. "He's almost arrogant in the net, but he's not cocky, and it suits him well. It's a fine line between confidence and cockiness. Luongo knows the difference between the two. He's the best rookie goalie in the league and a hot prospect," said Julien, whose team was taking on the Foreurs.

The New York Islanders, wowed by his deft glove hand and quick feet for a man of his size, took the hotshot keeper fourth overall in the 1997 NHL draft—then the highest-ever spot for a goalie. (Tom Barrasso and John Davidson had been number-five picks, Rick DiPietro would go number one in 2000, and Marc-André Fleury went number one three years later.)

Luongo continued to mature in the juniors, tying a record of seven shutouts in 1997–98, the same season his Foreurs won the President Cup as the QMJHL champions. In the Memorial Cup, however, the team did not win a game. The following year, he played just 21 games with Val D'Or before getting shipped to the Acadie-Bathurst Titan at the trade deadline in December 1998. For the second straight season, his club won the President Cup (the first Maritime team ever to capture it), but they also lost all their games in the Memorial Cup. Later, his brother Fabio would play for the Titan, and another brother, Leo, would become the goaltending coach there; Roberto's jersey, No. 1, was retired by Acadie-Bathurst in August 2012.

The pinnacle of Luongo's junior career was probably the 1999 World Junior Championship, as he was the starter for the silver medal–winning team in Winnipeg, losing to Russia in overtime. He was named the top goaltender and an All-Star, with a 1.92 GAA and two shutouts. But the picture most will remember is Luongo weeping on the ice as he accepted his awards.

"I'd trade the honours for the gold medal," he told the *Montreal Gazette* after returning home, adding, "I really wanted to win gold. The individual honours don't make a difference." In the previous year's tournament, he had been a backup to Mathieu Garon, making three appearances.

Luongo has always been there for international play, starting with the 1995 World U-17 Hockey Challenge, where he suited up for Team Quebec, winning bronze in Moncton, New Brunswick. Along with his two appearances with Team Canada's junior squad, Luongo has been on three Olympic teams and numerous World Championship teams—including leading Canada to gold in 2003 and 2004. Whether as a backup or a starter, he has been a team player.

"I love playing with that maple leaf on my jersey," he told ESPN .com's David Amber after the 2006 Games in Torino, Italy, where he was able to show off his mastery of the Italian language he had grown up speaking.

Luongo's entry deal with the Isles was $2.775 million over three years, and after starting with the American Hockey League's Lowell Lock Monsters, he made his NHL debut on November 28, 1999, a 2-1 win over Boston. Seemingly confident in Luongo's abilities, the Islanders sent starter Felix Potvin packing to the Canucks. But when GM Mike Milbury took goaltender Rick DiPietro with the first overall pick in the 2000 NHL entry draft, he opted to keep the newcomer and shipped Luongo, along with centre Olli Jokinen, to the Florida Panthers for Mark Parrish and Oleg Kvasha.

After the deal Luongo said, "I was shocked. I never expected to be traded. They had never talked about it, so it caught me off guard. But once it sunk in, I was excited to come to Florida."

Though the Panthers were better than the Isles, they played in an indifferent market, and during Luongo's five years there (plus sitting out the 2004–05 lockout), the squad never made the playoffs. Luongo was a workhorse, playing 65, 72, and 75 games in his last three seasons there; his second season, 2001–02, had been ended by a torn ligament in his right ankle. A good example of the team in front of him is the 2003–04 season, when Luongo set an NHL record for shots (2,475) and saves (2,303) in a season and was nominated for the Vezina Trophy as well as the Lester B. Pearson Award, given to the MVP as selected by the players. The losing ways of the Panthers factored into Luongo's decision not to extend his contract in the Sunshine State; he was reportedly offered a five-year, $30-million deal.

"He changed his mind when we said that we were prepared to trade him, but when he got back to us, he was asking for more money than we had talked about," Florida GM Mike Keenan said after sending Luongo to Vancouver along with defenceman Lukas Krajicek for Todd Bertuzzi, Bryan Allen, and Alex Auld at the draft on June 23, 2006.

Vancouver had been a "goalie graveyard" according to ex-GM Brian Burke, with 18 different netminders taking the stage after Kirk McLean left town. The Canucks immediately signed Luongo to a four-year, $27-million contract and, with the stability and success he brought to the net, ripped up the deal a year early and signed him to the now infamous September 2009 contract that promised $64 million over 12 years. The contract would eventually by the biggest obstacle to dealing Luongo.

At the time, GM Mike Gillis defended the massive contract, explaining that goaltenders should be exempt from the scrutiny that a forward would get for a similar deal, and he mentioned the longevity of Johnny Bower and Dominik Hasek as proof that Luongo could be a star for years to come. "We didn't have any of the discomfort we might have had with a skating defenceman or forward. Roberto plays a very cerebral type game, he's not making acrobatic saves and diving all over the place and relying on reflexes. He relies on intelligence and preparation and game planning . . . and that gives us a lot of confidence that he's going to be a top player for a long time," said Gillis.

For the most part, Luongo was a top goalie and subject to far more attention from the public and the media in Vancouver. He started with a bang, helping the club to a team-record 105 points and the playoffs, where he stopped 72 shots in his first ever post-season game, taking the team to the second round. Luongo finished second in voting for the Vezina Trophy, Lester B. Pearson Award, and Hart Memorial Trophy.

The following year was a bit of a letdown, as the Canucks didn't make the playoffs. Luongo's scant 54 appearances in 2008–09 were due to a groin injury, and, upon his return, the team was ousted in the second round by the Chicago Blackhawks—which would happen again in 2009–10, the year that Luongo was in net for the gold medal–winning Team Canada at the Vancouver Olympics.

The behind-the-scenes change of switching goaltending coach Ian Clark for Roland Melanson paid dividends as Luongo remade his game (though he still worked out with Clark during the summer). "Lou" played deeper in his net and didn't challenge shooters as often, dropped to the ice quicker to seal the bottom of the net, and switched up his footwork to change the way he moved laterally. Later, he altered his glove to a higher position, closer to his shoulder, meaning that he could get higher shots with his mitt, shots he used to get in his youth with a simple flex of his shoulders.

"He has always been a tremendous worker. I just tried to put a better plan in effect [for] the way he works. We're trying to get five per cent better. Louie is focused more on getting better at the weakest parts of his game because he knew his foundation was solid," Melanson told the *Vancouver Sun* in February 2011.

As 2010 turned into 2011, Luongo rode a 21-game regulation time unbeaten streak, but he also truly shared the net for the first time, with rookie backup Cory Schneider. They were awarded the Jennings Trophy for the league's lowest GAA. With Luongo's league-leading

38 wins, the Canucks won their first Presidents' Trophy as the NHL's top team, and they finally cracked the Hawks in the playoffs in a seven-game thriller and stormed into the Stanley Cup Final, with Luongo playing some of the best hockey of his career.

The 2011 final against the Bruins, though, was an odd one, with Luongo and the Canucks taking the first two games at home, including a 1-0 shutout in the first game. But in Game 3, in Boston, Luongo let in eight goals. In Game 4, with four goals on 20 shots, he was pulled. It was another loss. Back in Vancouver, Luongo stoned the Bruins for another 1-0 victory. During Game 6, in Boston, with the Cup within grasp, he was pulled again, giving up three goals in less than three minutes in the first period. For Game 7, the Canucks didn't show up at all, losing 4-0, and Luongo let in three goals on 20 shots.

Luongo was outplayed by his Bruins counterpart, Tim Thomas, who was named the Conn Smythe winner as playoff MVP.

The Hockey News's Ken Campbell wrote, "Bruins coach Claude Julien said before the series that the Stanley Cup Final would not be decided by goaltending. He could not have been more wrong. The championship went the way it did because one guy gave his team otherworldly goaltending when it needed it most and the other faltered at the most crucial time."

The next two seasons were marked by Canucks flame-outs in the playoffs and the ascension of Schneider as the starter for 2012–13, when Luongo got into 20 games during the lockout-shortened season. The awkwardness of two quality goalies in the salary-cap era couldn't continue, and, when Luongo couldn't be dealt by the trade deadline, GM Gillis instead dealt Schneider at the 2013 NHL entry draft.

In short, Luongo is among the most talented goaltenders of his generation and among the most perplexing.

Scott Morrison, executive producer of hockey at Rogers Sportsnet, argued that Luongo still ranks among the best: "I think Roberto has lived up to his billing. He has been a premier goaltender in the league for several years. Look at the success the Canucks have had over the years, finishing first overall a couple of times, finally making it to a seventh game in the Stanley Cup Final, he has been a huge part of that, no question. If he wins Game 7, he is a hero for life, not being second-guessed. Remember, he also won Olympic gold. So he has proven he can win important games."

ILYA BRYZGALOV It's a strange business, professional

hockey. A player can start as a rookie backup on a Stanley Cup winner only to be placed on waivers, or he can be traded for a third-round pick and a couple of years later become a reality TV celebrity with a massive nine-year deal, heralded as the saviour of a franchise.

And then be bought out and sent to the scrapheap.

No wonder Ilya Bryzgalov had to develop a strange, twisted sense of humour.

His off-ice comments—"I'm not afraid of anything; I'm afraid of bear, about bear in forest" in answer to a reporter's question about Pittsburgh's biggest offensive threats—have overshadowed his play on more than one occasion. But then the media attention is a little bit bigger in Philadelphia than in Phoenix, his previous home.

Sean Burke, the goalie coach with the Coyotes, doesn't think "Breeze" changed at all: "I'm sure he's the same guy, it just doesn't translate the same way. In Phoenix, you're in the desert. We have two beat writers who follow the team and Bryz is a colourful guy and he can say a lot of things that are probably never going to be printed or even if they are, nobody's going to read them."

When the HBO cameras arrived into the Flyers locker room, they found a uniquely honest, quirky figure in Bryz. He quickly became a talking point, just as he made his points, whether about the vastness of outer space or the death penalty for killing tigers.

National Post columnist Bruce Arthur wrote, "It is hard not to love Bryzgalov; even his failures are refreshing. While some athletes protect their own psyches by blaming circumstance, or glossing over what happened, or steeling themselves for the next time, Bryzgalov either laughs or slices open an artery, right there in front of you. He shows you who he is. He can't seem to help it."

Ilya Nikolaevich Bryzgalov was born on June 22, 1980, in Togliatti, Russia. His early successes came with the Lada Togliatti of the Russian Superleague and with Spartak Moscow, in the league below. He was on the Russian rosters for the 2000 World Junior Championship and World Championship as well as the 2002 Olympic squad.

The Mighty Ducks of Anaheim chose Bryzgalov in the second round, 44th overall, in the 2000 NHL entry draft. He got into one Anaheim game in 2002 but spent the next three seasons with the AHL's Cincinnati Mighty Ducks. His profile rose with his play in the 2004 World Cup and the 2006 Olympics (where he claimed the best part was the free McDonald's food). Unable to deny him any longer—Bryzgalov was among the top-ranked American Hockey League goaltenders in 2003–04 in games (64), minutes played (3,748), wins (27), and saves (1,644)—the Ducks brought him up as the backup in 2005, after the lockout.

He shone in the playoffs, however, when Jean-Sébastien Giguère was chased from the Ducks' net during the opening round of the 2006 playoffs against Calgary. Bryzgalov then proceeded to toss three straight shutouts, eliminating the Flames and taking two games against Colorado, tying Frank McCool's 1945 record for play as a rookie.

"I don't even think he realizes. He's just a guy who goes out there and has fun and doesn't take any pressure or anything," Anaheim's Teemu Selänne said of Bryzgalov's shutout streak of 249 minutes and 15 seconds, then the second longest in NHL playoff history.

Though the Ducks were eliminated by the Edmonton Oilers in the semifinals, their play built the foundation for the next season, when the team claimed the Stanley Cup.

After the championship, Ducks GM Brian Burke committed to Giguère with a long-term contract and, facing salary cap issues,

Ilya Bryzgalov has always made more sense in net than in interviews.
(George Tahinos)

promised to either find Bryz a new home or put him on waivers. The day after he was waived, November 17, 2007, the Phoenix Coyotes, who had been making due with Mikael Tellqvist and Alex Auld in net, grabbed him.

After the move, Bryzgalov said, "You have to earn this job. It's not a right to be a number one goalie. You have to earn this and prove this every day—in practice and in the game. It's so tough to get this job, to be number one, and it's so easy to lose it. You have to keep working hard."

His first two years in Phoenix, the team was pretty dismal, but 2009–10 marked the ascension of both the team and Bryzgalov, who had career bests in wins (42), games (69), shutouts (eight), goals-against average (2.29), and save percentage (.920) to lead the Coyotes to franchise records in wins (50) and points (107). Bryzgalov lost out to Buffalo's Ryan Miller for the Vezina. In the playoffs, the Coyotes took the Red Wings to a thrilling seven games in the opening round before bowing out.

The following season was the last of his three-year, $12.75 million deal with Phoenix, and after a decent 36-20-10 record with a 2.48 goals-against average and seven shutouts, the Coyotes, unable to pay him what he wanted and with their ownership in limbo, traded his negotiating rights to the Flyers.

Vowing "we are never going to go through the goalie issues we've gone through in the last couple of years again," Flyers chairman Ed Snider inked Bryzgalov to a nine-year, $51-million contract in June 2011.

After a rough start—"I have zero confidence in myself right now," he said—Bryz got into the groove and posted a 2.48 GAA and six shutouts over the season. However, his GAA exploded in the playoffs, ballooning to 3.46. Bryz was shelled by the Penguins, especially in the first round—but not as bad as Pittsburgh's keeper, Marc-André Fleury. Eliminated in the conference semifinals by the Devils, the next lockout-shortened year, the Flyers didn't even make the playoffs.

Negotiated into the new deal between the owners and the players after the lockout was an amnesty clause, and the Flyers chose to use it on Bryzgalov, meaning they were free of his contract against the salary cap but still had to pay him $23 million over the next 14 years.

Scott Hartnell of the Flyers praised the goalie for keeping things light in the dressing room: "You've got Ilya Bryzgalov, who talks about the universe, Husky dogs being like women, and things like that. It's a little quirky, but I like Bryz. He's a funny guy and a lot of people don't know how to take his sense of humour. He's a really good teammate."

On the way out of Philly, Bryzgalov was classy, thanking Snider "for the faith he showed in me when he committed to the long-term contract that has secured my family's financial future, and acknowledging his passion for the game of hockey."

Bryz's agent, Ritch Winter, was a little more explosive. "It's terrible for goaltenders in Philadelphia," Winter seethed on Edmonton's 630 CHED radio station. "There's more wrong with Philadelphia's goaltending than just the goaltending."

Bryzgalov would kick off the 2013–14 season in obscurity, attending the training camp of the East Coast Hockey League's Las Vegas Wranglers on a tryout. He did not, however, sign with the club and almost became a forgotten man.

His path back to the NHL was paved by the failure of Edmonton's goaltenders to keep the puck out of the net. Ranked last in the league in goals against with Devan Dubnyk, Jason LaBarbera, and Richard Bachman, a desperate Craig MacTavish reached out and plucked Bryzgalov from limbo to staunch the bleeding.

In an interview with AM-630 in Edmonton, MacTavish said, "I believe in the power of the potential of people. He's said and indicated all the right things to me in the conversations that I've had. I think he has a chance to come in here and make a real impact on our team."

After a conditioning stint with Oklahoma City of the AHL, Bryzgalov, wearing No. 80, proved he still had it, shutting out Nashville in his first start for the Oilers. This followed his impressive relief effort in a losing cause versus Chicago.

After the Nashville contest, Oilers coach Dallas Eakins said, "He picked up right where he left off last game. I thought he was solid. He looked big in the net, everything. Check marks right across the page for him."

Bryzgalov provided the goods as he stopped 92 of 98 shots against him in four appearances before his comeback was briefly cut short after a collision with a Dallas Stars forward left him with a concussion. He'd return, of course, and even got a shot at his former Flyers teammates; despite another stellar outing, the Oilers fell 4-3 in a shootout. None of his Oilers teammates, however, were hanging the loss around his neck, and not being cast as the goat must surely have been a refreshing change for Bryzgalov.

"Bryz played unreal. It's not an easy situation going against players in the jersey you used to wear. I'm proud of him and happy to have him," Oiler Taylor Hall told the *Edmonton Journal*.

"Bryz got us the point for sure. Look at the shots, they were pretty uneven," added Jordan Eberle about the 38 Flyers shots versus the Oilers' 16.

The old Bryz, it seemed, was back.

Despite playing on a club that was vying for worst with Buffalo, Bryzgalov put up a respectable .908 save percentage to go with his 3.01 GAA and a 5-8-5 record in 20 games.

But he became expendable once the Oilers signed recently acquired Ben Scrivens to a two-year contract. Just before the 2014 trade deadline, Bryzgalov was on the move again, this time to the Minnesota Wild, a team with two regular goalies down to injury, desperately seeking insurance.

Wild general manager Chuck Fletcher called Bryzgalov a quality veteran who'd add depth to his team's goaltending position. "He played well in Phoenix . . . Anaheim . . . Cincinnati. He's played in three Olympics, was Second-Team All-Star one year, he's won over 200 games in the NHL, so to add a goaltender of that calibre for what we felt was a very manageable price made a lot of sense to us," Fletcher told the *Star Tribune*.

JONATHAN QUICK Counted among the best of his peers,

Jonathan Quick rewrote Los Angeles Kings goaltending records, backstopped them to their first ever Stanley Cup in their nearly half-century of existence, and, maybe most remarkably, nobody *ever* saw him coming.

Selected in the third round, 72nd overall by the Kings, Quick was the eighth goalie chosen in the 2005 NHL amateur draft and was far from being heralded as joining the next generation of world beaters in net. In fact, he wasn't even pegged to become the Kings' goaltender of the future; rather, Quebec Major Junior Hockey League's Jonathan Bernier, whom L.A. chose with their first pick in 2006, would be slated for that role.

Clearly *someone* needed to emerge as the next Rogie Vachon or Kelly Hrudey, as the Kings were anything but stable in goal in those years, with Mathieu Garon, Sean Burke, Dan Cloutier, Jason LaBarbera, Jean-Sebastien Aubin, and Erik Ersberg taking turns blocking shots for L.A.

Quick managed to elbow his way through the crowd long enough to make his first start, which came on December 6, 2007, against the Buffalo Sabres.

Of the 8-2 home victory, Quick said, "You get out there and your nerves are going. But once you make a couple saves, it's just like another game. Obviously it's a little quicker than most games you ever played, but it's just another game, and you're just trying to take it one shift at a time, one shot at a time."

It was 2008–09 when Quick turned heads, starting 41 of the club's last 50 games. Although seemingly having earned the confidence of the coaching staff as the starter, Quick dismissed any notions he'd safely secured the number-one position: "While it was happening, you never really get the feeling like, 'I'm the guy.' You just every day try to prove to the coaches and teammates that you belong there."

There was no doubt where he belonged the following year, when he built on his previous season's accomplishments, breaking a Kings goaltending record by playing 72 games and winning 39.

He also earned a spot on the 2010 U.S. Olympic squad, behind Buffalo's Ryan Miller and Bruin Tim Thomas. At the time, U.S. coach Ron Wilson said, "I'm very impressed with him. Jonathan Quick's the future of USA goaltending right now."

Quick also earned positive reviews during the 2010 playoffs in the Kings' first-round match against Vancouver.

"He's just so fast post to post. And he covers the bottom of the net really well, which forces you to go upstairs," Canuck Alex Burrows marvelled after one game.

Daniel Sedin said, "He's got a quick glove hand. Really quick. So the best plan is to get a lot of pucks on him and get some traffic in front of him so he can't see the puck as well."

But it would be in 2011–12 that Quick did the seemingly impossible, given his modest origins, and challenged for the Vezina Trophy as best regular season goalie, winning playoff MVP honours, and capturing the Stanley Cup in L.A.'s first ever championship season in 45 years.

Born on January 21, 1986, in Milford, Connecticut, Quick's hockey roots began on the streets—literally. Quick related, "I got into it because I enjoyed playing street hockey. I was the goalie every time we played and I enjoyed that."

He talked his parents into taking him down to the local parks and rec department, where they rented goaltending equipment for him. By the time he was eight and a confirmed Mike Richter and New York Rangers booster, his parents recognized the seriousness of his intentions and bought him his own gear.

Tending goal in the Mid Fairfield Youth Hockey Association, Quick played on consecutive national championships. After two seasons at Hamden High, he transferred to Avon Old Farms, where he shone with a 53-8 record and 11 shutouts in three years. His Beavers also took consecutive New England championships, in 2004 and 2005.

The Kings drafted Quick in 2005, but he went Joe College before trying to go pro, heading to the University of Massachusetts Amherst. Quick played backup his freshman year on a losing team but took over the starting duties the next year, turning the club around while setting school records for single-season wins and games played. He also took the Minutemen to their first ever NCAA Ice Hockey Championship in his sophomore year.

Undoubtedly talented, Quick was still young and green, according to L.A. goaltending coach Bill Ranford. "When I went and saw Quickie play at UMass, I looked at a kid that was livin' the good life at the university level, and very raw from a technical standpoint, but super athletic. So he looked like a guy who just needed to clean up his game a little bit, but had some potential," Ranford said.

His transition to the NHL was gradual. Occasional 20-plus hour bus trips and rodents in hotel rooms weren't on the glamorous hockey lifestyle brochure, but such was life in the East Coast Hockey League, where Quick first cut his teeth. It was also where he wasn't necessarily making the greatest of impressions.

During the Kings' 2012 trip to the final, general manager Dean Lombardi told the *Los Angeles Daily News*, "All I think of with Jonathan Quick when I see him now is when he was in the ECHL, he fell asleep on the couch and Billy Ranford went down there to see him. He left the goalie coach with no goalie on the ice. Billy Ranford goes all the way down there, I don't know where the hell it was, to give him his tutoring. He's at the rink and Quicker's sleeping."

An admitted heavy sleeper, Quick looked wide awake the following year, 2008–09, when he graduated to the Manchester Monarchs of the American Hockey League before playing 44 games with the Kings in the second half of the year.

Quick left no doubt as to who occupied the Kings' throne, playing in over 60 games in each of the next three seasons. As Quick vied for the Vezina Trophy in 2011–12, Vachon endorsed him as the real deal: "He carried the team for months. He was absolutely phenomenal. The guy is very steady. He very rarely will give up a bad goal."

Quick rewrote the Kings record book that year with 10 shutouts—which led the league as well—and beat Vachon's single season team bests by compiling a 1.95 GAA and .929 save percentage. He also again demonstrated his durability with 69 games played, which he owed to a fastidious combination of healthful diet and training.

"If you eat properly, you're going to have an increase in energy and you'll feel better on the ice. The preparation you do in summertime goes a long way to making sure that you're in as great a shape as you can be for the long haul. It is a grind; 82 games and you hope for another 20 to 25 in the playoffs if you're lucky. You've got to be in as good a shape as you can be to go through that grind," Quick said.

His mentor Ranford played a part in Quick's consistency in all those games. "He brought a lot of control to my game. . . . Before I started playing pro, I didn't have too much goaltending coaching; I was getting help here and there from guys, but not too much," Quick said.

He cited Ranford's calming of his game so he could avoid being forced to make double and triple saves as the coach's biggest contribution: "I was tending to over-exert myself, making things more difficult than they needed to be. Obviously when the situation comes up when you do need to play outside the box, you use your athleticism. Use it when you need it, but not on routine saves."

Ranford said Quick's attention to detail and refining the technical side of his game served him well, and that he no longer needed to rely quite so much on his athletic ability alone: "Now it's a tool in the toolbox. When needed, you bring out the athletic aspect of the game, instead of athletics first and technique second. Mostly we just simplified his game more than anything."

What's caught Toronto Maple Leafs goaltending coach Rick St. Croix eye is Quick's ability to get an extra three or four inches on each side by going down to the splits.

St. Croix said, "Every goalie has something that's extra special, and his flexibility is extra special. He tracks pucks well and gets on them. He's obviously a pretty good goalie, he competes hard, but his flexibility is exceptional."

Although a championship year for Quick and the Kings, the club little resembled a Cup contender for part of 2011–12. Halfway through the season, the Kings fired coach Terry Murray and brought in Darryl Sutter, who'd recently been dismissed by the Calgary Flames. Under

Sutter, the Kings would turn their season around, going 25-13-11 in 49 games. They clinched eighth seed in an extremely tight Western Conference, where third-seeded Phoenix, which won the Pacific Division, finished only two points ahead of the Kings.

"We got a bit of confidence. Parts of the year we weren't playing as confident as we should have," said Quick.

The acquisition of scorer Jeff Carter marked another pivotal moment for the club, as he joined two other former Flyers in Mike Richards and Simon Gagné.

"The Jeff Carter trade ended up paying off big time for us as he came through in big games for us when we needed him to. I think when Jeff came in, it took a lot of pressure off guys. Even after Jeff came in and after Darryl was coaching, we went through stretches where we weren't playing our best hockey, but I think everybody was a little looser, and we were better able to break out of those slumps than earlier in the year," Quick said.

The Kings really came on by playoff time and dominated, first dispatching the Vancouver Canucks—the Presidents' Trophy winners as best regular season team—in only five games.

"He's an elite goaltender and it's been a real challenge for us," Canucks coach Alain Vigneault said.

"He's not just our best player, he's our most consistent. The quiet confidence filters down to the rest of the players. It's huge," said Kings captain Dustin Brown.

The Kings continued to steamroll their opponents, sweeping the St. Louis Blues and knocking off the Coyotes in five.

In the final, the Kings took their fourth straight three-games-to-none lead (an accomplishment no team had ever achieved before), but the Devils gave them a bit more fight than their other opponents, led by the league's long-time goaltending standard-bearer, veteran Martin Brodeur. They'd win two in a row to make it a series again, but Quick said he and the Kings at no point started losing their nerve: "No, not at all. We were confident we were going to go back home and win."

And they did, blowing the Devils out 6-1 in Game 6 to earn the victory and lift the Cup.

"He's in a class by himself as far as I'm concerned," the Kings' Dustin Penner said after the game.

Kings legend and president of business operations Luc Robitaille said, "Jonathan Quick's been like that. No one knows about it, but he's been playing this way. Look at his stats for the last three years— they're phenomenal."

It was also an accomplishment never achieved by an eighth-seeded team, but Quick dismissed the label: "I didn't buy into the whole eighth seed and we had to upset anybody, and I don't think the team did either. I think we knew going into Vancouver that we were just as good as them and we could play with them. We just had to do our system properly, take care of all the little details, and outwork them, and we have a big chance of winning."

Even more remarkable than the Kings' great play was the fact Quick was playing with a bad back. A herniated disc started pinching his sciatic nerve in March, and he'd feel discomfort whenever he sat down. In August 2012, he underwent surgery to repair a disc fragment and an inflammatory cyst that had formed in his back.

Quick returned in time for the lockout-shortened 2012–13 season and led the Kings all the way to the semifinals. They fell to eventual Cup winners, the Chicago Blackhawks. Quick and the Kings avenged that loss the following season, beating the Blackhawks on their way to the Finals. They defeated the New York Rangers in five closely contested games to win their second Stanley Cup in three years.

Also in 2014, Quick made Ron Wilson look prophetic when he took the Olympic starting reins from Ryan Miller to become the U.S. men's hockey team's No. 1 goalie in Sochi. Although a favourite to medal, the Americans finished a disappointing fourth, but that by no means reflected the play of Quick, who, if anything, kept his squad in contention. His stoning of the Canadians in what ended up a 1-0 loss in the semifinal had given his teammates the chance to steal a game from Team Canada, which dominated play

Jason LaBarbera's Pat Tillman mask was painted by Toronto artist David Arrigo. (Courtesy David Arrigo)

throughout. The Kings tweeted "Jonathan Quick 0, Canada 1 after 2 periods," which perfectly summed up the action and their man's outstanding efforts.

PAYING TRIBUTE WITH A MASK

Jason LaBarbera's masks have often drawn more attention than his work in net. The native of Prince George, BC, has bounced through a couple of teams (Rangers, Kings, Canucks, Coyotes, Oilers, Blackhawks) as a positive, team-first backup.

He is definitely enjoying the ride, and he thinks that the colourful head protection that he chooses speaks louder than he ever does: "I'm a pretty quiet guy as is, I'm not overly out there. I think I'm pretty normal for a goalie. With masks, as a kid, I always thought it was pretty cool that you got to have some kind of design on your helmet. Especially as masks evolved, it becomes your personality, stuff that you like, things that you want to show off of who you are. I've always enjoyed that aspect of coming up with something cool every year, something different every year, something for people to talk about."

There is the mask paying tribute to rock metal gods Metallica and a couple of WWE-themed ones with wrestlers CM Punk and The Undertaker.

"Barbs was one of my first goalies I ever painted for, it's been some five years now and I always look forward to working with him. Between his love of rock 'n' roll and wrestling, there's always something interesting to work with," said Toronto artist David Arrigo.

In the fall of 2011, while playing in Phoenix, he debuted a mask that paid tribute to Pat Tillman, the safety for the Arizona Cardinals who left his NFL contract to enlist in the U.S. Army after 9/11 and was killed by friendly fire in Afghanistan in April 2004.

LaBarbera said, "People thought it was pretty cool and were pretty touched by it. For me, I thought it was cool just because Pat Tillman played here and his story is incredible. To be a part of their organization and charity and stuff, people I think appreciated it. I just thought it was a nice gesture to do for someone who did something heroic."

CONCLUSION

WHERE GOALTENDING GOES FROM HERE

As the National Hockey League approaches its 100th anniversary in 2017, it begs the question of what goaltending will look like in the years to come. Hockey will always have a target of some sort, whether the nets end up bigger or in a different shape or, who knows, maybe in some sort of holographic projection that can automatically establish when a goal has been scored.

No other position receives the same focus (hassles?) as the goalie: goal scoring is down, blame the goalies; the nets need to be bigger; their equipment is gigantic; keep them in their creases so the defencemen have to play the puck more; the creases are too big; the European goalies are taking over; today's goalies get injured too much; they go down too quickly.

Get the picture?

John Davidson, one of the most respected minds in the game, said, "Every rule change seems to work against goaltenders. Everyone wants to open up play and increase scoring. There's no way a goaltender can carry the averages the greats used to get. You can't worry about average. You worry about winning." He said that in 1975.

If history is our guide, there will always be tinkering related to hockey and goaltenders, whether it is the legal width of the paddle of a stick or the proportional calculation of the height and width of the pads versus the goalie's height. Less obvious are the equipment manufacturers, who can tweak the angle of the board in a blocker to better serve an elite goalie's style, modify the thumb position in the catching glove, or offer pads with firmer foam for keepers who like to kick away rebounds and softer foam that keeps the puck closer to them. And the trainers don't just sharpen skates anymore; they can adjust the radius of the blade, changing the percentage of steel that touches the ice, and hone the edges to specifications to the eighth of an inch.

This is all fine and good, and today's netminders have the benefit of agents, goalie coaches, and trainers to help them through any adjustments.

Bob Sauvé is a goalie turned agent and is defensive yet grudgingly concessionary about changing the game. "Everybody keeps talking about the equipment . . . but then if they weren't protected well today, they wouldn't play the way they're playing right now, going down in front of those shots. Imagine if we had played like this with the equipment we had? We'd have been dead. Over the past two, three decades, it's probably the most improved position in sports," he said.

"They keep saying they're not scoring goals anymore. Hey, goalies just got so much better. They're going to have to double the scoring chances if they want to score more goals. Change the rules so they can get more scoring chances," said Sauvé.

Dallas Stars play-by-play man Ralph Strangis is on board with more scoring, even at the expense of the men in the nets:

This league crawls with progress. They put a premium on defending these guys. They talk about, "How are we going to shut down Alexander Ovechkin? Why doesn't he want to block shots like the rest of us and only then will he be a good teammate." That's friggin crazy. Michael Ryder scores 35 goals a year and "Well, he wasn't good in his own end of the rink." Who cares?! You know how many guys score 35 goals a year? Our focus should not be, "How do we shut down stars and how do we allow goalies to wear big pads," it should be, "How do we make the best players in the game able to do their thing on a nightly basis?" And, "How do we make the goalies less important?" Because they should not be this important.

Judging by his comment in December 2007, Canucks goaltender Roberto Luongo understands that fans crave more action. "I've said it a hundred times before: if you want to increase scoring, just open up the game more and there will be more scoring chances and there will be more goals. That's how you increase scoring," Luongo told the *Vancouver Sun*.

It is always interesting to talk to players from the past, as they have the benefit of having spent years watching the game and can express how it has changed. To Pete Conacher—a journeyman forward with a famous lineage (he's the son of Charlie Conacher and nephew to Lionel, Roy, and Bert Conacher)—who got into 229 NHL games in the 1950s, the actual game of hockey has changed so much that it is almost unrecognizable to him. Conacher, who still plays the occasional old-timer game, said,

The game was different then. They didn't shoot high. They tried to pick a corner down low, stick-side or long-side. That's just the way it was. These guys today, they just fire it right at the top every chance they get. But in our day, as a hockey player, a goal scorer, your shot was low to either corner. The first rule of thumb for goalies in those days was to keep your legs together. Stand up, keep your legs together. There was no such thing as a five-hole. Now it's just the opposite. You're butterflying, your legs are wide apart, trying to reach each post, and the hole is in the middle. As a goal scorer, to shoot low on either side, you'd be out of luck. There's nothing there. Plus, the sticks nowadays enable you to put that up there without any trouble. The sticks we used were like lumber. It definitely made a difference in your shot.

Scott Hartnell is one of those current players who aims for the upper corners. He said of the current crop of goaltenders, "They're athletic now. They have to compete. You have to be able to do the splits, go post to post. It's not easy to score goals in this league anymore. You watch in the 1980s when goals were just going in on the ice, goalies were standing up. Now it's butterfly, sprawling for saves. It's just a great game we've got going on now."

Hall of Fame sportswriter Frank Orr believes that the time of the butterfly goalie is at an end. "There's too many good high shooters now," he said, launching into a story that Patrick Roy once told him after being scored on high by Islanders Benoit Hogue and Pierre Turgeon: "I talked to him the next day at practice, and he opened up a bit; he said, 'It's funny, coaches crap all over you if you get beat low, but they never seem to say much if you get beat high. The butterfly is good because it forces guys to shoot high, and there aren't that many high shooters. If you force them to shoot high, often they'll beat themselves by shooting too high.' But now with the fiber sticks and all the new things, there's just some really good high shooters."

To be fair, goaltenders have the choice of composite sticks now too, which offer durability and are lighter, which in the vernacular of the manufacturers means "less stick arm fatigue." The foam core sticks absorb hard shots better than composites, allowing for better direction of rebounds.

The injuries suffered by butterfly goalies are different from those suffered by the goalies who preceded them in the nets. Hip ailments, in particular, seem to go hand in glove with the style, but there are groin pulls as well. The game is faster than it used to be, with more quality chances, and goalies have to react quicker and then get right back in the play; doing drills to mimic these challenges in practices doubles the pressures on the body.

"The game has opened up, the new rules mean goaltenders are a lot busier, the saves are harder and more spectacular, there's more stress on the joints. You have guys 25, 26 years old having hip operations, which never used to happen," said goaltending guru François Allaire in the *Globe and Mail* in 2009.

While there is much discussion about the equipment the goalies wear, the players have the use of custom-made composite sticks, a huge improvement over wood sticks, even if they can cost hundreds of dollars per stick.

"Everybody shoots the puck so hard today with those composite sticks. When I played, you had maybe two or three guys on each team that could really fire the puck with those wood sticks," said Bobby "the Chief" Taylor.

The other players have better equipment too, which has also had an influence on the game. A properly placed hit can now send an opposing player off the ice for weeks with a concussion or knee injury. The flip-side, though, are the defencemen that drop to the ice to block a shot far more frequently than their predecessors because of the better protection.

As a result, with everyone amped up physically and clad in suits of armour, the game is played at a higher level and the challenge to score is just that much greater.

It has created parity in the goaltending position, so an unheralded rookie or import can step into the role and perform equally well in the short-term as the star that they're replacing. In the lockout-shortened 2012–13 season, the Anaheim Ducks saw starter Jonas Hiller go down to injury and be replaced by Viktor Fasth, who never gave the net back.

John Ahlers, the TV play-by-play man for the Ducks, saw it all happen and believes there is a decided division between the very top keepers and the rest.

"I think there are five or six elite goalies in today's game, and a group of 10 or 12 that I think are all capable of winning the ultimate prize," he said, tossing around top names like Henrik Lundqvist, Pekka Rinne, and Roberto Luongo. Ahlers continued, "When you look at guys like Lundqvist, or if you consider guys like Luongo, the main thing for me is they're all bigger.... That, coupled with the fact that the equipment is bigger, whether or not we call it cheating or taking advantage of the rules nowadays, I think for a lot of goalies, that may be why there's a larger group that are capable of winning it all any given year, to get hot, because there's not that separation."

KING PATRICK

The rise of Patrick Roy has often been credited as the cause for the growth of goaltending as a glamour position. But one must also consider the timing of his ascension, 1986, and the expansion of cable television and all-sports stations like ESPN and TSN. Where once hockey was hard to find on TV other than on Saturday nights, programmers hungry for content exposed the game to new fans. VCRs were common in homes, and youngsters, like the 2013 Stanley Cup–winning goalie Corey Crawford, from Châteauguay, Quebec, wore out videotapes watching Roy's dramatics. Expansion to meet demand was inevitable, though the choice of franchises is a discussion for another day. The acquisition of Wayne Gretzky by the Los Angeles Kings in 1989 solidified hockey as a truly North American sport, especially in the Sun Belt.

But back to Roy.

Leading the Montreal Canadiens to a Stanley Cup as a rookie, and taking the Conn Smythe as playoff MVP in the process, hadn't been done since Ken Dryden came out of Cornell in 1971. Roy took the Habs to the final again in 1989, losing to Calgary, and to another win in 1993.

The general manager of the Canadiens was Serge Savard, who had played with Dryden. Savard said, "Sometimes one goalie can make a difference. Dryden won with us, but we had a great team. Patrick Roy won two Cups with not a great team. Patrick Roy was an outstanding goalie."

Philippe Sauvé's father, Bob, had been an NHL goalie, but it was watching Roy that convinced to take up the position. "I look at the guys my age, where we saw Patrick of '93. When we were younger and the butterfly style, it was very, very popular. It was the new thing in the game, the style of the goaltending," said Sauvé.

The apprenticeship Roy went through with the Granby Bisons of the QMJHL not only developed his skills, it encouraged others to follow in his wake.

Philippe Sauvé, now a player agent, said, "Why did we have a lot of goalies coming out of the 'Q' back then? I think you can look at a lot of reasons, but for sure Patrick, being here in Montreal and watching him play had a lot to do with it. You can look back then, and still is now, the Quebec league is a little more offensive as well. I'm a strong believer, if you're seeing a lot more action, a lot more scoring chances, you're going to get better when you're in your prime development. So that might have something to do with it as well."

In 2007, Quebec goaltending master François Allaire told the *Vancouver Sun*, "He was ahead of his time, a pioneer. Patrick played a style that wasn't common at the time [1980s]. With his flexibility, athleticism, passion, and blue-collar mentality, he was a genius at stopping the puck. All the French guys [goalies] in the NHL would all say they wanted to be like Patrick."

Brian Hayward was backup to Roy in Montreal from 1986 to 1990, and he helped him mature into his starting role, though the quirks stayed, like twitching, talking to his goalposts, and refusing to skate over any line on the ice.

"He'd already won a Cup, but he was still very raw, both in the way that he conducted his business, the way he took care of himself. He didn't eat properly. He didn't train probably as hard as he should have. He wasn't very strong physically. It was a perfect situation for me. I was the guy who went to practice every day and tried

Patrick Roy inspired a new generation of French-Canadian goaltenders.
(George Tahinos)

to outplay him, because I knew I needed to fight and do everything I could to get time in the net," said Hayward.

And Roy *did* improve as he went along, taking better care of himself and driving to be the best. With his two Stanley Cups in Colorado and three Vezina Trophies, he firmly put himself in the discussion as one of the greatest of all time. No one else has ever won three Conn Smythe Trophies as playoff MVP, proving he was the best when it mattered most. Roy set the bar very high for everyone who followed, and he firmly established that goalies could be the stars of a team—and the highest-paid players.

Goalie-turned-broadcaster John Davidson said,

> To be frank, a lot of the goalies in the old days weren't the best athletes on the team. Nowadays they certainly are. He [Roy] made a lot of the best athletes that were French Canadian want to be goalies, as opposed to centremen or right wingers or defencemen. So you could see when these guys came up they were good athletes. It's like in the States, a lot of times when you go into the Gretzky effect that you had in California. A lot of the best athletes in southern California instead of wanting to be football, baseball players, wanted to be hockey players, because of what Gretzky brought to them. You're seeing a lot of kids come out of there now that are drafted, players that are good players. But they became, growing up as kids, "I want to be a hockey player" even more so than a baseball player or a football player.

THE EUROPEAN INVASION

In 1963, the *Toronto Star*'s Jim Proudfoot derisively asked, "Swedish players in the National Hockey League?" During an October exhibition game against Chicago, the Maple Leafs had used Kjell Svensson of Sweden's national team in net and Carl Oeberg on the wing. "You'd have to rate them as fringe NHL players," said Punch Imlach, Toronto's coach and general manager, of the Swedes in his lineup.

Imlach, like many in the league, was ignorant of the game's international growth, and when the gates were finally open to a truly international roster, the European invasion of goaltenders took a little longer than for position players. It was defender Borje Salming, from Sweden, who firmly proved that a European could play the North American style, and, later, countrymen Anders Hedberg and Ulf Nilsson lit it up in the WHA.

As far as goalies are concerned, Markus Mattsson and Hannu Kamppuri blazed the trail for Finland, in the latter part of the 1970s in the WHA. Jiri Crha from Czechoslovakia replaced Mike Palmateer with the Leafs, Imlach having warmed to imports. Karl Friesen was a Winnipeg-born German for the '86–87 Devils. Russia's Sergei Mylnikov got into 10 games with the 1989–90 Quebec Nordiques. Swedes Hardy Åström and Göran Högosta both made NHL debuts in 1979.

There were prejudices to overcome, according to Ray Miron, who was the GM of the Colorado Rockies and brought in Åström to backstop the perennial loser and hired Don Cherry, a bombastic coach who spoke his mind.

Miron explained, "Cherry didn't like him at all, because he was Swedish for one thing. And he didn't try to help him. If Cherry had tried to help him a little bit, he might have improved. But Cherry didn't help him, he hurt him."

To be fair, Åström was no All-Star. Cherry can recall an early practice where the Rockies were blowing pucks past Åström, and he wondered whether he had a collection of awesome shooters or a sieve. And with a team that struggled to score, it was hugely deflating for the players to watch Åström let in soft goals and, worse yet, yank himself from the nets.

In an email from Sweden, Åström said he is proud of his pioneering role as a European goalie in North America, but he remains puzzled by Cherry. "Later he started to criticize me; some of it is true but most of them were his stories," he wrote. Åström was initially the property of the New York Rangers and chafed at having to play in New Haven in the American Hockey League. "The biggest challenge was the rink size. I was not used to fighting about the two goalie spots with the Rangers," he said. With no other Swedes on the team, the language and the culture were hard too.

A contemporary of Åström's, Sauvé said, "We had the European goalies in our day, but they weren't good. Now, they're all good."

While European goalies trickled in after the high-profile Åström failure, it wasn't until Dominik Hasek stood on his head in the early 1990s that the wall came tumbling down. Russian great Vladislav Tretiak was actually Hasek's goalie coach with the Blackhawks, but Tretiak never had a chance to play in the NHL.

It was a close thing, though, as the Montreal Canadiens took a flier on the Russian great, drafting him in the seventh round of the 1983 entry draft. Despite persistent attempts by Habs GM Serge Savard to secure his release, Russian officials—while perhaps initially considering allowing Tretiak to go—refused in the end.

"I would have loved to play in the Forum," Tretiak told the Hockey Hall of Fame. "I was hoping to one day play in the NHL. I would have liked to do it even for just one season. Unfortunately, it didn't work out that way. I regret not having the chance."

After Hasek came a funny little Latvian by the name of Arturs Irbe, who only turned around the fortunes of the San Jose Sharks with his unorthodox style, helping upset the powerhouse Detroit Red Wings before nearly doing likewise to Doug Gilmour and the Toronto Maple Leafs in the 1993–94 playoffs. The 5-foot-8 acrobat also took the Carolina Hurricanes to the franchise's first Stanley Cup Finals in a losing cause in 2002 against Hasek and the Red Wings. He and Hasek became the first European starting goalies to take their teams to the same final.

With the Iron Curtain permanently down, Nikolai Khabibulin provided the original NHL Winnipeg Jets the kind of goaltending they'd missed since Bob Essensa's heyday, and perhaps a caliber higher than that. He was the goalie of record at the last Jets game played at the Winnipeg Arena, and, in 2004, he became the first Russian netminder to win a Stanley Cup when he and the rest of the Tampa Bay Lightning defeated the Calgary Flames in seven games.

Now the Europeans are dominating. The last time there wasn't a non–North American in the top three was 2002–03, and in 2012–13, for the first time all three Vezina nominees were Europeans, and the winner was Russian, Sergei Bobrovsky.

Hardy Åström was one of the first European goalies to play in the NHL.
(IHA/Icon SMI)

The floodgates have opened and will not be closed, despite the protectionist efforts of the Canadian Hockey League to end the use of foreign goalies as one of two import spots allowed on rosters.

The inward-looking angst about the state of Canadian goaltending is misplaced, said Corey Hirsch, a former Team Canada goalie who recently worked with the netminders in St. Louis. He believes the gap between European and North American goalies has closed.

"All of the goalies now, the style is pretty similar globally, butterfly, tall goalies," said Hirsch, explaining that the styles really seemed to differ when he was playing in the 1980s. "With Canada, that's how we got an edge on teams, our goaltending was so much better. Now, if you look, everyone's like, 'What's wrong with Canada's goaltending?' Well, nothing. To me, other countries have just caught up. They've learned our systems and our styles. They've adapted their game."

Bruce Racine, who played 15 years as a pro, went in reverse and travelled to Finland to play in the Finnish Elite League with Lukko Rauma and Ilves Tampere. Now firmly entrenched in a second career with the Racine Goalie Academy in St. Louis, he finds himself sharing much of what he learned overseas.

"The training is great," he raved about Finland. A team will stick together through the years, so the players rise up through the ranks together, and given that most games were a bus trip away, there is a lot of time for team bonding—and teaching on the plentiful ice rinks. "Right from a young age, they're able to watch the junior teams and get training. It's a smaller, contained, winter country, so the focus is there. Kids right from a young age start getting the training," said Racine.

In an interview during the 2013 Stanley Cup Final, Jukka Ropponen, one of the top goaltending coaches in Finland, talked to the *Toronto Star* about how his country's national coaching standard, which stresses the importance of goalies playing with their hands out in front of their bodies, is the key factor in the success of today's Finnish keepers. Ropponen told columnist Dave Feschuk,

> If you look at the Quebec style, François Allaire and these guys, they just want to have every hole blocked and they want the hands tied close to the body—basically you're blocking the puck versus controlling the puck. The Finnish style—and the Swedes are following this path too—from a young age we put a lot of emphasis

on catching the puck and controlling the puck. We believe the more we bring the hands out front, the more we're catching the puck, the better we're seeing the puck and controlling the puck, and we're covering more space.

Ahlers lays part of the blame for the European goaltending trend and the decline in the development of homegrown talent on the copycat nature of the league, where one success encourages others to try to duplicate it exactly, constrained as teams are by the short lifespan of most coaches and general managers, who may not be around to see a prospect prosper.

Ahlers said, "Europe's the hot spot right now. Instead of developing your goalies, you just go over to Europe and find a guy who's had success over there and you plug him right in. It doesn't always work, but it's a quicker fix than drafting a kid, letting him play junior for two more years, and then letting him hone his trade for maybe two more years on the American League level."

THINKING ABOUT THE FUTURE

In a North American society where every player gets a participatory medal or trophy just for showing up and parents hire lawyers to fight for better grades, the mental makeup of kids coming up through the system is fundamentally different from that of their predecessors, said John Grahame, who succeeded in the NHL far longer than his father, Ron, did. He tries to get his students to stand up and acknowledge failure, which is not easy to do in a world quick to pass the blame.

Grahame said, "That's what I try to convey to these younger kids. It's your responsibility. Don't make excuses. It's your job to stop the puck. Don't blame it on anyone else. It's your responsibility. I think that's the mental side of things that will never change. Styles change and they're always going to, but that mental approach, it's your responsibility, don't make excuses, I don't think will ever change in order to be a successful goalie."

Sami Jo Small works with young goalies too, and she shares some of what helped her succeed as a goaltender on Canada's women's hockey teams. She explained,

> Parents always ask me how to tell if their kid's going to have potential or if they're going to be a great goaltender. I think one of the underlying factors that makes great goaltenders is the ability to deal with failure. People deal with failure in all different ways, whether it manifests through anger or they're internalizing it—whatever it is, they've developed a coping mechanism to be able to put that aside and move on to the next puck and stop the next puck.

We'll leave the last words to two of the Goaltenders' Union's greatest treasures, Hall of Fame members both.

Johnny Bower shared a lesson learned from Chuck Rayner when they were both with the New York Rangers: "He said, 'John, you've got to keep your eye on, not the player, but that little wee black thing. That's what you have to watch, no matter what you do. Whatever comes into your mind first, you do it. Don't hesitate. If you do hesitate, you're lost.' That was some good advice I got from him."

"Mr. Goalie" Glenn Hall reminds everyone to keep it simple: "The biggest thing to goalkeeping, as I see it, is get high position and back to post. They're giving them this stuff, you shuffle along, you go parallel, and everything else. It's a bunch of garbage. It's an easy position if you're capable of thinking."

Adrahtas, Tom. *Glenn Hall: The Man They Call Mr. Goalie.*
Vancouver: Greystone Books, 2002.

Allen, Kevin, and Bob Duff. *Without Fear: Hockey's 50 Greatest
Goaltenders.* Toronto: Monarch Books, 2002.

Bower, Johnny, with Bob Duff. *The China Wall: The Timeless
Legend of Johnny Bower.* Toronto: Fenn Publishing Company
Ltd., 2008.

Denault, Todd. *Jacques Plante: The Man Who Changed the Face of
Hockey.* Toronto: McClelland & Stewart, 2009.

Ferguson, John, Stan Fischler, and Shirley Fischler, *Thunder &
Lightning.* Scarborough, Ont.: Prentice-Hall Canada, 1989.

Hunter, Douglas. *A Breed Apart: An Illustrated History of
Goaltending.* Toronto: Viking, 1995.

Irvin, Dick. *Behind the Bench: Coaches Talk About Life in the NHL.*
Toronto: McClelland & Stewart, 1993.

Irvin, Dick. *In the Crease: Goaltenders Look at Life in the NHL.*
Toronto: McClelland & Stewart, 1995.

Irvin, Dick. *Now Back to You, Dick.* Toronto: McClelland &
Stewart, 1988.

Kendall, Brian. *Shutout: The Legend of Terry Sawchuk.* Toronto:
Viking, 1996.

Mahovlich, Ted. *The Big M.* Toronto: HarperCollins, 1999.

Mellanby, Ralph, with Mike Brophy. *Walking with Legends:
The Real Stories of Hockey Night in Canada.* Toronto: Fenn
Publishing Company Ltd., 2007.

Milton, Steve. *Hockey Hall of Fame Book of Jerseys.* Richmond Hill,
Ont.: Firefly Books, 2012.

Podnieks, Andrew. *Hockey Superstitions: From Playoff Beards to Crossed Sticks and Lucky Socks.* Toronto: McClelland & Stewart, 2010.

Proteau, Adam, ed. *The Hockey News Puck Funnies: Hockey, Humour, Hilarity & Hi-Jinx.* Montreal: Transcontinental Books, 2009.

Tretiak, Vladislav. *Tretiak: The Legend.* Edmonton: Plains Publishing Inc., 1987.

WEBSITES

www.sihrhockey.org
www.quanthockey.com
www.hockey-reference.com
www.greatesthockeylegends.com
www.hockeydb.com
www.hockeygoalies.org

The Goaltenders' Union would not exist without *Don't Call Me Goon*, which came out in the fall of 2013. That book proved to be a lot of fun to put together and spurred us on to do another collection of hockey stories. This one, however, was put together in a year, compared to the two years it took for *Goon*. The added benefit of a couple of years of contacts, sources, and better knowledge of the hockey world has helped tremendously, but man, there were times we thought we bit off more than we could chew. Having both freelanced articles for *The Hockey News* was a great ace in the hole too when contacting people. We did learn a lot about the need for photos with the previous book, and we relied on the goalies themselves for some of the unique shots in here.

Like with *Don't Call Me Goon*, Jeff Marek of Sportsnet gets a thank you for pointing us in the right direction along the way. It is proof that time spent drinking beer when you are young can pay off down the road.

As far as finding the goalies we talked to, we thank the public relations people at the teams, a couple of agents, and the NHL alumni association. The website LinkedIn, where hockey players try to be grown-ups after years playing a game, was invaluable. And to the especially passionate fans out there, who have kept the names of the players alive through their own interests, including card collecting and autographs, well, we hope your interest expands to buying a book about goalies!

The Society for International Hockey Research (SIHR) database was key to research, but perhaps more importantly, the friends and contacts made through SIHR have been fruitful but also encouraging when things looked rough. Thanks to Todd Denault in particular. The membership fee might just be the best tax writeoff ever.

The folks at ECW Press make up their own championship team, and it has been a fun one to be a part of for years now. Thanks especially to Michael Holmes, our editor, and Crissy Calhoun, for keeping us in line. Sarah Dunn spreads the word about us.

For Richard, this book wouldn't have been written without the music of GG Allin and the Murder Junkies. I again thank my parents, Sonja and Alex, and dog, Max, for keeping me grounded.

For Greg, a couple of friends in the schoolyard, Jay Petroff (a former goalie) and Mark Dillon (alas, a Bruins fan), deserve a thank you for their continued interest in this project. My brother, Chris, used to be a hockey guy (but now has the nerve to call during the Stanley Cup Final), and I spent a lot of time at the rinks watching him play. I found myself reflecting on that time recently, when one of the other "hockey siblings" that I would hang around with, Lori Kempel Heer, died way too soon, as did her brother, Shawn, who was a goalie. My son, Quinn, has always been fascinated by goalies and considers Roberto Luongo one of his heroes, up there with Captain Rex from *The Clone Wars* and, looking further back in time, Bob the Builder. My thanks to the hockey players like Glenn Hall, Johnny Bower, and Darryl Sittler, who talked to Quinn on the phone or left him messages, and to Pierre Pilote, who tried to teach Quinn to pitch and putt in his backyard. And, of course, thanks to Meredith, my long-suffering spouse, who now takes down a message with the notation, "Some old dude, and I don't know if it's a hockey or wrestling guy."

Richard Kamchen (Mike Mastrandrea)   Greg Oliver (Quinn Oliver)

RICHARD KAMCHEN still finds it hard to believe that he gets paid to talk hockey with some of his heroes from the past, including the Winnipeg Jets of his youth. It's a far cry from his regular writing gigs, which primarily focus on agriculture and the politics associated with it. To keep him sane, he takes his dog, Max, on long walks and listens to the likes of GG Allin, the Ramones, and Black Flag. If you dare, follow him on Twitter at @RKamchen.

GREG OLIVER has run the *SLAM! Wrestling* website since 1996 and was co-honoured with the James C. Melby Award alongside his frequent writing partner Steve Johnson for their work. After six books about pro wrestling, Greg has moved into the hockey world. *Don't Call Me Goon* hit the shelves in 2013, and *Written in Blue and White: The Toronto Maple Leafs Contracts and Historical Documents from the Collection of Allan Stitt* in fall 2014. Follow him on Twitter at @gregmep and read his *Pucks and Piledrivers* blog at blogs.canoe.ca/gregoliver.

Join the discussion about
The Goaltenders' Union
on Facebook at
http://bit.ly/Goaltenders